Pattern Calculus

Barry Jay

Pattern Calculus

Computing with Functions and Structures

Dr. Barry Jay
University of Technology, Sydney
Faculty of Engineering and Information Technology
School of Software
Broadway NSW 2007
Australia
cbj@it.uts.edu.au

ISBN 978-3-642-42601-8 ISBN 978-3-540-89185-7 (eBook)
DOI 10.1007/978-3-540-89185-7
Springer Dordrecht Heidelberg London New York

ACM Computing Classification (1998): D.1, D.2, D.3, F.3, F.4.

Cover design: KünkelLopka, GmbH

Printed on acid-free paper

Springer is part of Springer Science+Business Media (www.springer.com)

To my parents

Foreword

Over time, basic research tends to lead to specialization – increasingly narrow topics are addressed by increasingly focussed communities, publishing in increasingly confined workshops and conferences, discussing increasingly incremental contributions. Already the community of programming languages is split into various subcommunities addressing different aspects and paradigms (functional, imperative, relational, and object-oriented). Only a few people manage to maintain a broader view, and even fewer step back in order to gain an understanding about the basic principles, their interrelation, and their impact in a larger context.

The pattern calculus is the result of a profound re-examination of a 50-year development. It attempts to provide a unifying approach, bridging the gaps between different programming styles and paradigms according to a new slogan – computation is pattern matching.

It is the contribution of this book to systematically and elegantly present and evaluate the power of pattern matching as the guiding paradigm of programming. Patterns are dynamically generated, discovered, passed, applied, and automatically adapted, based on pattern matching and rewriting technology, which allows one to elegantly relate things as disparate as functions and data structures. Of course, pattern matching is not new. It underlies term rewriting – it is, for example, incorporated in, typically functional, programming languages, like Standard ML – but it has never been pursued as the basis of a unifying framework for programming.

It is surprising how this elementary principle allows one to uniformly and elegantly cover the various programming paradigms, not only concerning execution but also typing, which itself is also realized following the idea of pattern matching. The author plays this game of giving and extracting semantics from syntax with virtuosity.

Full appreciation of the mastery of this presentation requires deep knowledge of numerous theoretical areas of computer science, like lambda-calculus, term rewriting, and type theory. This is, however, not necessary to appreciate the fruits in terms of generalized typing and the new path and pattern polymorphisms. Even though the bondi environment presented is still in its infancy, it provides already a strong hint of its potential power.

Integrating the new technology in established settings in order to enhance their expressive power may well have a significant practical impact. People are much more prepared to accept new functionality in their known settings than totally changing paradigm. Another approach would be to use the pattern calculus as an "embedded technology" for dealing with matching and adaptation. Promising application scenarios for such an enterprise include Web Service discovery and mediation.

The described multiple dimensions of impact of the pattern calculus indicate the potential audience. It may range from students who want to get a deeper insight into the basic principles, to language designers interested in enhancing the power of their languages, to tool and service designers in need of new, powerful technologies. The "How to Read This Book" chapter shows that the author wants to address all these communities, and he stands a good chance of being successful.

It should not be forgotten, however, that the book focuses on foundations, and that it assumes a good theoretical background. Therefore interpreters will be needed so that the technology reaches the places where it will eventually have the largest impact, and I hope that the book will inspire this kind of technology transfer, whose value cannot be overestimated.

Dortmund,
March, 2009

Bernhard Steffen

Preface

The pattern calculus is a new foundation for computation, in which the expressive power of functions and of data structures are fruitfully combined within pattern-matching functions. The best of existing foundations focus on either functions (in the λ-calculus) or on data structures (in Turing machines) or compromise on both (as in object-orientation). By contrast, a small typed pattern calculus supports all the main programming styles, including functional, imperative, object-oriented and query-based styles. Indeed, it may help to support web services, to the extent that these are generic functions applied to partially specified data structures.

This book is an elaboration of the idea that computation is pattern matching. As with all such ideas, it must be made to work hard. New sorts of patterns and polymorphism are developed, culminating in the possibility that any term can be a pattern. Types and subtyping must be construed in novel ways, too. The development is incremental, using over a dozen calculi. Finally, the practicality of pattern calculus is illustrated in a programming language, **bondi**.

While the results could be spread over a series of papers, this would certainly diminish the overall impact, as experience shows that no one paper can be both formal enough to be convincing and comprehensive enough to be motivating. Rather, the book has been conceived as a whole, starting with an initial, motivating problem and ending with its implemented solution.

The primary audience for this book is thus the experts in fields related to the foundations of computation, including λ-calculus, rewriting theory, type theory or programming language design. The formal development is created with them in mind. However, it has also been used as the main reference in a course for research students and senior undergraduates. The many examples and the introduction to the **bondi** programming language are developed with them in mind. Some care has been taken to allow exploration of **bondi** without having to address the formalisms.

In addition, the book may come to be of interest to other communities interested in patterns. For example, it may be possible to represent some *design patterns* using the powerful patterns here. Also, since patterns can now be *computed* and not just written by a programmer, it should be possible to automate the process by which the patterns generated by pattern recognition software in, say, image processing or data mining, are used to produce pattern-matching functions.

My interest in pattern matching arose from the realisation that the *shapes* of data structures were best described as patterns. This led to a series of calculi of increasing sophistication: the *constructor calculus* (2001); the *higher-order pattern calculus* and the first version of **bondi** (2004); and, with Delia Kesner, the *pure pattern calculus* (2005-6). In the Fall of 2004, I gave a series of seminars on pattern calculus in North America and Europe, at which point the need for a book became clear. After some false starts, the initial draft of Parts I and II was produced while visiting Simon Peyton Jones at Microsoft Research (Cambridge) in the second half of 2006. Part III was produced in 2007 at the University of Technology, Sydney. Most of the material was presented to the pattern calculus seminar in Sydney, in 2007, and in the subject *Recent Advances in Software Engineering* at the the University of Technology, Sydney in 2008.

Assumed Knowledge

For the most part, the book is self-contained, aside from some rudimentary knowledge of set theoretical notation. Of greater importance is mathematical or logical maturity. Prior knowledge of λ-calculus, type theory or programming will be an advantage.

Acknowledgements

Many people have provided useful feedback on both the ideas in this book and its drafting, especially Marco Bakera, Henk Barendregt, Luca Cardelli, Germain Faure, Marcelo Fiore, Thomas Given-Wilson, Daniele Gorla, Bob Harper, Ryan Heise, Freeman Huang, Neil Jones, Simon Peyton Jones, Jean-Pierre Jouannaud, Delia Kesner, Robin Milner, Eugenio Moggi, Clara Murdaca, Tony Nguyen, Jens Palsberg, Richard Raban, Matt Roberts, Don Sannella, David Skillicorn, Tony Sloane, Bernhard Steffen, Eelco Visser, Joost Visser, Yiyan Wang and members of the pattern calculus seminar. My special thanks go to Eugenio Moggi and Bernhard Steffen for their careful reading of the second draft, and to David Broman for his painstaking efforts while reading the final draft. All remaining errors are the sole responsibility of the author.

I am particularly indebted to Microsoft Research (Cambridge) for their support while writing this book, and to the University of Technology, Sydney for giving me the freedom to pursue my thoughts.

Sydney,
December, 2008

Barry Jay

Contents

List of Figures

Part I
Terms

Chapter 1
Introduction

Abstract This book develops a new programming style, based on pattern matching, from pure calculus to typed calculus to programming language. It can be viewed as a sober technical development whose worth will be assessed in time by the programming community. However, it actually makes a far grander claim, that the pattern-matching style subsumes the other main styles within it. This is possible because it is the first to fully resolve the tension between functions and data structures that has limited expressive power till now. This introduction lays out the general argument, and then surveys the contents of the book, at the level of the parts, chapters and results.

1.1 Programming Styles

Why are there so many programming styles? Functional, imperative, relational and object-oriented styles are all widespread, running on the same hardware, and yet hardly interacting. Since a large project typically employs several programming styles, it has been necessary to link them through fragile middleware that, over time, grows in complexity and cost. These difficulties are compounded when producing web services, which in turn motivate the creation of yet more styles. Thus, any progress in relating programming styles may have substantial practical implications.

Stylistic differences are most obvious in syntax, but this is not, of itself, a barrier to communication, but rather a reflection of deeper differences. It is productive to identify each programming style with its central concept, whose manipulation supports a distinctive approach to program reuse, or polymorphism. For example: functional languages such as Lisp, ML and Haskell apply functions; imperative languages such as FORTRAN and C assign to locations holding data; relational languages such as SQL access fields; object-oriented languages such as C++ and Java invoke methods. In this light, the original question can be re-expressed more positively. How compatible are the central concepts of programming? Can these various forms of polymorphism coexist?

B. Jay, *Pattern Calculus*,
DOI 10.1007/978-3-540-89185-7_1, © Springer-Verlag Berlin Heidelberg 2009

There are three tempting reasons to dismiss the question. Perhaps it was answered at the very beginning, in the 1930s, when Alonzo Church and Alan Turing showed the equivalence of λ-calculus (for functions) and Turing machines (for imperative programming). However, this equivalence says merely that both approaches support the same functions on natural numbers, without in any way addressing programming style or program reuse. Indeed, the latter concepts did not properly arise until the late 1950s with the advent of the high-level languages Lisp and FORTRAN.

Perhaps stylistic differences arise only in practice. However, the differences are well established in theory, too. Over and above the communities devoted to each style, there is the more fundamental division between those studying program complexity, as measured by Turing machines, and those concerned with program meaning, as emphasised in λ-calculus.

Finally, perhaps the fragmentation of styles is caused by differences between type systems. After all, since any one computation can be expressed in λ-calculus, a programming language can do no more than restrict the expressive power of pure λ-calculus. However, supporting individual computations is not the same as supporting a style. Also, types did not become important in programming until after the stylistic differences were well established. Again, types are not diverse enough to generate the variety of polymorphic styles, as will be discussed in Sect. 1.4.

The oldest source of stylistic tension appears to be that between functions and data structures. At one extreme, functional programming considers everything to be a function, even a number or a pair. At the other extreme, imperative programming considers everything, even a function, to be a structure built from assignable components, such as squares on a tape. In between are various compromises or mixtures. For example, relational programming combines a limited range of data structures (tables of records) with a limited range of functions (queries and updates). Again, object-orientation wraps a mixture of data and functionality into a self-contained object. Thus, the original question can be further narrowed. Is there a single concept able to support a uniform treatment of both functions and structures, within which the various other styles can be expressed?

The desired concept is pattern matching, as embodied in pattern calculus. Patterns describe data structures while matching supports functionality. By making the class of patterns sufficiently generous, all the main programming styles can be expressed within a single, small calculus.

Although pattern matching is a very well known programming technique, it has generally been used to add convenience without increasing expressive power. By contrast, the most general pattern calculus allows any term to be a pattern, so that patterns are dynamic: they can be generated by an algorithm for pattern recognition, or discovery, passed as parameters, and then applied in a pattern-matching function. This is expressive enough to support the existing programming styles, and to suggest some new ones, based on new forms of polymorphism.

1.2 A Motivating Problem

The importance of balancing functions and structures can be illustrated through an example. The problem is to award a salary increase to all employees of a large organisation. Salaries are represented by floating point numbers, which are to be increased according to some formula.

The possibilities for the formula are determined by the style. Query programming would limit the formula to those expressible as queries. Object-orientation is more flexible, allowing any existing method to be used. The functional style allows the formula to be represented by a parameter, which can be instantiated by functions yet to be defined.

Now consider the data structure representing the organisation. Of concern is the location of employees within the structure, and the representation of employees therein. In a relational database, or using the functional style, the location and representation must both be given in almost complete detail. This can be quite a burden. In a large organisation, employees are likely to appear in departments, units or divisions, etc. which must be handled explicitly. Similarly, employees may have different roles, or belong to different classes, e.g. of managers or temporary employees, with corresponding differences in the way their salaries are reckoned. The resulting programs are complex, and must be maintained. This is a significant burden since dynamic organisations restructure fairly frequently. Object-oriented languages can reduce the representation issues by using a root class of employees, whose subclasses describe different roles. This requires prior agreement on the employee class, and employee locations within departments, etc. must still be encoded explicitly. Recent work on programming with semi-structured data, such as XML, addresses the location problem, but still struggles to represent employees and the formula in a flexible manner.

In short, none of the existing styles are able to provide a solution to the salary update problem without additional information about the data structures involved. The curious thing is that this structural detail is absent from the original problem. The specification itself is unambiguous, since it is easy to check any particular solution. What is lacking is a sufficiently general programming style.

This is achieved by providing a uniform account of data structures. The necessary account is surprisingly simple. Every data structure is either an indivisible *atom* or a *compound* built from two components. Hence a program that is to act on an arbitrary data structure requires just two cases, one for atoms and one for compounds. This style is used to produce *generic queries*.

This approach can be used to define a generic iterator that recursively applies its procedure argument to every component of a structure. When applied to a procedure for increasing salaries, the location problem is solved. When this procedure is defined using an object-oriented method for increasing salaries, the representation problem is also solved within the employee class framework. Finally, by allowing the pattern for an employee to be generated dynamically, the nature of the employee class itself (its ontological status) can be described using a program parameter. This yields a completely general solution to the salary update problem. It is able to handle arbitrary employee subclasses within a dynamically determined employee class within an arbitrary company structure. This problem is typical of those that can be solved using pattern matching in its most general form.

1.3 Pattern Matching

To find the balance between functions and structures, let us begin with the theory of functions, the λ-calculus. In brief, every term of the pure λ-calculus is either a variable, application or λ-abstraction. Evaluation is given by a single rule that substitutes the function argument for the bound variable. Pure λ-calculus is able to encode data structures as abstractions, but the encoding is not uniform since there is no means of distinguishing atoms from compounds.

The first step is thus to add some *constructors* c which are atoms from which data structures can be built, by application. Then add some operations that act on data structures, e.g. to compare constructors, or recover components. The resulting *compound calculus* is enough to define the generic queries of interest.

Actually, the required operations are already present in Lisp. For example, its `car` and `cdr` recover the components of a compound (there called a pair). So compound calculus can be seen as a core of Lisp, in which the variables and constructors are carefully distinguished. While effective, the compound calculus looks rather ad hoc, since it is not quite clear whether the new operations are well chosen.

An alternative means of acting on data structures is to use pattern matching. Patterns can be used to describe the internal structure of data, i.e. its shape, and to name its parts, which are then available for use.

Till now, patterns have been used to represent particular sorts of data, such as pairs or lists. For example, the pattern for an employee in a small business might be `Employee` $n\ s$ where n represents their name and s represents their salary. In this approach, a nontrivial pattern is always headed by a constructor, such as `Employee`.

More generally, the pattern $x\ y$ can be used to represent an arbitrary compound, where `car` and `cdr` yield x and y, respectively. Now x can match against any (partially applied) constructor such as `Employee` n without knowing anything more of its nature. In this manner, all of the seemingly ad hoc operations of the compound calculus are subsumed within the single process of matching. The pattern $x\ y$ above is a typical *static pattern*, in that it is ready to be matched without being evaluated. When used in a recursive function, such patterns allow for traversal of an arbitrary data structure, by following all paths. This *path polymorphism* is enough to find all employee records within an arbitrary database, provided the pattern for an employee is known to the programmer. Static patterns offer more expressive power than existing, constructor patterns, at little cost to the programmer.

Even greater expressiveness comes from *dynamic patterns*, which contain a mix of *variable symbols* and *matchable symbols*. A typical example is given by the pattern $x\ \hat{y}$ in which y is a matchable symbol, or *matchable* (that is among the *binding symbols* of the enclosing case) and x is a variable symbol or *variable*. If y is to represent a salary then x can be instantiated by a (partial) pattern for an employee, worker, or other salary earner. Pursuing this approach to its limit yields *pattern polymorphism*, in which any term can be a pattern. Now patterns are first-class citizens which can be taken as arguments, evaluated, and returned as results, just like any other term. For example, patterns generated by data mining to identify, say, high-value customers could be exploited directly by pattern-consuming functions without any programmer intervention, thus allowing for a positive feedback loop from pattern generation to pattern consumption and back again. To the extent that pattern generation and matching are fundamental to intelligence, one can speculate about the development of software agents and web services, whose exploration, interaction and strategies are all expressed in the language of patterns, the pattern calculus.

1.4 Types

Given that the compound calculus, or Lisp, is able to express such useful queries, it is natural to wonder why this expressive power is not more widely available. Perhaps the main reason was that later languages are predominantly typed, and it was not clear how to type components in a uniform manner. To put this more sharply, the importance of types in computation has been buttressed by a variety of principles that have served us well, but are now inhibiting development. This section explores some of the issues while trying to keep technicalities to a minimum.

As noted earlier, pure λ-calculus has been viewed as the acme of expressiveness, in that it supports all computation, whether meaningful or not. From this viewpoint, known as the *Curry style*, types serve to characterise the meaningful terms. For example, an abstraction may have a function type. An alternative approach is the *Church* style, in which the types come first, and the terms are used to describe the types. For example, an abstraction is just a means of introducing a function type. Here the only well-formed terms are those that have a type, so the expressiveness of the type system determines that of the terms, and the nature of any polymorphism. For example, type variables can be used to support parametric polymorphism, while subtyping supports inclusion polymorphism. In its strongest form, the types are identified with the propositions of a logic, and the terms with their proofs, using the so called Curry–Howard Correspondence. Since Curry is already represented, we may call this the *Howard* style. Now a function type corresponds to an implication in the logic, a product type to logical conjunction, etc.

Unfortunately, the latter approaches have had the effect of excluding some forms of polymorphism. For example, path and pattern polymorphism are not expressible in λ-calculus which is, after all, a theory of functions. Further, they can be typed using the existing machinery of type variables and function types introduced for the λ-calculus. For example, the size of a data structure is given by a function of type $X \to \mathtt{nat}$ where X is a type variable and $\mathtt{nat}$ is a type of natural numbers. This make no sense in the Church and Howard styles, where this type supports constant functions only.

This raises an interesting point. Data structures are intrinsic to the pattern calculus and yet *need not* have their own types (or their own logic). That said, there are significant benefits to be had by introducing such data types, built from type constants, such as `Int` (for integers) and `List` (for lists), and type applications such as `List Int`. Here are three such benefits.

First, the *query calculus* supports path polymorphic versions of the queries and updates familiar from query languages such as SQL. Unfortunately, this path polymorphism can also be used to define fixpoints as pattern-matching functions, so that functions need not terminate. This is an unattractive feature for a database language to have. The difficulties arise when constructors have higher types, such as $(X \to X) \to X$. When all types are function types, such things cannot be avoided, but with data types available the necessary restrictions are easily enforced.

Second, the data types themselves suggest a new form of polymorphism, called *functor polymorphism* in which terms are polymorphic in the choice of functor, or structure used to hold the data. In this manner, the familiar mapping for lists, of type $(X \to Y) \to \mathtt{List}\ X \to \mathtt{List}\ Y$ can be generalised to $(X \to Y) \to F\ X \to F\ Y$ where F is a type variable representing the unknown structure type. Once again, the terms are not merely a reflection of the type structure, since the generic mapping is a complex pattern-matching function developed from the representation theory of data types.

Third, the most popular accounts of subtyping focus on the function types, which leads to numerous difficulties, especially concerning argument types. However, since objects now have data types, it is natural to make function argument types *invariant* under subtyping, so that the difficulties with argument types all vanish. Now specialised methods can be represented as pattern-matching functions, so that inclusion polymorphism can be added with a minimum of disruption.

Thus, a fairly simple type system, rather similar to those well known for decades, can support a variety of old, neglected, and new forms of polymorphism. To the path and pattern polymorphism visible in the untyped calculi can be added parametric polymorphism (from type variables), plus two forms of polymorphism that combine elements from both the types and the terms, namely inclusion polymorphism (from subtyping) and functor polymorphism (from data types). This makes a total of five sorts of polymorphism that can be supported by the pattern calculus.

1.5 bondi

The programming language **bondi** is based on an implicitly typed pattern calculus called *extension calculus*. Its source code is freely available. Much of the syntax will be familiar to functional programmers. For example, the generic size function is given by

```
let rec (size : a -> Int) =
| x y -> (size x) + (size y)
| x -> 1
```

It declares `size` to be a recursive function of type `a -> Int` (here a is a type variable) defined as a pattern-matching function with two cases, as indicated by the symbol `|`. The first case has pattern `x y` to handle an arbitrary compound, while the second case has pattern `x` that matches anything else.

Also, data types can be declared in the usual manner. For example,

```
datatype List a = Nil  | Cons of a and List a
```

introduces a type constant `List` and two constructors `Nil: List a` for empty lists and `Cons: a -> List a -> List a`. for adding new entries.

Object-orientation is supported through classes whose syntax is similar to that of Java. For example,

```
class Name {
name : String;
get_name = { | () -> !this.name }
set_name = { fun n -> this.name = n }
with
toString += | Name x y -> !y
}
```

declares a class of names, with a field `name` of type `String` and the usual get- and set- methods. Note the use of the assignment `this.name = n` and the use of `!` to de-reference fields. Also, the syntax `+-` is used to add a case to an existing *function* `toString` that does not belong to any class.

This shows that **bondi** is able to augment existing functions (e.g. `toString`) with cases for new data structures (e.g. names), as well as augment existing data structures with new functions, as is usual with algebraic data types. Of course, augmenting existing functions changes their meaning, so that this violates *referential transparency*. However, by restricting this capacity for adding cases to newly declared structures, this can be achieved without ever changing the behaviour of existing programs, so that one has *behavioural continuity*. In the past, the difficulty of achieving both sorts of augmentation has been seen as evidence that one must choose between a data-centric or a function-centric programming style, but **bondi** provides more evidence that functions and data structures are fully compatible.

This brings us back to the original question of programming styles. There will always be a need for syntax that is customised to simplify different sorts of program reuse. However, the pattern calculus and **bondi** show that the main existing styles are all quite compatible. They can be realised in a single, small, typed calculus, based on pattern matching, and be combined freely. Indeed, the potential of this approach to support new programming styles is not exhausted. In sum, pattern calculus provides a foundation for computing that does more than just describe the computable functions, as it is able to account for the polymorphism of programming styles in a quite general manner, allowing them to be combined freely and confidently.

1.6 Synopsis

Part I considers terms without types. It starts with a brief introduction to the well known pure λ-calculus in Chap. 2.

Chapter 3 introduces data structures. They are built from *constructors*, a class of inert term constants. While commonly viewed as syntactic sugar for the corresponding λ-terms, the compound calculus shows how they may support additional expressive power, such as the ability to compute the size of a data structure. The compound calculus provides a new account of the core of Lisp, which describes its data structures as well as its functions, the main point of difference being that compound calculus maintains a clear distinction between variables and constructors.

Chapter 4 introduces pattern matching through a class of static patterns. The static pattern calculus generalises the standard approaches to pattern matching by allowing a pattern that matches an arbitrary compound. Hence it is able to support algorithms that traverse arbitrary data structures.

In passing from λ-calculus to compound calculus to static patterns, the size of the calculus has expanded to include new term constants, and then a new syntactic class of patterns. Chapter 5 purifies the syntax while further increasing expressive power, by identifying constructors with *matchable symbols*, and patterns with terms, in the dynamic pattern calculus. The main challenge then is to control matching, so it cannot get stuck, and so its results are stable under reduction of either pattern or argument (reduction is confluent), as established in joint work with Delia Kesner.

Chapter 6 shows how pure static pattern calculus can support records and objects. There is a translation to it from Abadi and Cardelli's pure object calculus.

Part II develops type systems that can support the program reuse introduced in Part I. The main theorems in Part II show that reduction is confluent, preserves typing and progresses. There are also some results on termination of reduction.

Chapter 7 describes the type variables (or parameters) of the typed λ-calculus, System **F** with its parametric polymorphism. Jean-Yves Girard's proof of strong normalisation is recalled.

Chapter 8 describes functor polymorphism, in which functions that are able to act on general collections are defined by giving cases for each sort of primitive structure. By contrast with earlier accounts, the combination of cases is here given by a *typecase* which branches according to the value of a type argument. In turn, typecases can be seen as performing pattern matching on types. This is described in a new account of type variable quantification in which instantiation is handled by type matching, in System **FM**.

Chapter 9 uses the typecases to type a variant of the compound calculus as the query calculus. It generalises queries from records to arbitrary data structures. By controlling the types of constructors in ranked query calculus, it can be proved that reduction always terminates, an important property for a query language. The same types can be used to type the static pattern calculus.

Chapter 10 types the dynamic pattern calculus, introducing matchable type symbols in parallel with the matchable term symbols.

Chapter 11 introduces a structural *subtyping* relation. This provides a radical alternative to existing approaches, which is simpler (subtyping is structural), more expressive (type variables are in play) and more closely aligned with class-based approaches to object-oriented programming (no contravariance in function argument types). This is exploited by the method calculus, in which method choices are added to λ-calculus, and then in the subtyped pattern calculus.

Chapter 12 introduces the extension calculus. It is an implicitly typed calculus that underpins **bondi**. It can be seen as a dynamic variant of the pattern calculus that preceded all the calculi presented here. It surrenders a little expressive power of the (sub)typed pattern calculus to eliminate the need for types during evaluation.

Part III presents the main examples of the earlier parts within the **bondi** programming language. Chapter 13 introduces the language, which is based on the extension calculus, and illustrates higher-order functions and parametric polymorphism. Chapter 14 introduces algebraic data types and pattern-matching functions upon them. Generic functional programming is also introduced. Chapter 15 introduces generic queries. Chapter 16 introduces dynamic patterns. Chapter 17 adds state in the form of references. Chapter 18 adds classes to support *object-orientation*.

Perhaps surprisingly, the proof techniques in the book are all adapted from λ-calculus and rewriting theory. The most delicate of these is the proof of strong normalisation for the ranked query calculus, which adapts the familiar technique of reducibility candidates to the presence of data structures. The chief contribution of the work lies in the novelty of the definitions, of constructors and data structures, of type invocation and specialisation, etc., which in turn derive from pursuit of a single observation, that functions and data structures are not interchangeable, but rather can be related through pattern matching.

1.7 How to Read This Book

The book is designed to be read in a number of ways. Of course, the clearest account is obtained by reading from the beginning to the end. Other approaches provide shorter routes to the most developed systems, leaving some explanations behind along the way. For example, each of the three parts, on terms, types and programs, may be read in isolation. As well as this "horizontal" structure, there is also a "vertical" structure, exhibited by the following table of chapters:

Concept	2 functions	3 data	4 static	5 dynamic	6 objects
Polymorphism	7 parametric	8 functor	9 path	10 pattern	11 inclusion
Style	13 functional	14 algebraic	15 query	16 pattern	18 object-or.

Here, "static" and "dynamic" refer to patterns,"algebraic" is a contraction of "algebraic data types" and "object-or." contracts "object-oriented." For example, Chaps 4, 9 and 15 address static patterns, showing how they behave as terms, how their path polymorphism can be typed, and their use in defining generic queries in **bondi**. A safe approach is to read all of the chapters above and to the left of the chapter of interest. For example, before Chap. 9, read Chaps. 2, 3, 4, 7 and 8. It may even be possible to read advanced chapters in isolation, if one is after the main ideas only. Highlights among the calculi include those of Chaps. 5, 10 and 11. Three chapters do not appear in the table above: Chap. 1 provides an overview of the book as a whole; Chap. 12 provides a bridge from the calculi to programming, and Chap. 17 introduces imperative features. Finally, the appendix contains a brief account of each calculus that appears in Parts I and II and a technical summary of all the shared syntactic definitions, e.g. of free variables.

Chapter 2
Functions

Abstract This chapter provides an overview of the pure theory of functions, the pure λ-calculus. It is used to introduce general notions that will recur throughout the book. Grammars, meta-variables, free variables, substitutions and α-equivalence are all necessary to define the term syntax precisely. Computation is characterised by reduction rules. Unique results of computation are guaranteed by confluence of reduction. In λ-calculus, reduction is defined using the β-rule, which evaluates functions by substitution. Its expressive power is illustrated by some basic examples, culminating in the characterisation of general recursion through fixpoints.

2.1 Substitution

The use of functions is so familiar that on first consideration they may appear unworthy of serious study. This view is understandable if the functions involved have simple arguments which are, say, numbers or words, but there are many situations in which functions are themselves the arguments of other, *higher-order* functions. One of the commonest examples in mathematics is the differential operator of differential calculus, which converts a function producing values into a function producing the rate of change of values. Similarly, in playing games or proving theorems, one may develop complex tactics (functions from game positions to moves) built from simpler tactics. Within programming, *routines* may be viewed as functions, so that subroutines become function arguments. Again, database queries are commonly built by applying an operator to, say, a predicate (a boolean function) that tests values. In such settings, the functional machinery must be described with more care.

Further, when functions are *first-class*, i.e. able to be passed as parameters, evaluated and returned as results, then the functional machinery can represent both natural numbers, and any function on them which is (Turing) computable. That is, the pure functional view is not only compact but self-contained.

The elements of a theory of functions can be illustrated by a trivial example. Consider a function f that is defined by the equation

B. Jay, *Pattern Calculus*,
DOI 10.1007/978-3-540-89185-7_2, © Springer-Verlag Berlin Heidelberg 2009

$$f(x) = x + 1$$

so that $f(1)$ is 2 and $f(3)$ is 4, etc. This declaration combines the description of the function for adding one, and its naming as f. The issues can be separated by considering nameless functions, using the Greek letter λ instead of the symbol f and rearranging the syntax to produce

$$\lambda x.x + 1\ .$$

Now the definition of f above can be rewritten as

$$f = \lambda x.x + 1$$

in which the function construction (by λ) and naming (by $=$) are clearly separated.

When this function is *applied* to, say, 3 to get

$$(\lambda x.x + 1)\ 3$$

then its evaluation, or *reduction* replaces x by 3 in $x+1$ to get $3+1$ which evaluates to 4.

The naming of functions is useful for reasoning about them, or for creating an environment for programming, but is not central to the study of functions in computation, whose key elements are abstraction, application and reduction. The reduction has two aspects, *substitution* of 3 for x and simplification of the addition. In the pure theory of functions, the nature of terms such as, say, 3 or $+$ is put to one side (until Chap. 3) to focus on the application of abstractions to arguments, and the nature of substitution.

2.2 Pure λ-Calculus

Throughout the book, calculi will be introduced by first giving their syntax and then their semantics. The syntax will be given by one or more grammars followed by a description of basic syntactic manipulations, such as substitution, and perhaps an equivalence relation which determines when two syntactic forms represent the same term, e.g by renaming of bound symbols. Since much of this machinery is shared between calculi, repetition is avoided by providing a complete account of the syntax in the appendix. The semantics will describe how evaluation is to proceed. This will typically be given by a reduction relation. No attempt will be made to consider *denotational semantics* in which the meaning of terms is described without reference to evaluation. Although denotational semantics is well developed for the λ-calculus it has not yet been addressed for the pattern calculi. The phrase "Throughout the book" at the beginning of this paragraph is used to flag conventions that apply throughout. They are listed in the index, under the heading "conventions."

The *term syntax* of the *pure λ-calculus* is described by the following grammar:

$$\begin{array}{rl} t ::= & \text{(term)} \\ x & \text{(variable symbol)} \\ t\ t & \text{(application)} \\ \lambda x.t & \text{(abstraction).} \end{array}$$

Its first line asserts that t is a *meta-variable* for a term. Meta-variables appear in meta-languages that are used to describe object languages. In logic, object languages make statements about the world while meta-languages make statements about object languages. They can be used to resolve paradoxes arising from statements such as "This sentence is false." Here, the calculus or programming language is the object language, which is described using a meta-language.

Throughout the book, the meta-variables b and m,n,o,p,q,r,s,t,u and v may be used for terms, as may their subscripted variants such as s_3 and t_5 and their primed versions s' and t''. Typically, b will represent a boolean, m and n will represent object-oriented methods, and p and q will represent patterns.

Each succeeding line in the grammar above describes a possible form for terms, and its name. The system requires a countable collection of *symbols* which must be easily distinguished from each other, but apart from that, their exact nature does not matter as they are merely identifiers, or place-holders. Throughout the book, the meta-variables for symbols are the italic lower case roman letters f,g,h,i,j,k and w,x,y,z. The latter carry no particular associations, but f,g and h will be used when they are to be thought of as functions, and i,j and k are typically used for numbers.

In the pure λ-calculus every symbol is also a term, namely a *variable symbol* or *variable*. The distinction between symbols and variables is not crucial here, but later calculi will admit *matchable symbols* as well as variable symbols.

If r and u are terms then $r\ u$ is the *application* of the *function* r to the argument u. The *head* $\mathsf{head}(t)$ of a term t is the term at the root of the (possibly empty) sequence of applications that make t. More precisely, it is given by

$$\begin{aligned} \mathsf{head}(r\ u) &= \mathsf{head}(r) \\ \mathsf{head}(t) &= t \text{ otherwise.} \end{aligned}$$

For example $\mathsf{head}((\lambda x.x)\ u\ v) = \lambda x.x$.

If s is a term then $\lambda x.s$ is an abstraction, the *abstraction* of s obtained by *binding* the symbol x. Although every term of the pure λ-calculus may be used as a function, this is not true of λ-calculi in general, so it is sometimes useful to characterise the abstractions as *explicit functions*, since their structure reveals their nature. Variants of this concept will be important in later calculi.

To the extent that binding symbols are place-holders, their actual name is not important. For example, $\lambda x.x$ and $\lambda y.y$ are both the identity function. The actual terms will be defined as equivalence classes in the term syntax under renaming of binding symbols, once the machinery for renaming has been introduced. However, the distinction between the terms and their syntax will not be emphasised in the development unless relevant.

Application is left-associative, so that $s\ t\ u$ is $(s\ t)\ u$. Also, it binds tighter (has a higher precedence) than abstraction, so that $\lambda x.t\ u$ is $\lambda x.(t\ u)$ not $(\lambda x.t)\ u$.

The basic reduction rule of λ-calculus is that an application $(\lambda x.s)\ u$ yields the substitution of u for x in s. The first step is to determine which occurrences of x are to be replaced. For example, if s is $x\ (\lambda x.x)$ then the substitution yields $u\ (\lambda x.x)$ and not $u\ (\lambda u.u)$ or $u\ (\lambda x.u)$ since the copy of x in the body of $\lambda x.x$ is bound locally, and not by the outer binding of $\lambda x.s$. To clarify this, it is necessary to specify the *scope* of bindings, by defining the free variables of a term (those available for substitution).

The *free variables* $\mathsf{fv}(t)$ of a term t is the set of symbols defined by

$$\begin{aligned} \mathsf{fv}(x) &= \{x\} \\ \mathsf{fv}(r\ u) &= \mathsf{fv}(r) \cup \mathsf{fv}(u) \\ \mathsf{fv}(\lambda x.s) &= \mathsf{fv}(s) \setminus \{x\} \end{aligned}$$

where $\{x\}$ is the singleton set containing x and $\mathsf{fv}(r) \cup \mathsf{fv}(u)$ is the *union* of the sets $\mathsf{fv}(r)$ and $\mathsf{fv}(u)$ and $\mathsf{fv}(s) \setminus \{x\}$ is the *set-theoretic difference* of $\mathsf{fv}(s)$ and $\{x\}$ given by removing x from $\mathsf{fv}(s)$ if it is present. The key point is that the binding symbol is *not free* in an abstraction, i.e. x is not free in $\lambda x.s$ as λx *binds* all free occurrences of x in s. Throughout the book, a term t is *closed* if it has no free variables. Here, this means $\mathsf{fv}(t) = \{\}$ but later when terms contain type variables, they must not have free type variables either.

Throughout the book, a *term substitution* (meta-variable σ) is a partial function from term symbols to the relevant term syntax. If its *domain* $\mathsf{dom}(\sigma)$ is given by the symbols $x_1, \ldots, x_n$ and maps x_i to u_i then it may be written $\{u_1/x_1, \ldots, u_n/x_n\}$. The set of *free variables* of σ is given by the union of the sets $\mathsf{fv}(\sigma x)$ where $x \in \mathsf{dom}(\sigma)$. The *symbols* $\mathsf{sym}(\sigma)$ of a substitution σ are given by $\mathsf{dom}(\sigma) \cup \mathsf{fv}(\sigma)$. The substitution σ *avoids* a symbol x (respectively, a set of symbols B) if $x \notin \mathsf{sym}(\sigma)$ (respectively, $B \cap \mathsf{sym}(\sigma) = \{\}$).

The *application* of a substitution σ to syntax t of the pure λ-calculus is given by

$$\begin{aligned} \sigma x &= u && \text{if } \sigma \text{ maps } x \text{ to } u \\ \sigma x &= x && \text{if } x \notin \mathsf{dom}(\sigma) \\ \sigma(r\ u) &= (\sigma r)\ (\sigma u) && \\ \sigma(\lambda x.s) &= \lambda x.\sigma s && \text{if } \sigma \text{ avoids } x. \end{aligned}$$

The *composition* $\sigma_2 \circ \sigma_1$ of two substitutions σ_1 and σ_2 is defined by the function $(\sigma_2 \circ \sigma_1)x = \sigma_2(\sigma_1 x)$.

The requirement above that σ avoid x is necessary to avoid a *symbol clash* that will cause *symbol capture* or *scope violations*. The necessity of the restriction is illustrated by two examples. $\{u/x\}(\lambda x.x)$ is not $\lambda x.u$ since the inner occurrence of x is bound. Also, $\{y/x\}(\lambda y.x)$ is not $\lambda y.y$ since the free occurrence of y in the substitution would become bound by the abstraction with respect to y. It follows that, as a function on term syntax, the application of a substitution to a term is a partial operation. However, it will prove to be a total operation on terms since the clashes can be avoided by renaming binding symbols as follows.

The actual terms are to be defined as equivalence classes of term syntax under renaming of binding symbols. In set theory an *equivalence relation* $\equiv$ is a relation that is *reflexive, symmetric* and *transitive*. That is:

- $t \equiv t$;
- if $s \equiv t$ then $t \equiv s$; and
- if $r \equiv s$ and $s \equiv t$ then $r \equiv t$.

The *equivalence class* of some t is the set of all s such that $s \equiv t$.

A relation R is a *congruence* if it is also closed under the relevant formation rules. For term syntax of the pure λ-calculus this means:

- if $r_1 R r_2$ and $u_1 R u_2$ then $(r_1\ u_1) R (r_2\ u_2)$; and
- if $s_1 R s_2$ then $(\lambda x.s_1) R (\lambda x.s_2)$.

Define the α*-equivalence* relation $=_\alpha$ to be the congruence generated by

$$\lambda x.t =_\alpha \lambda y.\{y/x\}t \text{ if } y \notin \mathsf{fv}(t)$$

(assuming that the right-hand side is defined). The *terms* of the pure λ-calculus are equivalence classes of term syntax under α-equivalence.

The definitions of free variables and of substitution extend naturally from term syntax to terms. Further, substitution is always defined on terms since α-equivalence can always be applied to avoid symbol clashes. For example

$$\{u/x\}(\lambda x.x) =_\alpha \{u/x\}(\lambda y.y) = \lambda y.y$$

and

$$\{y/x\}(\lambda y.x) =_\alpha \{y/x\}(\lambda z.x) = \lambda z.y\ .$$

Lemma 2.1. *For every substitution σ and term t_1 there is a term t_2 that is α-equivalent to t_1 such that σt_2 is defined. If t_1 and t_2 are α-equivalent terms then* $\mathsf{fv}(t_1) = \mathsf{fv}(t_2)$ *and if $u_1 = \sigma t_1$ and $u_2 = \sigma t_2$ are both defined then $u_1 =_\alpha u_2$.*

Proof. The proofs are by straightforward inductions. □

2.3 β-Reduction

Now let us consider the semantic equality of terms. The β*-equality*

$$(\lambda x.s)\ u = \{u/x\}s$$

formalises the original description of abstractions as functions. The η-equality rule

$$t = \lambda x.t\ x \text{ if } x \notin \mathsf{fv}(t)$$

asserts that every pure λ-term is a function. The $\beta\eta$-equality of terms is the congruence relation $s = t$ generated by these rules.

In computation, the η-rule is not so interesting, since it does not hold when data structures are added as primitives. Rather than study full $\beta\eta$-equality, let us focus on β*-reduction* as the basis of computation. It is given by the rule

$$\frac{t_1 \longrightarrow_r t_2}{t_1 \longrightarrow t_2} \qquad \frac{r_1 \longrightarrow r_2}{r_1\ u \longrightarrow r_2\ u} \qquad \frac{u_1 \longrightarrow u_2}{r\ u_1 \longrightarrow r\ u_2} \qquad \frac{s_1 \longrightarrow s_2}{\lambda x.s_1 \longrightarrow \lambda x.s_2}$$

Fig. 2.1 Rewriting for pure λ-terms

$$(\lambda x.s)\ u \longrightarrow_r \{u/x\}s \quad (\beta)$$

which says that the left-hand side, or *redex* $(\lambda x.s)\ u$ can be replaced by the right-hand side, or *reduct* $\{u/x\}s$.

From this rule can be built a *rewriting relation* $t_1 \longrightarrow t_2$ which holds if t_2 is obtained by applying the rule to an arbitrary subterm of t_1 as described in Fig. 2.1. That is, the rewriting relation is the *congruence* generated by the reduction rule(s). A similar process will be applied with each calculus in the book. Each rule can be used as a step in a proof: given *derivations* of all the *premises* appearing above the line there is a derivation of the *conclusion* appearing below the line. For example, a derivation of $(\lambda x.x)\ u\ v \rightarrow u\ v$ is given by

$$\frac{\dfrac{(\lambda x.x)\ u \longrightarrow_r u}{(\lambda x.x)\ u \longrightarrow u}}{(\lambda x.x)\ u\ v \longrightarrow u\ v}\ .$$

Further, one may chain together zero or more such rewrites or *reductions* $t_1 \longrightarrow t_2 \rightarrow \ldots \longrightarrow t_n$ to get a *general reduction* $t_1 \longrightarrow_* t_n$ as defined in Fig. 2.2. When discussing general reductions, a mere rewrite may be called a *one-step reduction* for emphasis. Unless it is relevant, the notation $\longrightarrow$ will be used indiscriminately for the rule, the relation and general reduction.

Now a computation can be defined as a general reduction $t \longrightarrow_* v$ where v cannot be reduced any further, i.e. v is *irreducible* or a *normal form*.

It often happens that a single term will contain two or more subterms that are available for reduction, so that there is some choice in how to proceed. Does one choice preclude the other? Can a single term have two normal forms?

2.4 Confluence

Without knowing if a term has *any* normal forms, the question of their uniqueness must be generalised to arbitrary terms.

A reduction relation $\longrightarrow$ is *confluent* if for any term t and pair of reductions $t \longrightarrow_* t_1$ and $t \longrightarrow_* t_2$ there is a term t_3 and a pair of reductions $t_1 \longrightarrow_* t_3$ and $t_2 \longrightarrow_* t_3$. It follows that if t_1 and t_2 are both irreducible then they must both be t_3. That is, if reduction produces a normal form then it is unique.

One of the simplest ways of establishing confluence is to show the *diamond property*, namely if t reduces to both t_1 and t_2 *in one step* then there are one-step

$$\frac{}{t \longrightarrow_* t} \qquad\qquad \frac{t \longrightarrow t_1 \quad t_1 \longrightarrow_* t_n}{t \longrightarrow_* t_n}$$

Fig. 2.2 General reduction

reductions from t_1 and t_2 to some t_3:

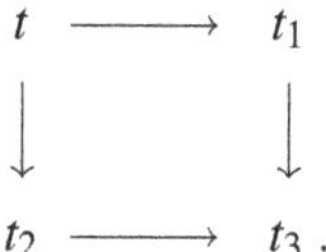

Lemma 2.2. *If a reduction relation satisfies the diamond property then it is confluent.*

Proof. The proof begins with a sub-lemma. If $t \longrightarrow t_1$ in one step and $t \longrightarrow_* t_2$ for some terms t and t_1 and t_2 then there is a term t_3 such that $t_1 \longrightarrow_* t_3$ and $t_2 \longrightarrow t_3$. The proof is by induction on the length of the reduction from t to t_2. If this takes no steps then let t_3 be t_1. Suppose that the reduction sequence is of the form $t \longrightarrow s$ and $s \longrightarrow_* t_2$. By the diamond property, there is a term s_3 such that t_1 and s both reduce to it in one step. Now apply induction to s and s_3 and t_2.

The main result is now by induction on the length of the derivation of $t \longrightarrow_* t_1$. □

Unfortunately, one-step reduction for the λ-calculus does not satisfy the diamond property since β-reduction may multiply redexes. For example, if $u \longrightarrow u_2$ then $(\lambda x.f\ x\ x)\ u \longrightarrow f\ u\ u$ (if x is not free in f) which now takes two steps to reduce to $f\ u_2\ u_2$. The argument can be repaired by replacing reduction by *simultaneous reduction* in which the two reductions of u above can be performed in one step.

The *simultaneous reduction relation* $\gg$ for pure λ-calculus is given in Fig. 2.3. It allows distinct subterms to be reduced simultaneously (by the first rule for applications) and also allows identical subterms to be reduced within a term that is itself being reduced (in the rule that generalises β-reduction).

Lemma 2.3. *The reflexive-transitive closure $\gg_*$ of $\gg$ is the general reduction relation $\longrightarrow_*$.*

Proof. The point is that every one-step reduction is a simultaneous reduction, while every simultaneous reduction is a general reduction. The proofs are by straightforward induction on the definitions. □

Lemma 2.4. *Let s_1, s_2, u_1 and u_2 be terms. If $s_1 \gg s_2$ and $u_1 \gg u_2$ then $\{u_1/x\}s_1 \gg \{u_2/x\}s_2$.*

Proof. The proof is by a straightforward induction on the structure of s_1. □

$\overline{x \gg x}$	$\dfrac{r_1 \gg r_2 \quad u_1 \gg u_2}{r_1\, u_1 \gg r_2\, u_2}$	$\dfrac{s_1 \gg s_2}{\lambda x.s_1 \gg \lambda x.s_2}$	$\dfrac{s_1 \gg s_2 \quad u_1 \gg u_2}{(\lambda x.s_1)u_1 \gg \{u_2/x\}s_2}$

Fig. 2.3 Simultaneous reduction for pure λ-calculus

Theorem 2.5. *The relation $\gg$ has the diamond property.*

Proof. Suppose that $t \gg t_1$ and $t \gg t_2$. The proof is by induction with respect to the derivation of $t \gg t_1$. If t is x then let t_3 be t_2. If t is of the form $\lambda x.s$ then t_1 is of the form $\lambda x.s_1$ and t_2 is of the form $\lambda x.s_2$ where $s \gg s_1$ and $s \gg s_2$. Hence, by induction, there is a term s_3 such that $s_1 \gg s_3$ and $s_2 \gg s_3$ and so let t_3 be $\lambda x.s_3$. Suppose that t is of the form $r\ u$ and t_1 is $r_1\ u_1$ where $r \gg r_1$ and $u \gg u_1$. If t_2 is of the form $r_2\ u_2$ where $r \gg r_2$ and $u \gg u_2$ then, by induction, there are terms r_3 and u_3 such that r_1 and r_2 both simultaneously reduce to r_3 and u_1 and u_2 both simultaneously reduce to u_3 so let t_3 be $r_3\ u_3$. Suppose that r is an abstraction $\lambda x.s$ and t_2 is of the form $\{u_2/x\}s_2$ where $s \gg s_2$ and $u \gg u_2$. Then r_1 must be of the form $\lambda x.s_1$ where $s \gg s_1$. By induction, there are terms s_3 and u_3 such that $s_1 \gg s_3$ and $s_2 \gg s_3$ and $u_1 \gg u_3$ and $u_2 \gg u_3$ and so let $t_3 = \{u_3/x\}s_3$. Finally, suppose that t is of the form $(\lambda x.s)\ u$ and t_1 is of the form $\{u_1/x\}s_1$ where $s \gg s_1$ and $u \gg u_1$. If t_2 is of the form $r_2\ u_2$ where $\lambda x.s \gg r_2$ and $u \gg u_2$ then the previous case applies, with the roles of t_1 and t_2 reversed. The remaining alternative is that t_2 is $\{u_2/x\}\ s_2$ where $s \gg s_2$ and $u \gg u_2$. By induction there are terms s_3 and u_3 such that $s_1 \gg s_3$ and $s_2 \gg s_3$ and also $u_1 \gg u_3$ and $u_2 \gg u_3$. Now apply Lemma 2.4. □

Corollary 2.6 (Confluence). *The reduction relation is confluent.*

Proof. The relation $\gg$ has the diamond property and so Lemma 2.2 implies that $\gg$ is confluent. Hence $\gg_*$ is confluent and so $\longrightarrow_*$ and $\longrightarrow$ are too, by Lemma 2.3. □

Confluence holds for all of the calculi and systems presented in Parts I and II. Throughout the book, it can be proved by a variant of the simultaneous reduction technique above but usually the proof is omitted.

2.5 Fixpoints

Here are some examples of pure λ-terms, including some that do not have normal forms. Throughout the book, words in monospace font with a leading lower-case letter will be used in examples, either as meta-variables for terms, such as `compose` or `fix`, or as *keywords* such as `if`, `then` and `else` in `if` b `then` s `else` t.

Example 2.7. Function Composition

The identity function has already been mentioned. The *composition* of two functions f and g can be defined by $\lambda x.g\ (f\ x)$. More generally, composition can be represented by the term $\texttt{compose} = \lambda g.\lambda f.\lambda x.g\ (f\ x)$. It is convenient to write this as

$$\texttt{compose}\ g\ f\ x = g\ (f\ x)$$

in which the initial bindings on the right are converted to applications (to symbols) on the left.

Example 2.8. Conditionals

Define the booleans

$$\begin{aligned} \texttt{true} &= \lambda x.\lambda y.x \\ \texttt{false} &= \lambda x.\lambda y.y \end{aligned}$$

to be the functions that return the first or second of two arguments. Then the *conditional*

$$\texttt{if}\ b\ \texttt{then}\ s\ \texttt{else}\ t$$

is just $b\ s\ t$ since $\texttt{true}\ s\ t$ reduces to s and $\texttt{false}\ s\ t$ reduces to t. Boolean operators can then be defined in the usual way. For example, the *conjunction* of terms s and t is given by

$$\texttt{conjunction}\ s\ t = \texttt{if}\ s\ \texttt{then}\ t\ \texttt{else}\ \texttt{false}.$$

Example 2.9. Non-termination

The simplest example of a term without a normal form is

$$(\lambda x.x\ x)\ (\lambda x.x\ x)$$

which reduces to itself. It contains two examples of self-application, of x to itself, and then of $\lambda x.x\ x$ to itself. The nature of self-application is rather curious. Is it reasonable for a function to be able to self-apply? One way of investigating this is by considering type systems, the subject of Part II, since they can be used to block such constructions.

Example 2.10. Recursion

Non-termination is not always bad, however, as it is essential for general recursion. This can be expressed in various ways but the focus here is on fixpoints. Mathematically, t is a *fixpoint* for a function f if

$$t = f\ t\ .$$

Here, it is enough that both sides have a common reduct. To get a fixpoint $\texttt{fix}\ f$ of a λ-term f define

$$\begin{aligned} \texttt{fix0} &= \lambda f.\lambda x.f\ (x\ x) \\ \texttt{fix} &= \lambda f.(\texttt{fix0}\ f)\ (\texttt{fix0}\ f)\ . \end{aligned}$$

Now $\texttt{fix}\ f$ reduces to $(\texttt{fix0}\ f)\ (\texttt{fix0}\ f)$ which reduces to $f\ ((\texttt{fix0}\ f)\ (\texttt{fix0}\ f))$ i.e. to f applied to itself.

It is convenient to write

$$f\ x = \ldots f \ldots$$

instead of $\texttt{fix}\ (\lambda f.\lambda x.\ldots f\ldots)$. That is, if the declared symbol f appears free in the right-hand side then it refers to the defined function itself, so that the definition is given by a fixpoint.

Of course, reduction of $\texttt{fix}\ f$ need not terminate since expansion of $\texttt{fix}\ f$ can be repeated indefinitely. In practice, one must adopt an evaluation strategy in which one seeks to evaluate f first, only evaluating the inner copy of $\texttt{fix}\ f$ if forced to do so. A curious aspect of this construction is the self-application $x\,x$ appearing in `fix`.

2.6 Notes

The first paper to use the λ-binding was written by Alonzo Church in 1932 [18]. The following quotation gives the flavour of the work, and its relationship to logic ($\sim$ denotes negation):

> The formula which leads to the paradox may be written, in the notation explained below, $\{\lambda\phi.\sim\phi(\phi)\}(\lambda\phi.\sim\phi(\phi))$. It has the property that if we assume $\sim\mathbf{P}$ then we can infer $\mathbf{P}$ and if we assume $\mathbf{P}$ then we can infer $\sim\mathbf{P}$.

He reformulated the ideas in 1936 [19] as an approach to computation, to produce an undecidability result. It also established the Church–Rosser theorem on uniqueness of normal forms. At about the same time, Turing published his seminal paper on computability by Turing machines [99] which was seen to be computationally equivalent to the λ-calculus, as expressed by Church's Theorem [100]. The first book on λ-calculus was published by Church in 1941 [21]. The most comprehensive book on λ-calculus is by Barendregt [6]. Other, more accessible books are by Hindley and Seldin [42] and Hankin [38]. Rosser [91] wrote a history of the subject.

λ-calculus underpins the design of the untyped programming language Lisp in 1958 (but see also Chap. 3). Its theoretical importance for functional programming was crystallised by Landin [71] whose language ISWIM was described using the SECD machine. Later developments tended to emphasise typed λ-calculus.

Finding mathematical models of pure λ-calculus is not easy since there is nothing to stop a function being applied to itself. Set-theoretic models are not adequate, but Dana Scott developed models using lattices and ordered sets, which became the mathematical (or denotational) semantics of [93].

Although the original proof of the Church–Rosser property by Church and Rosser was reported by Church [19] there have been many other proof techniques developed since then. The use of simultaneous reduction was developed by Tait and Martin-Löf in the late 1960s, as explained in [6].

Reduction in the λ-calculus can be seen as an important example of *term rewriting* (e.g. [3, 102]) in which the concepts of confluence, the Church–Rosser property, etc. can be explored in a way that allows general results to be established for classes of calculi.

There are many ways of defining fixpoint functions in pure λ-calculus. The one given here is Curry's Y combinator [25].

Chapter 3
Data Structures

Abstract This chapter begins with a basic account of data structures, with their constructor and operators. These can be encoded in pure λ-calculus by treating a data structure as a higher-order function that acts on functions that require the data in the structure. Compound calculus simplifies the presentation by using generic operations (derived from Lisp) to provide a uniform collection of operators.

3.1 Constructors and Operators

Having introduced functions, the next step is to consider data structures upon which functions can act, such as numbers, pairs, lists and various sorts of trees (but not arrays, sets or graphs). The simplest way to add data structures to the λ-calculus is by introducing an ad hoc collection of term constants, which are a mix of *constructors* and *operators*. Operators come with associated reduction rules in which they appear at the head of the redex (the left-hand side of a reduction rule). All other constants are *constructors*. This approach has the disadvantage that each new operator increases the number of reduction rules. Hence, to prove results about such a system, e.g. confluence, it is necessary to make assumptions about the operators.

One way to avoid this is to encode the data structures within the λ-calculus. The most direct approach is to treat each data structure as a higher-order function using the *Church encoding*. For example, a pair can service any function needing two arguments while a list can service any function accepting a finite sequence of arguments. This approach does away with additional reduction rules, so that properties of the pure λ-calculus suffice. However, it is quite unable to support operations that apply uniformly to all data structures, unless these also apply uniformly to all functions. In particular, operations such as equality, or searching or querying, that make perfectly good sense for arbitrary data structures, cannot be defined for arbitrary abstractions, so that these must be defined separately for pairs, lists and trees.

Another way of containing the calculus is to accept an unspecified collection of constructors but to act on them using a fixed collection of operators. The result is the

DOI 10.1007/978-3-540-89185-7_3,

compound calculus. Its operators correspond to the fundamental operations of the programming language Lisp, the main difference being that in Lisp *symbols* serve as both variables and constructors, so that its notion of data structure is not stable. Although the collection of constructors is unspecified, it is possible, in principle, to manage with just one constructor, since its compounds can be used to encode all the others.

3.2 Ad Hoc Operators

Throughout the book, constructors and operators will be represented by words in monospace font: constructors will have a leading upper-case letter, as in `True` or `Nil`, while operators will lead with a lower-case letter, as in `isZero`. The letter c is a meta-variable for a constructor. Church encodings of the booleans, `true` and `false`, conditionals, fixpoints etc. are as given in Sect. 2.5.

Here are some examples of constructors and operators and their use in λ-calculus. The notation exploits the conventions developed in Sect. 2.5.

Example 3.1. Pairs

Pairs can be constructed using the constructor `Pair` so that the pair of terms s and t is given by `Pair` $s\,t$. The corresponding *eliminators* are `fst` and `snd` (the first and second projections, respectively) with the reduction rules

$$\begin{aligned} \texttt{fst}\ (\texttt{Pair}\ s\,t) &\longrightarrow s \\ \texttt{snd}\ (\texttt{Pair}\ s\,t) &\longrightarrow t\,. \end{aligned}$$

Example 3.2. Natural Numbers

The *unary natural numbers* can be constructed from a *constructors* `Zero` representing zero, and a constructor `Successor` for creating successors, so that the numeral two can be defined as `Successor (Successor Zero)`. Let $\overline{n}$ be shorthand for the nth numeral, so that $\overline{0} = \texttt{Zero}$ and $\overline{1} = \texttt{Successor Zero}$, etc. The most fundamental query for numbers is the *zero test* operator `isZero` with reduction rules

$$\begin{aligned} \texttt{isZero Zero} &\longrightarrow \texttt{true} \\ \texttt{isZero}\ (\texttt{Successor}\ t) &\longrightarrow \texttt{false}\,. \end{aligned}$$

The other basic operator is the *predecessor* given by the constant `pred` whose reduction rule is

$$\texttt{pred}\ (\texttt{Successor}\ t) \longrightarrow t\,.$$

Now *addition* can be defined by the recursive function

$$\texttt{plusNat}\ x\ y = \texttt{if isZero}\ y\ \texttt{then}\ x\ \texttt{else plusNat}\ (\texttt{Successor}\ x)\ (\texttt{pred}\ y)\,.$$

An example of the use of `plusNat` is given by

$$\begin{aligned}\texttt{plusNat}\ \overline{1}\ \overline{2} &\longrightarrow_* \texttt{plusNat}\ \overline{2}\ \overline{1}\\ &\longrightarrow_* \texttt{plusNat}\ \overline{3}\ \overline{0}\\ &\longrightarrow_* \overline{3}\,.\end{aligned}$$

Example 3.3. Lists

Every list is either an *empty* or *nil* list, given by the constructor `Nil` or has a head and a tail, combined using the constructor `Cons`. The associated operators are `isNil`, `head` and `tail` with reduction rules

$$\begin{aligned}\texttt{isNil}\ \texttt{Nil} &\longrightarrow \texttt{true}\\ \texttt{isNil}\ (\texttt{Cons}\ h\ t) &\longrightarrow \texttt{false}\\ \texttt{head}\ (\texttt{Cons}\ h\ t) &\longrightarrow h\\ \texttt{tail}\ (\texttt{Cons}\ h\ t) &\longrightarrow t\,.\end{aligned}$$

For example, the *append* of lists is given by

$$\texttt{append}\ x\ y = \texttt{if}\ \texttt{isNil}\ x\ \texttt{then}\ y\ \texttt{else}\ \texttt{Cons}\ (\texttt{head}\ x)\ (\texttt{append}\ (\texttt{tail}\ x)\ y)$$

so that, for example, append $(\texttt{Cons}\ \overline{2}\ \texttt{Nil})\ (\texttt{Cons}\ \overline{1}\ (\texttt{Cons}\ \overline{0}\ \texttt{Nil}))$ reduces to the list $\texttt{Cons}\ \overline{2}\ (\texttt{Cons}\ \overline{1}\ (\texttt{Cons}\ \overline{0}\ \texttt{Nil}))$.

Example 3.4. Binary Trees

Binary trees can be built from constructors `Leaf` and `Node` with eliminators `isLeaf`, `getLeaf`, `left` and `right` with reduction rules

$$\begin{aligned}\texttt{isLeaf}\ (\texttt{Leaf}\ t) &\longrightarrow \texttt{true}\\ \texttt{isLeaf}\ (\texttt{Node}\ s\ t) &\longrightarrow \texttt{false}\\ \texttt{getLeaf}\ (\texttt{Leaf}\ t) &\longrightarrow t\\ \texttt{left}\ (\texttt{Node}\ s\ t) &\longrightarrow s\\ \texttt{right}\ (\texttt{Node}\ s\ t) &\longrightarrow t\,.\end{aligned}$$

Example 3.5. Alternatives

Just as natural numbers are either zero or successors, lists are either empty or have a head, and trees are either leaves or nodes, one may consider *alternatives* in a more general way, by introducing constructors `Inl` and `Inr` (*left* and *right inclusion*, respectively) and an *alternative* operator `alt` with reduction rules

$$\begin{aligned}\texttt{alt}\ f\ g\ (\texttt{Inl}\ s) &\longrightarrow f\ s\\ \texttt{alt}\ f\ g\ (\texttt{Inr}\ t) &\longrightarrow g\ t.\end{aligned}$$

3.3 Data Structures as Abstractions

Although the pure λ-calculus is a theory of functions, it supports encodings of data structures. The traditional encoding describes data structures as functions that describe how to use the data stored within them. Here are some examples.

Example 3.6. Pairs

The pair of the term s and t is given by $\texttt{pair}\ s\ t$ where

$$\texttt{pair} = \lambda x.\lambda y.\lambda f.f\ x\ y\ .$$

If f acts on two arguments then it can be converted into a function that acts on a pair, namely

$$\lambda z.z\ f\ .$$

Note how the constructor `Pair` (with a leading uppercase letter) is represented by the function `pair` (with a leading lowercase letter). For example, the *first and second projections* are given by

$$\begin{aligned} \texttt{fst} &= \lambda z.z\ \texttt{true} \\ \texttt{snd} &= \lambda z.z\ \texttt{false} \end{aligned}$$

since $\texttt{fst}\ (\texttt{pair}\ s\ t) \rightarrow_* (\lambda f.f\ s\ t)\ \texttt{true} \rightarrow_* \texttt{true}\ s\ t \rightarrow_* s$.

Example 3.7. Alternatives

Similarly, define coproduct inclusions and alternatives by

$$\begin{aligned} \texttt{inl} &= \lambda x.\lambda f.\lambda g.f\ x \\ \texttt{inr} &= \lambda y.\lambda f.\lambda g.g\ y \\ \texttt{alt} &= \lambda f.\lambda g.\lambda z.z\ f\ g\ . \end{aligned}$$

Then

$$\begin{aligned} \texttt{alt}\ f\ g\ (\texttt{inl}\ s) &\rightarrow_* \texttt{inl}\ s\ f\ g \rightarrow_* f\ s \\ \texttt{alt}\ f\ g\ (\texttt{inr}\ t) &\rightarrow_* \texttt{inr}\ t\ f\ g \rightarrow_* g\ t \end{aligned}$$

as expected.

Example 3.8. Natural Numbers

The natural numbers can be represented as *Church numerals* where the numeral n is represented by the nth *iterator*, so that

$$\overline{n} = \lambda f.\lambda x.f^n(x)$$

where $f^n(x)$ is $f\ (f\ \dots (f\ x)\dots)$ that applies f some n times. In this way, `Zero` and `Successor` are represented by

$$\begin{aligned} \texttt{zero} &= \lambda f.\lambda x.x \\ \texttt{successor} &= \lambda n.\lambda f.\lambda x.f\ (n\ f\ x)\ . \end{aligned}$$

Now addition can be defined by

$$\texttt{plusNat} = \lambda m.\lambda n.\lambda f.\lambda x.m\ f\ (n\ f\ x)$$

since this gives the iterator which applies f n times and then m times. Similarly, multiplication is given by

$$\texttt{times} = \lambda m.\lambda n.\lambda f.m\ (n\ f)$$

as it iterates the n-fold iterate of f some m times.

The operator isZero is given by $\lambda m.m\ (\lambda x.\texttt{false})\ \texttt{true}$ in which the iterated function will convert true to false if it is applied at all. The predecessor of a number m is surprisingly hard to define by iteration. A naive attempt would be like the following instructions for leaving a train: "Upon arrival at station m, get off at the previous stop." For this to work, you need two co-ordinated trains, one travelling a station behind the other. Now the instructions become "When the first train gets to station m, get off the second train." That is, the iterated function must act on pairs. Define

$$g = \lambda z.z\ (\lambda x.\lambda y.\texttt{pair}\ y\ (\texttt{successor}\ y))$$

so that g (pair s t) reduces to pair t (successor t) from which s has been discarded. Then, given a Church numeral m it follows that

$$(\texttt{successor}\ m)\ g\ (\texttt{pair zero zero})$$

reduces to pair m (successor m) whose first component is the predecessor of successor m. In general, the predecessor is given by

$$\texttt{pred} = \lambda m.\texttt{fst}\ (m\ g\ (\texttt{pair zero zero}))\ .$$

For example, subtraction is defined by $\texttt{minus} = \lambda m.\lambda n.n\ \texttt{pred}\ m$ which maps m and n to the nth *predecessor* of m. Also, the factorial function can be defined by

$$\texttt{factorial}\ n = \texttt{if isZero}\ n\ \texttt{then}\ \overline{1}\ \texttt{else times}\ n\ (\texttt{factorial}\ (\texttt{pred}\ n)))\ .$$

Its behaviour is illustrated by:

$$\begin{aligned}\texttt{factorial}\ \overline{2} &\longrightarrow (\lambda n.\texttt{if isZero}\ n\ \texttt{then}\ \overline{1}\\ &\qquad \texttt{else times}\ n\ \texttt{factorial}\ (\texttt{pred}\ n))\ \overline{2}\\ &\longrightarrow \texttt{if isZero}\ \overline{2}\ \texttt{then}\ \overline{1}\\ &\qquad \texttt{else times}\ \overline{2}\ (\texttt{factorial}\ (\texttt{pred}\ \overline{2}))\\ &\longrightarrow \texttt{times}\ \overline{2}\ (\texttt{factorial}\ \overline{1})\\ &\longrightarrow \texttt{times}\ \overline{2}\ \overline{1} \longrightarrow \overline{2}\ .\end{aligned}$$

Example 3.9. Lists

Lists are constructed using

$$\begin{aligned}\texttt{nil} &= \lambda z.\lambda f.z\\ \texttt{cons} &= \lambda x.\lambda y.\lambda z.\lambda f.f\ x\ (y\ z\ f)\ .\end{aligned}$$

Thus `cons` $x\ y$ is a function of two arguments z and f. The term z acts as a seed value, to be returned if the list is empty, while f acts on the head x of the list, and then the result $y\ z\ f$ of "iterating" f over y. For example, `cons` x `nil` $z\ f$ reduces to $f\ x\ z$. The corresponding operators are defined much as are those for natural numbers, with the tail of the list being defined much like the predecessor.

Example 3.10. Binary Trees
Similarly, binary trees can be constructed using

$$\begin{aligned}\texttt{leaf} &= \lambda z.\lambda f.z\\ \texttt{node} &= \lambda x.\lambda y.\lambda z.\lambda f.f\ (x\ z\ f)\ (y\ z\ f).\end{aligned}$$

Now "iteration" employs a function of two arguments, representing the results coming from the left and right subtrees of a tree.

3.4 Compound Calculus

The approaches of the last two sections are able to handle all pairs in a uniform manner, and all lists in a uniform manner, etc. but are not able to handle all data structures together in a uniform manner. For example, there is no mechanism for computing the size of an arbitrary structure that could be a pair or a list or a tree.

Such examples require a uniform account of data structures, which arises from the following observation. Every data structure is either an *atom* (such as `Zero`, `Nil`, `Cons`, `Leaf` or `Node`) or a *compound* (such as `Cons` u or `Cons` $u\ v$ or `Leaf` u) built by application. This structure can be exploited by operations that test for constructor equality, for being a compound, and for extracting the components of a compound.

For example, the second component operator, `cdr`, recovers the second projection from a pair, the tail of a list, a leaf value, or the right branch of a tree. Binary constructors require a little more work. For example, `car` (`Cons` $u\ v$) is `Cons` u so that `cdr` must be applied to recover the head u of the list. Constructors with more arguments can be handled similarly. Of course, `car` and `cdr` are famous as operators of Lisp, but the treatment here will be slightly different.

As well as extracting components, it is necessary to be able to recognise constructors and compounds. For each constructor c and term t the term c `eqa` t tests to see if t is c. Also, `pair?` t is true if t is a compound. This is enough to proceed.

The *term syntax* of the *compound calculus* is given by

$$
\begin{array}{lll}
t ::= & & \text{(term)} \\
& x & \text{(variable)} \\
& t\ t & \text{(application)} \\
& \lambda x.t & \text{(abstraction)} \\
& c & \text{(constructor)} \\
& c\ \mathtt{eqa}\ t & \text{(constructor equality)} \\
& \mathtt{pair?}\ t & \text{(compound test)} \\
& \mathtt{car}\ t & \text{(first component)} \\
& \mathtt{cdr}\ t & \text{(second component).}
\end{array}
$$

The novel term forms do not bind any symbols, so that the syntactic machinery generalises that of the pure λ-calculus in the obvious manner, as described in the appendix. Once again the *explicit functions* are the abstractions. The key point is to characterise the atoms and compounds. This is not quite trivial as application is now being used to *build* data structures as well as to *eliminate* abstractions. In principle, one could distinguish these two uses of application. For example, the compound of terms u and v could be written $u.v$ but actually the "dot" then behaves just like a constructor (written between its two arguments), so it seems more natural not to give it a special status.

Throughout the book, the *data structures* (meta-variable d) are given by the terms whose head is a constructor. For untyped calculi these are given by

$$
\begin{array}{lll}
d ::= & & \text{(data structure)} \\
& c & \text{(constructor)} \\
& d\ t & \text{(compound).}
\end{array}
$$

Throughout the book, a *matchable form* is either a data structure or an explicit function. Matchable forms which are not compounds are *atoms*. Note that any term can appear within a data structure simply by applying a constructor to it. This allows pairs or lists of functions to be data structures. Also, every explicit function is an atom. This is a little counter-intuitive, but it is appropriate here since, unlike compounds, explicit functions are indivisible. The alternative names, of "divisibles" and "indivisibles", don't have the same ring. A *pure data structure* is a data structure built purely from constructors. Many generic operations, such as equality, will only succeed on pure data structures.

The *reduction rules* of the compound calculus are given in Fig. 3.1. Then the reduction relation is the corresponding congruence (defined by augmenting the rewriting relation of Fig. 2.1 with rules for the new term forms) and general reduction are defined as in Figs. 2.1 and 2.2.

Theorem 3.11 (Confluence). *Reduction in the compound calculus is confluent.*

Proof. The proof is by simultaneous reduction, much as in Theorem 2.6. Note that the side conditions on the reduction rules are essential here. For example,

$$\mathtt{pair?}\ ((\lambda x.\mathtt{false})\ \mathtt{false}) \longrightarrow \mathtt{pair?}\ \mathtt{false} \longrightarrow \mathtt{false}$$

$$
\begin{array}{rlll}
(\lambda x.s)\ u & \longrightarrow \{u/x\}s & & (\beta) \\
\texttt{car}\ (u\ v) & \longrightarrow u & \text{if } u\ v \text{ is a compound} & (\text{car}) \\
\texttt{cdr}\ (u\ v) & \longrightarrow v & \text{if } u\ v \text{ is a compound} & (\text{cdr}) \\
\texttt{pair?}\ (u\ v) & \longrightarrow \texttt{true} & \text{if } u\ v \text{ is a compound} & (\text{ispair}) \\
\texttt{pair?}\ u & \longrightarrow \texttt{false} & \text{if } u \text{ is an atom} & (\text{isatom}) \\
c\ \texttt{eqa}\ c & \longrightarrow \texttt{true} & & (\text{same}) \\
c\ \texttt{eqa}\ u & \longrightarrow \texttt{false} & \text{otherwise, if } u \text{ is matchable} & (\text{different}).
\end{array}
$$

Fig. 3.1 Compound calculus

but this would also so reduce to `true` if rule (ispair) were unrestricted. □

3.5 Defined Operators

The operators of the compound calculus are expressive enough to represent the various operators considered in Sect. 3.2. For example, the second projection of a pair t is given by `cdr` t. Of course, this does not check to see if the argument actually *is* a pair, so that `cdr Zero` is "stuck", being an irreducible closed term that is not a matchable form. This can be avoided by defining some error term `error` and replacing `cdr` t by

$$\texttt{if pair? } t \texttt{ then cdr } t \texttt{ else error.}$$

Of course, this approach quickly becomes cumbersome. For example, to safely obtain the head of a list (built using `Cons`) requires

```
λx. if pair? x
    then if pair? (car x)
         then if Cons eqa (car (car x))
              then cdr x
              else error
         else error
    else error.
```

In the next chapter, the compound calculus will be shown to be equivalent to the static pattern calculus, in which the head of a list can be written as the case

$$\texttt{Cons}\ x\ y \rightarrow x\,.$$

Given the dramatic simplification of terms that this entails, all further examples will be postponed until Sect. 4.6.

3.6 Notes

The encodings of pairs, etc. as abstractions formed part of the original account of λ-calculus, as described by Church in 1936 [19]. The Lisp programming language was developed by McCarthy in 1958 [74]. The second oldest programming language still in use, it has had a major impact in diverse areas of computing, and has given rise to various dialects, such as Scheme [92, 27]. Although the syntax is almost identical, Lisp uses symbols for both variables and constructors, so that the latter are not stable under reduction.

A distinction between constructors and operators can be found in *constructor term rewriting systems* [78] which constrain their rewriting rules to have redexes of the form $f(t_1,\ldots,t_n)$ where f is an operator and each t_i is either a variable or a constructor. Here it is enough to ensure that f is not a constructor. A detailed treatment of the compound calculus has been developed by Given-Wilson in [36].

Chapter 4
Static Patterns

Abstract Traditional accounts of pattern matching require nontrivial patterns to be headed by a constructor, but these are not expressive enough to model the compound calculus. The static pattern calculus admits a pattern that can match an arbitrary compound, and so can model generic queries. A new class of examples is introduced, led by generic mapping that generalises mapping on lists and trees. The static pattern calculus is slightly superior to compound calculus since its notation is more compact, and its treatment of match failure is more comprehensive. Also, it supports developments in subsequent chapters.

4.1 Patterns

Patterns provide a concise means of describing data structures of unlimited complexity, such as lists having at least three entries, or pairs of nonempty lists. Patterns are used to build *cases* of the form $p \rightarrow s$ where p is the pattern and s is the body. When such a case is applied to an argument u then p is matched against u to find a substitution that maps p to u. If successful, the substitution is applied to s. More generally, pattern-matching functions are built from sequences of cases. Then matching is attempted with each case in turn, until successful.

Pattern matching for data structures appears to have emerged as a mechanism to handle data of algebraic data type, so that pattern matching was constrained to fit the current understanding of types. In particular, all cases in a pattern-matching function were required to have the same type, and all nontrivial patterns were headed by a constructor. Unfortunately, this excludes the generic queries defined in the compound calculus, and much else besides. This chapter will show how the expressive power of the compound calculus can be captured by static patterns, i.e. patterns that are not evaluated, postponing the typing issues to Part II. The main novelty here will be showing how careful management of match failure allows a sequence of cases in a pattern-matching function to be represented by a single case, much as conditionals may be represented by an abstraction in pure λ-calculus.

B. Jay, *Pattern Calculus*,
DOI 10.1007/978-3-540-89185-7_4,

4.2 Static Pattern Calculus

The *static pattern calculus* has *pattern syntax* (meta-variables p,q) given by the grammar

$$\begin{array}{rll} p ::= & & \text{(static pattern)} \\ & x & \text{(matchable symbol)} \\ & c & \text{(constructor)} \\ & p\ p & \text{(application).} \end{array}$$

As patterns are partial descriptions of data structures, they should include the constructors and be closed under application. Also, there must be symbols to represent those components of the data structure which are not specified. Such symbols are not available for substitution – they are static – and so are *not* variables, but *matchable symbols* or *matchables* used in matching to create substitutions. In most calculi and programing languages, the context makes it clear whether a symbol is variable or matchable, but in Chap. 5 they will appear together, in dynamic patterns, so it is best to separate them clearly from the beginning.

The *term syntax* (meta-variables r,s,t,u,v) is given by the grammar

$$\begin{array}{rll} t ::= & & \text{(term)} \\ & x & \text{(variable)} \\ & c & \text{(constructor)} \\ & t\ t & \text{(application)} \\ & p \to t & \text{(case).} \end{array}$$

Most of the syntax is the same as in the λ-calculus and compound calculus. A case $p \to s$ has *pattern* p and *body* s. The *explicit functions* are the cases. The *free matchable symbols* $\mathsf{fm}(p)$ of a pattern p are defined in the obvious way. Note that it is a set of *symbols*, just as the free variables of a term form a set of symbols. The *free variables* of a case are given by

$$\mathsf{fv}(p \to s) = \mathsf{fv}(s) \setminus \mathsf{fm}(p).$$

α-equivalence is the congruence generated by

$$p \to s =_\alpha \{y/x\}p \to \{y/x\}s \quad \text{if } x \in \mathsf{fm}(p) \text{ and } y \notin \mathsf{fm}(p) \cup \mathsf{fv}(s).$$

A case of the form $x \to s$ corresponds to the abstraction $\lambda x.s$. A case of the form $c \to s$ has a pattern c which successfully matches only with itself. The pattern `Pair` $x\ y$ represents a pair, and `Cons` $x\ y$ represents a nonempty list. Most approaches to pattern matching are limited to the sorts of patterns above. By contrast, the static pattern calculus also allows patterns headed by a matchable symbol. These are used to represent `car` and `cdr` by

$$\begin{array}{ll} x\ y \to x & \text{and} \\ x\ y \to y & \end{array}$$

respectively. That is, the pattern $x\ y$ represents an arbitrary compound.

$$\begin{aligned}
\{u/x\} &= \mathsf{some}\ \{u/x\} \\
\{c/c\} &= \mathsf{some}\ \{\} \\
\{u\,v/p\,q\} &= \{u/p\} \uplus \{v/q\} && \text{if } u\,v \text{ is a compound} \\
\{u/p\} &= \mathsf{none} && \text{otherwise, if } u \text{ is matchable} \\
\{u/p\} &= \mathsf{undefined} && \text{otherwise}
\end{aligned}$$

Fig. 4.1 Static matching

4.3 Static Matching

Reduction is based on the match rule, which first generates a match and then applies it. A *match* is either a *successful match*, of the form some σ where σ is a term substitution, or a *failure*, denoted by none. A failed match is distinct from an undefined match, which may evolve to a success or failure. The application of a match to a term is defined by

$$\begin{aligned}
\mathsf{some}\ \sigma\ t &= \sigma t \\
\mathsf{none}\ t &= \mathtt{Nomatch}
\end{aligned}$$

where `Nomatch` is a designated constructor.

It may happen that a pattern contains two occurrences of the same matchable symbol, as in `Pair` x x. It is tempting to allow this to match any term of the form `Pair` u u but this is more trouble than it is worth. If u is a case then it is hard to determine its equality with another term while if u is a pure data structure then the equality test can be incorporated into the body of the case. On top of this, such nonlinearity can break confluence of reduction. For these reasons, unions of matches are required to be disjoint, as will now be defined.

If σ_1 and σ_2 are term substitutions with disjoint domains then their *disjoint union* $\sigma_1 \uplus \sigma_2$ is the substitution whose action on a symbol x is given by $\sigma_1(x)$ if defined, and by $\sigma_2(x)$ otherwise. The *disjoint union* of two matches (written using infix $\uplus$) is given as follows. $\mathsf{some}\ \sigma_1 \uplus \mathsf{some}\ \sigma_2 = \mathsf{some}\ (\sigma_1 \uplus \sigma_2)$ if σ_1 and σ_2 have disjoint domains. Otherwise, the disjoint union of (defined) matches is none. If either match is undefined then so is their disjoint union.

As in the compound calculus, a matchable form is either a data structure (headed by a constructor) or an explicit function (a case).

The *matching* $\{u/p\}$ of a pattern p against a term u is defined by applying the rules in Fig. 4.1 in order: In the middle three rules, the term must be a matchable form, i.e. either a data structure or an explicit function. This restriction is not imposed in the first rule as it corresponds to β-reduction in the λ-calculus, where any term u may be substituted for x. If none of the first four rules apply then matching is (temporarily) stuck, until evaluation of u produces a matchable form.

The reduction rule of the static pattern calculus is the *match rule*

$$(p \to s)\ u \longrightarrow \{u/p\}\ s \qquad \text{(match).}$$

Throughout the book, if the reduct of a rule is undefined then the rule cannot be applied. In particular, if the match $\{u/p\}$ is undefined then the rule above does not apply. The rule induces a corresponding reduction relation and rewriting relation in the usual way.

Theorem 4.1 (Confluence). *The reduction relation of the static pattern calculus is confluent.*

Proof. Use the simultaneous reduction technique as in Sect. 2.4. Alternatively, the later proof of Theorem 5.4 can be simplified. □

Theorem 4.2 (Progress). *Every closed irreducible term of the static pattern calculus is a matchable form. In particular, a closed term of the form* $(p \to s)\ u$ *is always reducible. That is, pattern matching cannot get stuck.*

Proof. The proof is by induction on the structure of the term. The only nontrivial situation is an application of a case as in the theorem. Now u is a closed irreducible term and so is matchable by induction, as are all of its components. Hence $\{u/p\}$ is defined. □

Note, by contrast, that reduction of the compound calculus can become stuck, as when evaluating `cdr` c for some constructor c.

4.4 Constructor Patterns

The most common sorts of patterns are constructor patterns, being those which are headed by a constructor. Here are some examples.

Example 4.3. Fixpoints Through Patterns

Clearly, the pure λ-calculus embeds into the static pattern calculus. However, many features can be expressed in novel ways. For example, any constructor can be used to define fixpoints, as follows. Let `Rec` be a designated constructor. Define

$$\texttt{omega} = \texttt{Rec}\ x \to x\ (\texttt{Rec}\ x).$$

Now `omega (Rec omega)` reduces to itself. This can be used to define a fixpoint operator, by

$$\texttt{fix} = f \to \texttt{omega}\ (\texttt{Rec}\ (x \to f\ (\texttt{omega}\ x)))$$

since then

$$\begin{aligned}\texttt{fix}\ f &\longrightarrow \texttt{omega}\ (\texttt{Rec}\ (x \to f\ (\texttt{omega}\ x)))\\ &\longrightarrow (x \to f\ (\texttt{omega}\ x))\ (\texttt{Rec}\ (x \to f\ (\texttt{omega}\ x)))\\ &\longrightarrow f\ (\texttt{omega}\ (\texttt{Rec}\ (x \to f\ (\texttt{omega}\ x))))\end{aligned}$$

which is a reduct of $f\ (\texttt{fix}\ f)$.

This will be of particular interest in Part II, since, unlike the fixpoint functions of pure λ-calculus, `Rec` will have a type, the same type as the fixpoint function it defines.

Example 4.4. Extensions

Pattern matching functions are frequently built from several cases. If the first case produces a successful match then it is used, else the next case is attempted. This can be expressed as a sequence of cases

$$\begin{array}{l} p_1 \to s_1 \\ \mid p_2 \to s_2 \\ \quad \dots \\ \mid p_n \to s_n \end{array}$$

where $\mid$ binds less strongly that application, and associates to the right so that this pattern-matching function is just $p_1 \to s_1 \mid r$ where r is given by the remaining cases. Hence it is enough to consider *extensions* of the form $p \to s \mid r$. Here p is the *pattern*, s is the *body* which together make the *special case* $p \to s$ and r is the *default*. Extensions should support the following reductions

$$\begin{array}{lll} (p \to s \mid r)\ u & \longrightarrow \sigma s & \text{if } \{u/p\} = \mathsf{some}\ \sigma \\ (p \to s \mid r)\ u & \longrightarrow r\ u & \text{if } \{u/p\} \text{ is } \mathsf{none}. \end{array}$$

This behaviour can be captured by defining extensions as follows:

$$p \to s \mid r = x \to (\texttt{Nomatch}\ y \to y)\ ((p \to z \to \texttt{Nomatch}\ s)\ x\ (r\ x))$$

where x, y and z are fresh symbols, i.e. not free in p, s or r. When applied to a matchable term u it reduces via

$$\begin{array}{ll} (p \to s \mid r)\ u & \longrightarrow (\texttt{Nomatch}\ y \to y)\ ((p \to z \to \texttt{Nomatch}\ s)\ u\ (r\ u)) \\ & \longrightarrow (\texttt{Nomatch}\ y \to y)\ (\{u/p\}(z \to \texttt{Nomatch}\ s)\ (r\ u)). \end{array}$$

Now if $\{u/p\}$ is $\mathsf{some}\ \sigma$ for some substitution σ then the term reduces to

$$\begin{array}{ll} (\texttt{Nomatch}\ y \to y)\ ((z \to \texttt{Nomatch}\ \sigma s)\ (r\ u)) & \longrightarrow (\texttt{Nomatch}\ y \to y)\ (\texttt{Nomatch}\ \sigma s) \\ & \longrightarrow \sigma s \end{array}$$

as desired. Alternatively, if $\{u/p\}$ is none then this reduces to

$$(\texttt{Nomatch}\ y \to y)\ (\texttt{Nomatch}\ (r\ u)) \longrightarrow r\ u$$

as desired. When using implicit types in Chap. 12, extensions will replace cases as the primitive term form, since they can carry more type information.

Example 4.5. Pairing

The projections associated to the constructor Pair can be given by

$$\begin{aligned}\texttt{fst} &= \texttt{Pair}\;x\;y \to x\\ \texttt{snd} &= \texttt{Pair}\;x\;y \to y.\end{aligned}$$

Example 4.6. Lists

Now introduce constructors Nil for the empty list and Cons for adding a new entry to the head of a list. For example, $\texttt{singleton} = x \to \texttt{Cons}\;x\;\texttt{Nil}$ builds singleton lists and the *append* of lists is defined by

$$\begin{aligned}&\texttt{append} =\\ &\quad \texttt{Nil} \to z \to z\\ &\mid \texttt{Cons}\;x\;y \to z \to \texttt{Cons}\;x\;(\texttt{append}\;y\;z)).\end{aligned}$$

For example,

$$\texttt{append}\;(\texttt{Cons}\;r\;\texttt{Nil})\;(\texttt{Cons}\;s\;(\texttt{Cons}\;t\;\texttt{Nil})) \longrightarrow \texttt{Cons}\;r\;(\texttt{Cons}\;s\;(\texttt{Cons}\;t\;\texttt{Nil})).$$

Mapping over a list is given by

$$\begin{aligned}&\texttt{mapList}\;f =\\ &\quad \texttt{Nil} \to \texttt{Nil}\\ &\mid \texttt{Cons}\;x\;y \to \texttt{Cons}\;(f\;x)\;(\texttt{mapList}\;f\;y).\end{aligned}$$

For example, $\texttt{mapList}\;f\;(\texttt{Cons}\;s\;(\texttt{Cons}\;t\;\texttt{Nil})) \longrightarrow \texttt{Cons}\;(f\;s)\;(\texttt{Cons}\;(f\;t)\;\texttt{Nil}))$.

Folding over a list is given by

$$\begin{aligned}&\texttt{foldleftList}\;f\;x =\\ &\quad \texttt{Nil} \to x\\ &\mid \texttt{Cons}\;y\;z \to \texttt{foldleftList}\;f\;(f\;x\;y)\;z\end{aligned}$$

For example, $\texttt{foldlefList}\;f\;r\;(\texttt{Cons}\;s\;(\texttt{Cons}\;t\;\texttt{Nil})) \longrightarrow f\;(f\;r\;s)\;t$.

Example 4.7. Binary trees

Given constructors Leaf and Node for binary trees then one may define mapTree analogously to mapList by

$$\begin{aligned}&\texttt{mapTree}\;f =\\ &\quad \texttt{Leaf}\;x \to \texttt{Leaf}\;(f\;x)\\ &\mid \texttt{Node}\;x\;y \to \texttt{Node}\;(\texttt{mapTree}\;f\;x)\;(\texttt{mapTree}\;f\;y)\end{aligned}$$

so that $\texttt{mapTree}\;f\;(\texttt{Node}\;(\texttt{Leaf}\;5)\;(\texttt{Leaf}\;6)) \longrightarrow \texttt{Node}\;(\texttt{Leaf}\;(f\;5))\;(\texttt{Leaf}\;(f\;6))$.

4.5 Generic Mapping

The two mapping functions mapList and mapTree of Sect. 4.4 can be combined into a single function

```
mapListTree f =
  Leaf x → Leaf (f x)
| Node x y → Node (mapListTree f x) (mapListTree f y)
| Nil → Nil
| Cons x y → Cons (f x) (mapListTree f y)
```

that will map over lists or trees. Of course, this is rather ad hoc. There is no apparent reason why the list and tree cases should be combined in this way, and it will create challenges for the type systems (see Sect. 8.6). More generally, it would seem that each new data type will require yet more cases, so that the terms like that for mapping will be large and unstable.

However, it is possible to define a single mapping function that works for a large class of data structures. This will be achieved by *deconstructing* the data structure to its representing data structure, then applying a structural version of mapping, called map0, and finally *reconstructing* the resulting data structure from its representation. Let us consider this through the example of lists.

If the list is of the form Cons x y then the mapping should apply f to x and *map* f over y. Introduce a constructor

Ths

to indicate that its argument is data to be acted on. That is, mapping f over the representing structure Ths x returns Ths $(f\ x)$. For the tail, y apply the constructor

Ok

so that applying map0 f to Ok y returns Ok (map f y) in which the standard mapping is applied to y. That is, y must now be deconstructed, etc.

The representations of x and y are combined by applying the parametrised pairing

ParamPair

both of whose arguments are to have mapping applied. Thus, the underlying data structure representing Cons x y is

ParamPair (Ths x) (Ok y).

Although this has captured the structure of the data, it fails to distinguish data structures that have the same representation. The structure must be tagged with this information, using the constructor

Tag

so that the representation of our cons-list is

$$\texttt{Tag Cons\_name (ParamPair (Ths } x\texttt{) (Ok } y\texttt{))}.$$

Now the mapping ignores the tags so that map0 f (Tag n x) is Tag n (map0 f x).

Finally, consider the representation of Nil. That it contains no data to be acted upon is expressed by the constructor

$$\texttt{Evr}$$

so that the representation of Nil is

$$\texttt{Tag Nil\_name (Evr Un)}$$

where Un is used to indicate that Nil does not contain any data at all, whether to be acted upon or not.

Summarising, the *representing*, or *primitive* constructors required for lists are

$$\texttt{Evr, Ths, ParamPair, Ok, Tag.}$$

This list is not truly comprehensive, since it only considers the most common uses of data to be mapped.

The definition of map and of map0 are given by mutual recursion. That of map is

$$\texttt{map } f\ x = \texttt{reconstruct (deconstruct } x\ \texttt{(map0 } f\texttt{))}.$$

The terms deconstruct and reconstruct are given by pattern-matching functions with a case for each constructor. Their nature will be discussed in more detail when describing algebraic data types in **bondi**. The definition of map0 is given by

$$
\begin{array}{l}
\texttt{map0 } f = \\
\quad \texttt{Evr } x \rightarrow \texttt{Evr } x \\
\mid \texttt{Ths } x \rightarrow \texttt{Ths } (f\ x) \\
\mid \texttt{Ok } x \rightarrow \texttt{Ok (map } f\ x) \\
\mid \texttt{ParamPair } x\ y \rightarrow \texttt{ParamPair (map0 } f\ x\texttt{) (map0 } f\ y) \\
\mid \texttt{Tag } n\ x \rightarrow \texttt{Tag } n\ \texttt{(map0 } f\ x).
\end{array}
$$

Many other list functions, such as foldleftList, can be similarly generalised, as described in Chap. 14.

4.6 Generic Queries

Till now, the examples in this chapter have all involved patterns headed by a constructor, so that a nontrivial pattern may match against a pair or a list, but not both. Here are some examples of queries that treat all compounds uniformly.

Example 4.8. Size

The simplest measure of a data structure is given by

```
size =
  x y → plusNat (size x) (size y)
| x → 1̄.
```

As mentioned before, this can be modified so that natural numbers all have size $\overline{1}$ by

```
size =
  Successor x → 1̄
| x y → plusNat (size x) (size y)
| x → 1̄ .
```

Example 4.9. Selecting

Selecting is achieved by

```
select f x =
(if f x
then Cons x
else (y → y)) ((
  z y → append (select f x z) (select f x y)
| y → Nil) x) .
```

The last two lines perform the path polymorphism. For example, if the argument is a compound then the results of selecting on each component are appended. Then the test f is applied to the whole term x. If $f\ x$ holds then x is added to the head of the list of results.

Example 4.10. Applying to All

The function `apply2all` is given by

```
apply2all f =
  x y → f ((apply2all f x) (apply2all f y))
| f.
```

This is like `select` in that the function f is applied to the whole argument, as well as any components it might have.

Example 4.11. Updating Salaries

When f is a function for increasing salaries, as in the motivating example of Sect. 1.2, then `apply2all` f could increase all employee salaries in the organisation's data structure. In a sense, this is the heart of the solution, but there are several unresolved issues. One is that this solution makes a copy of the data, rather than updating it, as will be addressed in Chap. 17. A second is that the solution is not typed, as will be addressed in Part II. A third is that it does not accept an object-oriented method for increasing salaries, as developed in Chap. 6.

Example 4.12. Folding

The examples size and select and apply2all can all be thought of as *folds* in the following sense. Define a generic fold operation

$$\begin{aligned}&\texttt{fold}\, f\, g =\\ &\quad x\, y \to f\ (\texttt{fold}\, f\, g\, x)\ (\texttt{fold}\, f\, g\, y)\\ &\mid x \to g\, x.\end{aligned}$$

Now, we have the derived reduction rules

$$\begin{aligned}\texttt{fold}\, f\, g\, (u\, v) &\longrightarrow f\ (\texttt{fold}\, f\, g\, u)\ (\texttt{fold}\, f\, g\, v) \quad \text{if } u\, v \text{ is a compound}\\ \texttt{fold}\, f\, g\, u &\longrightarrow g\, u \text{ if } u \text{ is an atom}\end{aligned}$$

and the examples above can be redefined by

$$\begin{aligned}\texttt{size} &= \texttt{fold plusNat}\ (\lambda x.\overline{1})\\ \texttt{apply2all}\, f &= \texttt{fold}\ (\lambda x.\lambda y.f\ (x\, y))\ f\, .\end{aligned}$$

Further, select can be defined by

$$\texttt{select}\, f\, x = \texttt{snd}\ (\texttt{fold}\, g\, h\ (\texttt{Pair}\, x\, \texttt{Nil}))$$

where

$$h = \texttt{Pair}\, x\, xs \to \texttt{if}\ f\, x\ \texttt{then Cons}\, x\, \texttt{Nil else Nil}$$

but g is a little harder to define. Informally, it is given by

$$\begin{aligned}g = {}&\texttt{Pair}\, x\, xs \to \texttt{Pair}\, y\, ys \to\\ &\texttt{Pair}\ (x\, y)\\ &\quad ((\texttt{if}\ f\ (x\, y)\ \texttt{then Cons}\ (x\, y)\ \texttt{else}\ \lambda z.z)\\ &\qquad (\texttt{append}\, xs\, ys))\, .\end{aligned}$$

That is, if both its arguments are pairs, then extract their components x, xs, y and ys and proceed as in the right-hand side. Otherwise, return error. The pairs are here used to maintain information about the argument of select as well as the results, so that components are available for recombination and testing. This is in the spirit of the earlier encoding of predecessor.

Although the generic fold is here defined using fixpoints it can be thought of as a form of primitive recursion, in which special cases for zero and successors are generalised to atoms and compounds. This will be formalised in the *query calculus* of Chap. 9.

4.7 Relating to Compound Calculus

The operators of the compound calculus can be interpreted in the static pattern calculus by

$$\begin{aligned}
c\ \texttt{eqa}\ t &= (c \rightarrow \texttt{true} \mid x \rightarrow \texttt{false})\ t \\
\texttt{pair?}\ t &= (x\ y \rightarrow \texttt{true} \mid x \rightarrow \texttt{false})\ t \\
\texttt{car}\ t &= (x\ y \rightarrow x)\ t \\
\texttt{cdr}\ t &= (x\ y \rightarrow y)\ t.
\end{aligned}$$

Conversely, there is a translation of the static pattern calculus into the compound calculus so that the two calculi are almost identical in expressive power. The main benefit of the pattern calculus is that a single mechanism, pattern matching, supplants a family of (apparently, ad hoc) operators in the latter calculus, while providing a more compact notation.

Theorem 4.13. *There is a translation of the static pattern calculus to the compound calculus that preserves reduction and maps distinct normal forms to distinct normal forms.*

Proof. In the translation below, compound patterns will be decomposed in a way that risks losing track of matchable symbols that appear twice in a pattern. Call such patterns *nonlinear.*

The translation is given by

$$\begin{aligned}
[\![x]\!] &= x \\
[\![c]\!] &= c \\
[\![r\ u]\!] &= [\![r]\!]\ [\![u]\!] \\
[\![p \rightarrow s]\!] &= \lambda x.\texttt{Nomatch} \quad \text{if } p \text{ is nonlinear} \\
[\![x \rightarrow s]\!] &= \lambda x.[\![s]\!] \\
[\![c \rightarrow s]\!] &= \lambda x.\texttt{if}\ c\ \texttt{eqa}\ x\ \texttt{then}\ [\![s]\!]\ \texttt{else Nomatch} \\
[\![p\ q \rightarrow s]\!] &= \lambda x.\texttt{if pair?}\ x \\
&\qquad \texttt{then}\ [\![p \rightarrow q \rightarrow s]\!]\ (\texttt{car}\ x)\ (\texttt{cdr}\ x) \\
&\qquad \texttt{else Nomatch}.
\end{aligned}$$

If σ is a term substitution then $[\![\sigma]\!]$ is the substitution defined by $[\![\sigma]\!](x) = [\![\sigma(x)]\!]$.

That the translation preserves reduction amounts to showing that $[\![(p \rightarrow s)\ u]\!]$ reduces to $\{[\![u/p]\!]\}[\![s]\!]$. The proof is by induction on the structure of p. If the match $\{u/p\}$ is none or p is a variable or constructor or is nonlinear then the result follows directly. If p is a linear application $p_1\ p_2$ and u is an application $u_1\ u_2$ then

$$\begin{aligned}
[\![(p \rightarrow s)\ u]\!] &\longrightarrow [\![(p_1 \rightarrow p_2 \rightarrow s)\ u_1\ u_2]\!] \\
&\longrightarrow \{[\![u_1/p_1]\!]\}[\![(p_2 \rightarrow s)\ u_2]\!] \\
&\longrightarrow \{[\![u_1/p_1]\!]\}\{[\![u_2/p_2]\!]\}[\![s]\!] \\
&= \{[\![u/p]\!]\}\ [\![s]\!]
\end{aligned}$$

by two applications of induction.

That the translation preserves (distinct) normal forms follows by induction on the structure of the form which is a matchable form by Theorem 4.2. □

4.8 Notes

Patterns are a popular concept in computing and programming. This chapter is concerned with *pattern matching* as distinct from *pattern recognition* (which extracts patterns from data, commonly by means of heuristics) or *design patterns* (semi-formal programming paradigms) [32].

The earliest work on pattern matching concerned string matching, which will be addressed in the Sect. 5.5.

The logic programming language **Prolog** [73] developed around 1972 is based on resolution of Horn clauses, which can also be viewed as a form of pattern matching.

Pattern matching on trees [46] arose to support the use of algebraic data types, which will be addressed in Chap. 14. Partly in response to the work in typed languages, pattern matching was encoded in Scheme [107]. By this time, the typed view was so entrenched that the connection to `car` and `cdr` was not noticed.

Pattern matching is also central to rewriting theory [102, 3] when developed as a basis for programming. Given a rewriting rule $l \rightarrow r$ then $\sigma l \rightarrow \sigma r$ for any substitution σ. To base a programming language on this requires pattern matching to discover the appropriate substitution. Such languages include **Mathematica**, first released in 1988 [106] and also **Maude** developed in the early 1990s [24]. In the same spirit, **Tom** [98, 5] allows rewriting rules to be added to existing languages, especially Java.

In the 1990s there were various attempts to put pattern matching on a more general footing. These will be considered in the notes for Chap. 5.

Stratego [101] supports a rich class of strategies for traversing data structures, especially syntax trees of programs. Many of these, if not all, will be representable in static pattern calculus.

The definition of fixpoints by pattern matching can be found in [23].

Folding began as a concept in list programming where it comes in two flavours: `foldleft` is tail-recursive and `foldright` is head-recursive [9]. The `fold` of this chapter is a form of `foldleft` since the left component of a compound is used first. One could equally employ a right fold.

Chapter 5
Dynamic Patterns

Abstract This chapter simplifies the conceptual framework of pattern calculus by identifying the syntactic classes of patterns and terms, and of constructors and symbols. Now patterns are first-class entities that may be passed as parameters, evaluated and returned as results. Since variable scope is required to be static, this requires that symbol binding be handled separately from pattern formation. Also, extra care is required to ensure confluence of reduction. Examples include generic functions for equality, elimination, and for string matching. Wildcards and views are also considered.

5.1 First-Class Patterns

The static pattern calculus is able to handle some key aspects of the salary update problem. The generic `apply2all` is able to act on employees wherever they are found. Now let us add a new twist. Suppose that salary increases are to be limited to employees within groups. If groups are a fixed part of the organisation's structure, represented by a constructor `Group`, then it is enough to write patterns of the form `Group` x just as before. The more interesting possibility is that the concept of group is dynamic. At one time it may be a department, at another time it may be a division, or even a department within a division. Using the existing, static patterns, each notion of a group must have its own case, so that all possibilities must be addressed explicitly, in an ad hoc manner. The alternative developed here is to replace the constructor `Group` by a *variable* `group` in the pattern.

Once patterns contain variables, it is natural to ask what they can be replaced by, what syntactic class they refer to. One option is to maintain the separation of patterns and terms present in the static pattern calculus, using two sorts of symbols. Although feasible, this option is conceptually unattractive and limits our ability to compute patterns. The decision as to the meaning of `group` may be as complex as any other computation, drawing on contextual information, dynamic inputs, and perhaps other calculations. For this reason, we are led to identify the syntactic class

DOI 10.1007/978-3-540-89185-7_5,

of patterns with that of terms, so that any term can be a pattern. Patterns are now first-class, able to be passed as arguments, evaluated, and returned as results.

This treatment of patterns is quite similar to the treatment of first-class functions that underpins λ-calculus. Along with a dramatic reduction in syntactic overheads comes a number of subtle issues, especially concerning symbol scope, as can be seen when considering patterns involving `group`.

A first attempt at a pattern for a group is `group` x. Now substitution for the variable `group` can replace it by constructors such as `Department` or `Division` to produce the familiar static patterns. The difficulty is that while `group` and x are both symbols, `group` is to be a variable while x is to be a matchable. In the static calculus, all symbols in a pattern are matchable but now both kinds of symbols are terms in their own right (patterns are terms) and so must be clearly distinguished. The solution adopted is to allow each symbol x to appear as either a *variable* x or as a *matchable* $\hat{x}$. For example, the dynamic pattern for a group is now

$$\texttt{group}\ \hat{x}$$

in which `group` is free and x will be bound. Much of the flexibility of this approach comes from the ability to compute patterns, but this brings the possibility of eliminating matchable symbols. In the static pattern calculus, the free matchables of the pattern are used for both matching and binding, but this is unacceptable when reduction can eliminate bindings, as this would change the scope of the affected symbols. That is, bindings must be static, even though patterns are dynamic. To reflect this, each case is now of the form

$$[\theta]\ p \rightarrow s$$

where θ is a sequence of distinct binding symbols. If the pattern p is for the group above, then this becomes

$$[x]\ \texttt{group}\ \hat{x} \rightarrow s\ .$$

This notation may seem a little heavy. If x is known to be binding, then perhaps this is enough to isolate the matchable symbols. While true of simple examples, recall that any term can appear in a pattern now. For example, consider

$$[x]\ ([\,]\ \hat{x} \rightarrow p)\ \hat{x} \rightarrow s$$

in which the pattern is itself the application of a case. Now $\hat{x}$ is able to match itself, so that the pattern reduces to p. However, without the markings, there is no local mechanism for determining that it is safe to match x with itself. For this to happen would require reduction to be context sensitive. To avoid this it is necessary for variables and matchables to be distinguished as terms, and not just within the context of a case.

Actually, the match rules for matchables are identical to those for constructors. This leads to another identification, of constructors with matchables. That is, a constructor is a matchable symbol which is not bound in the current context.

Summarising, greater expressive power, and simplicity, comes by identifying the syntactic classes of constructors and symbols, and of patterns and terms. The resulting calculus can be seen as an heir to the λ-calculus in which abstractions are generalised to cases, and matchable symbols are used to seed data structures. These small changes nevertheless generate a significant increase in polymorphism.

5.2 Dynamic Pattern Calculus

Let θ be a meta-variable for a finite sequence of distinct term symbols. A sequence may also be used to denote the underlying set, when convenient. The *term syntax* of the *dynamic pattern calculus* is given by

$$\begin{array}{lll} t ::= & & \text{(term)} \\ & x & \text{(variable symbol)} \\ & \hat{x} & \text{(matchable symbol)} \\ & t\,t & \text{(application)} \\ & [\theta]\,t \to t & \text{(case).} \end{array}$$

The case $[\theta]\,p \to s$ has *binding symbols* θ and *pattern* p and *body* s. The λ-abstraction $\lambda x.s$ is shorthand for $[x]\,\hat{x} \to s$. Similarly, `car` $= [x,y]\,\hat{x}\,\hat{y} \to x$. A matchable $\hat{x}$ may also be called a *constructor* if its binding is not under consideration. As before, these may be represented by capitalised words in monospace font. For example, `Pair` is $\hat{x}$ for some unspecified symbol x, as is `Nomatch`. *Well-formed* term syntax does not bind the symbol for `Nomatch`. Throughout the book, we shall restrict our attention to well-formed syntax. The *explicit functions* are the cases.

Free variables of the new term forms are defined by:

$$\begin{aligned} \mathsf{fv}(\hat{x}) &= \{\} \\ \mathsf{fv}([\theta]\,p \to s) &= \mathsf{fv}(p) \cup (\mathsf{fv}(s) \setminus \theta). \end{aligned}$$

Hence the binding symbols of a case bind their free variable occurrences in the body but not those of the pattern. For example, in $[x]\,\hat{x}\,x \to x$ the occurrence of the matchable $\hat{x}$ in the pattern and the variable x in the body are both bound by $[x]$ but the occurrence of the variable x in the pattern is free in the case as a whole.

Similarly, the *free matchable symbols* $\mathsf{fm}(t)$ of terms are defined by

$$\begin{aligned} \mathsf{fm}(x) &= \{\} \\ \mathsf{fm}(\hat{x}) &= \{x\} \\ \mathsf{fm}(r\,u) &= \mathsf{fm}(r) \cup \mathsf{fm}(u) \\ \mathsf{fm}([\theta]\,p \to s) &= (\mathsf{fm}(p) \setminus \theta) \cup \mathsf{fm}(s)\,. \end{aligned}$$

Note that the free matchables of the body are always free in its case. Also, the definition of *closed terms* is unchanged: they may have free matchables even though they have no free variables. The *symbols* $\mathsf{sym}(\sigma)$ of a substitution σ are given by $\mathsf{dom}(\sigma) \cup \mathsf{fv}(\sigma) \cup \mathsf{fm}(\sigma)$.

The application of a term substitution σ is defined as before, with rules for the new term forms given by

$$\begin{array}{lll} \sigma\hat{x} & = \hat{x} & \\ \sigma([\theta]\ p \to s) & = [\theta]\ \sigma p \to \sigma s & \text{if } \sigma \text{ avoids } \theta. \end{array}$$

Since binding symbols appear as matchables in patterns, it is necessary to be able to substitute for matchables, as well as variables, when renaming binding symbols. Given a substitution σ define the function $\hat{\sigma}$ on terms as follows.

$$\begin{array}{lll} \hat{\sigma}z & = z & \\ \hat{\sigma}\hat{x} & = \sigma x & \text{if } x \in \mathsf{dom}(\sigma) \\ \hat{\sigma}\hat{x} & = \hat{x} & \text{if } x \notin \mathsf{dom}(\sigma) \\ \hat{\sigma}(r\ u) & = (\hat{\sigma}r)\ (\hat{\sigma}u) & \\ \hat{\sigma}([\theta]\ p \to s) & = [\theta]\ \hat{\sigma}p \to \hat{\sigma}s & \text{if } \sigma \text{ avoids } \theta. \end{array}$$

When σ is of the form $\{u_i/x_i\}$ we may write $\{u_i/\hat{x}_i\}$ for $\hat{\sigma}$.

To define α-equivalence requires a little more machinery. Let θ be a sequence of symbols and let x and y be symbols. Then $\{y/x\}\theta$ is defined to be the set obtained by replacing x by y in θ if $x \in \theta$ and $y \notin \theta$, and to be undefined otherwise. *α-equivalence* is the congruence relation generated by the following axiom

$$[\theta]\ p \to s =_\alpha [\{y/x\}\theta]\ \{\hat{y}/\hat{x}\}p \to \{y/x\}s \quad \text{if } y \notin \mathsf{fm}(p) \cup \mathsf{fv}(s).$$

For example, $[y]x\,\hat{y} \to x\ (f\ y) =_\alpha [z]x\,\hat{z} \to x\ (f\ z)$ if z is not free in x or f. A *term* is an α-equivalence class in the term syntax.

5.3 Matching

Matching is similar to that of the static pattern calculus but modified to take into account the explicit binding of symbols, and generalising from constructors to matchable symbols. In particular, the successful match of a term p against a term u with respect to binding symbols θ will yield a substitution σ whose domain is θ such that $\hat{\sigma}p = u$

The *data structures* are defined by

$$d ::= \hat{x} \mid d\ t$$

where the head is now a matchable symbol. Note that this symbol may either play the role of a constructor or be bound if the data structure is used as a pattern. Thus, typical patterns are themselves data structures. The matchable forms are the data structures and cases, as before.

In the static pattern calculus, binding variables in patterns were guaranteed to appear in patterns, and so to appear in the domain of a successful match. Now this must be checked explicitly after the matching rules have been applied.

$$\begin{array}{rcll}
\{u \,/\!/ [\theta]\, \hat{x}\} &=& \mathsf{some}\ \{u/x\} & x \in \theta \\
\{\hat{x} \,/\!/ [\theta]\, \hat{x}\} &=& \mathsf{some}\ \{\} & \text{if } x \notin \theta \\
\{u\, v \,/\!/ [\theta]\, p\, q\} &=& \{u \,/\!/ [\theta]\, p\} \uplus \{v \,/\!/ [\theta]\, q\} & \text{if } p\ q \text{ and } u\ v \text{ are matchable} \\
\{u \,/\!/ [\theta]\, p\} &=& \mathsf{none} & \text{otherwise, if } p \text{ and } u \text{ are matchable} \\
\{u \,/\!/ [\theta]\, p\} &=& \mathsf{undefined} & \text{otherwise.}
\end{array}$$

Fig. 5.1 Dynamic matching

The *basic matching* $\{u \,/\!/ [\theta]\, p\}$ of a term p (called the *pattern*) against a term u (called the *argument*) relative to a sequence θ of *binding symbols* is the partial operation defined by applying the rules in Fig. 5.1 in order. A matchable which is a binding symbol matches anything. Any other matchable matches itself only. Matching of compound data structures is component-wise, using disjoint union as before. If these rules do not apply then match failure occurs provided that the pattern and argument are matchable forms. Otherwise basic matching is undefined.

These rules correspond to those of the static pattern calculus, which may be a little surprising since there are many more patterns than before. These new patterns can be used during pattern computation, but successful matching has been limited to the familiar static patterns used to match against data structures. It is worth digressing to consider the alternative possibilities, if successful matching is to extend to arbitrary patterns.

It may well be feasible to match cases, provided sufficient care is taken with *their* binding symbols. Another possibility is to allow free variables to match themselves, by adding the rule $\{x \,/\!/ [\theta]\, x\} = \mathsf{some}\ \{\}$. However, without additional restrictions this will destroy confluence. For example, if x, y and z are distinct symbols then $\{x\, \hat{z} \,/\!/ []\, x\, \hat{y}\}$ would be none but substitution of $\lambda y.\hat{z}$ for x would cause both pattern and argument to reduce to $\hat{z}$ so that matching would succeed.

Even though successful matching is limited to patterns for data structures, it is also necessary to check that all binding symbols are accounted for. Let μ be a meta-variable for a match. The *check* of a match μ on a set of symbols θ is μ if μ is some substitution whose domain is exactly θ and is none otherwise.

Let p and u be terms and let θ be a sequence of symbols. Define the *matching*

$$\{u \,/\, [\theta]\, p\}$$

of p against u with respect to binding symbols θ to be the check of $\{u \,/\!/ [\theta]\, p\}$ on θ. The check is necessary to ensure that reduction does not allow bound symbols to become free. For example, $\{\hat{x} \,/\, [y]\, \hat{x}\} = \mathsf{none}$ since the basic matching is not defined on y.

By requiring that unions of term substitutions be disjoint and applying the check, successful matching guarantees that each binding symbol appears exactly once in the pattern, i.e. that the pattern is *linear* in the binding symbols. It is tempting to make this a requirement of a well-formed case, but if arbitrary terms are to be al-

$$\frac{}{x \gg x} \qquad \frac{}{\hat{x} \gg \hat{x}} \qquad \frac{r_1 \gg r_2 \quad u_1 \gg u_2}{r_1\, u_1 \gg r_2\, u_2}$$

$$\frac{p_1 \gg p_2 \quad s_1 \gg s_2}{[\theta]\, p_1 \to s_1 \gg [\theta]\, p_2 \to s_2} \qquad \frac{p_1 \gg p_2 \quad s_1 \gg s_2 \quad u_1 \gg u_2}{([\theta]\, p_1 \to s_1)\, u_1 \gg \{u_2\,/[\theta]\, p_2\}\, s_2}$$

Fig. 5.2 Simultaneous reduction for dynamic patterns

lowed in pattern then it is very difficult to enforce, and ends up excluding some perfectly good nonlinear patterns that reduce to a linear form.

The dynamic pattern calculus has *match rule*reduction given by

$$([\theta]\, p \to s)\; u \longrightarrow \{u\,/[\theta]\, p\}\; s \quad \text{(match)}.$$

That is, if matching of the pattern against the argument produces a substitution whose domain is the binding symbols then apply this to the body. If the matching fails then return Nomatch as in the static calculus. Of course, if $\{u/[\theta]p\}$ is undefined (because p or u needs to be evaluated) then the match rule does not apply.

Theorem 5.1 (Progress). *Every closed irreducible term of the dynamic pattern calculus is a matchable form. Hence, pattern matching cannot get stuck.*

Proof. The proof is by induction on the structure of the term. Without loss of generality, it suffices to consider the form t given by $([\theta]\, p \to s)\; u$. Neither p nor u has free variables since these would be free in the overall form. Similarly, p and u are irreducible. So, by induction, p and u are matchable forms. Hence the basic matching of p against u is defined and so t is reducible. □

5.4 Confluence of Matching

Confluence of reduction is established using the *simultaneous reduction* technique as in Sect. 2.4. As before, it is enough to prove confluence of simultaneous reduction, as defined in Fig. 5.2.

The *simultaneous reduction relation* $\gg$ *between matches* is defined as follows. Given two substitutions σ_1 and σ_2 then some $\sigma_1 \gg$ some σ_2 if $\mathsf{dom}(\sigma_1) = \mathsf{dom}(\sigma_2)$ and $\sigma_1 x \gg \sigma_2 x$ for every $x \in \mathsf{dom}(\sigma)_1$. Also none $\gg$ none.

Lemma 5.2. *Let μ be a match and let θ be a sequence of symbols that are avoided by μ. If p and u are terms such that $\{u\,//[\theta]\, p\}$ is defined then so is $\{\mu\; u\,//[\theta]\;\mu\, p\}$ and $\{\mu\; u\,//[\theta]\;\mu\, p\} \circ \mu = \mu \circ \{u\,//[\theta]\, p\}$. Hence*

$$\{\mu\; u\,/[\theta]\,\mu\; p\} \circ \mu = \mu \circ \{u\,/[\theta]\, p\}\,.$$

Proof. The second statement follows directly from the first, so consider the latter. If μ is none then both sides are none. So without loss of generality, assume that

μ is some substitution σ. The proof is by induction on the structure of p. If p is a matchable symbol $\hat{x}$ where $x \in \theta$ then both sides map x to σu and behave as σ on all other symbols since μ avoids θ. If p is some other matchable symbol and u is the same then both sides are μ. If p and u are compounds then apply induction twice. If $\{u\,//[\theta]\;p\} = \mathsf{none}$ then $\{\sigma u\,//[\theta]\,\sigma p\} = \mathsf{none}$ and so both sides of the match equation are none.

□

Lemma 5.3. *If $u_1 \gg u_2$ is a simultaneous reduction on terms and $\{u_1\,/[\theta]\,p\}$ is defined then so is $\{u_2\,/[\theta]\,p\}$ and $\{u_1\,/[\theta]\,p\} \gg \{u_2\,/[\theta]\,p\}$.*

Proof. The proof is by induction on the structure of p. If p is a matchable (whether binding or not) then the result follows directly. If p is a case then both matches will fail. Otherwise p must be a compound $q_1\;q_2$ and u must be a matchable form. If u is an atom then both matchings will fail. Alternatively, if $u = v_1\;v_2$ is a compound then v_1 is a data structure and thus $u_2 = v_3\;v_4$ where $v_1 \gg v_3$ and $v_2 \gg v_4$. Hence induction applies.

□

Lemma 5.4. *If $\mu_1 \gg \mu_2$ and $t_1 \gg t_2$ are simultaneous reductions of matches and terms respectively then $\mu_1\;t_1 \gg \mu_2\;t_2$.*

Proof. If μ_1 is none then μ_2 is none and so the result is immediate. So assume that μ_1 and μ_2 are some σ_1 and σ_2 respectively. The proof is by induction on the derivation of $t_1 \gg t_2$. The only nontrivial case is when $t_1 = ([\theta]\,p_1 \to s_1)\;u_1 \gg \{u_2\,/[\theta]\,p_2\}\;s_2$ where $p_1 \gg p_2$ and $u_1 \gg u_2$ and $s_1 \gg s_2$. Without loss of generality, assume σ_1 and σ_2 both avoid θ. Thus, $\sigma_1(([\theta]\,p_1 \to s_1)u_1) = ([\theta]\,\sigma_1(p_1) \to \sigma_1(s_1))\;(\sigma_1(u_1)) \gg \{\sigma_2(u_2)\,/[\theta]\,\sigma_2(p_2)\}(\sigma_2(s_2))$ by three applications of induction. In turn, this result is also $\sigma_2(\{u_2\,/[\theta]\,p_2\}s_2)$ by Lemma 5.2.

Theorem 5.5. *The relation $\gg$ has the diamond property. That is, if $t \gg t_1$ and $t \gg t_2$ then there is t_3 such that $t_1 \gg t_3$ and $t_2 \gg t_3$.*

Proof. The proof is by induction on the definition of simultaneous reduction. Suppose $([\theta]\,p \to s)\;u \gg \{u_1\,/[\theta]\,p_1\}s_1$ and $([\theta]\,p \to s)\;u \gg \{u_2\,/[\theta]\,p_2\}\,s_2$ where $p \gg p_1$ and $p \gg p_2$ and $s \gg s_1$ and $s \gg s_2$ and $u \gg u_1$ and $u \gg u_2$. By induction, there are terms p_3 and s_3 and u_3 such that $p_1 \gg p_3$ and $p_2 \gg p_3$ and $s_1 \gg s_3$ and $s_2 \gg s_3$ and $u_1 \gg u_3$ and $u_2 \gg u_3$. Now $\{u_1\,/[\theta]\,p\} \gg \{u_3\,/[\theta]\,p_3\}$ by Lemma 5.3 and so $\{u_1\,/[\theta]\,p\}s_1 \gg \{u_3\,/[\theta]\,p_3\}s_3$ by Lemma 5.4. Similarly, $\{u_2\,/[\theta]\,p_2\}\,s_2 \gg \{u_3\,/[\theta]\,p_3\}s_3$ which completes the diamond. The other cases are equally straightforward. □

Corollary 5.6 (Confluence). *The reduction relation of the dynamic pattern calculus is confluent.*

Proof. Theorem 2.5 shows that $\gg$ has the diamond property and so the reflexive-transitive closure of $\gg$ is confluent. Hence the reduction relation is confluent, too.

□

5.5 String Matching

Example 5.7. Generic Eliminator

Static patterns can be used to eliminate any particular constructor. This "design pattern" can be captured within a single term, namely the generic eliminator given by

$$\texttt{elim} = [x]\,\hat{x} \to [y]\,x\,\hat{y} \to y.$$

Equally, it may be written as $\lambda x.[y]\,x\,\hat{y} \to y$ or

$$\texttt{elim}\,x = [y]\,x\,\hat{y} \to y.$$

Note how the first argument x is used as a free variable in the pattern $x\,\hat{y}$. For example, let `'a'` be a constructor for the character 'a'. Then

$$\texttt{elim}\,(\texttt{Cons 'a'})\,(\texttt{Cons 'a' (Cons 'b' Nil)}) \longrightarrow \texttt{Cons 'b' Nil}.$$

Allowing the usual string syntax in which the list of characters above is given by "ab" this example becomes

$$\texttt{elim}\,(\texttt{Cons 'a'})\;\texttt{"ab"} \longrightarrow \texttt{"b"}.$$

The generic eliminator can be iterated to yield

$$\texttt{elim*}\,x = ([y]\,x\,\hat{y} \to \texttt{elim*}\,x\,y \mid \lambda y.y)\,.$$

For example,

$$\texttt{elim*}\,(\texttt{Cons 'a'})\;\texttt{"aaabca"} \longrightarrow^{*} \texttt{"bca"}\,.$$

Now consider a pathological example.

$$\texttt{elim}\,(\lambda x.\texttt{Nil})\;\texttt{Nil} \longrightarrow ([y]\,\texttt{Nil} \to y)\;\texttt{Nil}.$$

If matching did not check that all binding symbols are given values then this closed term would reduce to the variable y!

Example 5.8. Extensions

These are defined as in Sect. 4.4, using

$$[\theta]\,p \to s \mid r = \lambda x.([y]\,\texttt{Nomatch}\,\hat{y} \to y)\;(([\theta]\,p \to \lambda z.\texttt{Nomatch}\,s)\;x\;(r\,x))$$

where x, y and z are fresh symbols.

Example 5.9. Generic Equality

This is given by

$$\texttt{equal} = \lambda x.([\,]\,x \to \texttt{true} \mid \lambda y.\texttt{false})\,.$$

For example, if u and v are pure data structures then equal $(\texttt{Pair}\ u\ v)$ $(\texttt{Pair}\ u\ v)$ reduces to true since $\{\texttt{Pair}\ u\ v/[\,]\ \texttt{Pair}\ u\ v\} = \{\}$.

Example 5.10. Updating

The functions select and apply2all of the static pattern calculus can equally be supported here. A common application of apply2all is to a function of the form

$$\begin{aligned}&[x]\ c\ \hat{x} \rightarrow c\ (f\ x)\\ |\ &\lambda y.y\end{aligned}$$

in which terms built from c have their argument modified by f. This algorithm can be described exactly by update $c\ f$ where update is defined by

$$\begin{aligned}&\texttt{update}\ z\ f =\\ &\quad [x]\ z\ \hat{x} \rightarrow z\ (f\ x)\\ &\ |\ [x,y]\ \hat{y}\ \hat{x} \rightarrow (\texttt{update}\ z\ f\ y)\ (\texttt{update}\ z\ f\ x)\\ &\ |\ [x]\ \hat{x} \rightarrow x.\end{aligned}$$

Note how the variable z is used in the pattern instead of a matchable. Updating at a constructor is easily defined in the static pattern calculus, but here it is more general. For example, if singleton $= \lambda x.\texttt{Cons}\ x\ \texttt{Nil}$ creates singleton lists then update singleton f reduces to an extension whose first case is

$$[x]\ \texttt{Cons}\ \hat{x}\ \texttt{Nil} \rightarrow \texttt{Cons}\ (f\ x)\ \texttt{Nil}\ .$$

Special forms of selecting can be defined in the same manner.

For example, consider the problem of updating salaries by some function f. If salaries are represented by terms of the form Salary s where s is a number then the updated salary should be Salary $(f\ s)$. In this setting update Salary f does the job. However, if salaries are represented by terms such as Wage Euro s or Wage Dollar s then the required function is update (Wage Euro) f or perhaps update (Wage Dollar) f.

The general solution is to use update salary f where salary is a *variable* that can be instantiated to Salary or Wage Euro or Wage Dollar.

5.6 Encoding Static Patterns

There is a translation of the static pattern calculus into the dynamic pattern calculus. Define the alphabet of symbols of the dynamic pattern calculus to be the disjoint union of the alphabets of symbols and constructors of the static pattern calculus. The translation $[\![p]\!]_p$ of a pattern p and $[\![t]\!]_t$ of a term t are given by

$$\begin{array}{rcl} [\![x]\!]_p &=& \hat{x} \\ [\![c]\!]_p &=& \hat{c} \\ [\![p\ q]\!]_p &=& [\![p]\!]_p\ [\![q]\!]_p \end{array} \qquad \begin{array}{rcl} [\![x]\!]_t &=& x \\ [\![c]\!]_t &=& \hat{c} \\ [\![r\ u]\!]_t &=& [\![r]\!]_t\ [\![u]\!]_t \\ [\![p \to s]\!]_t &=& [\mathsf{fm}(p)]\ [\![p]\!]_p \to [\![s]\!]_t \end{array}$$

where $\mathsf{fm}(p)$ is here used informally to denote the *sequence* of free matchables of p given in order of first occurrence in p, from left to right. Similarly, the translation $[\![\sigma]\!]$ of a substitution σ is given by the substitution that maps a variable x to $[\![\sigma x]\!]_t$.

Lemma 5.11. *Let $\{u/p\}$ be a defined match in the static pattern calculus. Then $\{[\![u]\!]_t/[\mathsf{fm}(p)]\ [\![p]\!]_p\}$ is defined in the dynamic pattern calculus and is $[\![\{u/p\}]\!]$.*

Proof. The proof is by straightforward induction on the structure of p. □

Lemma 5.12. *If t is a term and σ is a substitution of the static pattern calculus then $[\![\sigma t]\!]_t = [\![\sigma]\!][\![t]\!]_t$.*

Proof. The proof is by straightforward induction on the structure of t. □

Theorem 5.13. *The translation from the static pattern calculus to the dynamic pattern calculus preserves reduction and (distinct) normal forms.*

Proof. Consider the translation of the match rule:

$$\begin{array}{rcl} [\![(p \to s)\ u]\!]_t &=& ([\mathsf{fm}(p)]\ [\![p]\!]_p \to [\![s]\!]_t)\ [\![u]\!]_t \\ &\longrightarrow& \{[\![u]\!]_t/[\mathsf{fm}(p)]\ [\![p]\!]_p\}[\![s]\!]_t \\ &=& [\![\{u/p\}]\!][\![s]\!]_t \\ &=& [\![\{u/p\}s]\!]_t \end{array}$$

where the last two equations are applications of Lemmas 5.11 and 5.12. It is easy to verify that normal forms are preserved and distinct normal forms remain distinct. □

5.7 Wildcards

This section and the next introduce some useful additions to the calculus.

It is interesting to add a new constant denoted _ to the dynamic pattern calculus, the *wildcard*. It has no free variables or matchables, and is unaffected by substitution. It is a data structure and has the basic matching

$$\{u /\!/ [\theta]\,\_\} = \{\}$$

for any θ. That is, it behaves like a fresh binding symbol in a pattern but like a constructor in a body. For example, the second and first projections from a pair can be encoded as `elim` (`Pair` _) and `elim` ($\lambda x.$`Pair` x _).

The following example uses recursion in the pattern. Define the function for the extracting list entries by

$$\begin{array}{l}\texttt{entrypattern} = \\ \quad [n]\ \texttt{Successor}\ \hat{n} \rightarrow \lambda x.\texttt{Cons}\ \_\ (\texttt{entrypattern}\ n\ x) \\ \ |\ \texttt{Zero} \quad\ \rightarrow \lambda x.\texttt{cons}\ x\ \_\end{array}$$

$$\texttt{entry}\ n = \texttt{elim}\ (\texttt{entrypattern}\ n)\,.$$

For example, $\texttt{entry}\ \overline{2}$ reduces to $[x]\,\texttt{Cons}\ \_\ (\texttt{Cons}\ \_\ (\texttt{Cons}\ \hat{x}\ \_)) \rightarrow x$ which recovers the second entry from a list (counting from 0). Note that the standard approach, in which each occurrence of the wildcard represents a distinct binding symbol, cannot support such recursion.

5.8 Views

Views allow a data structure to support virtual constructors. For example, suppose floating-point arithmetic is given, and the usual trigonometric operations such as sine `sin` and cosine `cos`. Consider a constructor `Cart` for building complex numbers from their real and imaginary parts. It is easy to define addition of complex numbers in this representation, by

$$[x_1, y_1]\ \texttt{Cart}\ \hat{x}_1\ \hat{y}_1 \rightarrow [x_2, y_2]\ \texttt{Cart}\ \hat{x}_2\ \hat{y}_2 \rightarrow \texttt{Cart}\ (x_1 + x_2)\ (y_1 + y_2)$$

but multiplication is given by the more complicated formula

$$[x_1, y_1]\ \texttt{Cart}\ \hat{x}_1\ \hat{y}_1 \rightarrow [x_2, y_2]\ \texttt{Cart}\ \hat{x}_2\ \hat{y}_2 \rightarrow \texttt{Cart}\ (x_1 * y_1 - x_2 * y_2)\ (x_1 * y_2 + x_2 * y_1)\,.$$

However, every complex number can be represented in *polar* coordinates, in terms of their length r and their angle θ (not to be confused with the meta-variable for binding symbols). The corresponding cartesian coordinates are given by

$$\texttt{polar2cart} = [r, \theta]\ \texttt{Pair}\ \hat{r}\ \hat{\theta} \rightarrow \texttt{Pair}\ (r\cos\ \theta)\ (r\sin\ \theta).$$

For convenience, let us write (s,t) for $\texttt{Pair}\ s\ t$. The polar coordinates can be recovered by

$$\texttt{cart2polar} = [x, y]\ (\hat{x}, \hat{y}) \rightarrow (\sqrt{x^2 + y^2},\ tan^{-1}(y/x)) \quad \text{if } x \neq 0$$

with special cases for when x is 0 that need not concern us here.

Given two complex numbers with polar coordinates (r_1, θ_1) and (r_2, θ_2) then their product has polar coordinates $(r_1 * r_2, \theta_1 + \theta_2)$. The goal is to be able to write a pattern-matching function for multiplying complex numbers, as follows

$$\begin{array}{l}[r_1, \theta_1]\ \texttt{polar2cart}\ (\hat{r}_1, \hat{\theta}_1) \rightarrow [r_2, \theta_2]\ \texttt{polar2cart}\ (\hat{r}_2, \hat{\theta}_2) \rightarrow \\ \texttt{polar2cart}\ (r_1 * r_2, \theta_1 + \theta_2))\end{array}$$

in which the conversion between views is hidden from the programmer. The problem is that the arithmetic functions used to define polar2cart will fail when applied to the matchables such as $\hat{r}_1$ as they only evaluate when given floating-point numbers to act upon. The desired behaviour is that the *arguments* to this pattern-matching function be converted to polar coordinates, rather than attempt to convert the pattern to cartesian coordinates, so that

$$\{u/[r,\theta]\ \texttt{polar2cart}\ (\hat{r},\hat{\theta})\} = \{\texttt{cart2polar}\ u/[r,\theta]\ (\hat{r},\hat{\theta})\}\ .$$

This is achieved by replacing polar2cart in the pattern by view cart2polar and the rule

$$\{u/[r,\theta]\ \texttt{view cart2polar}\ (\hat{r},\hat{\theta})\} = \{\texttt{cart2polar}\ u/[r,\theta]\ (\hat{r},\hat{\theta})\}\ .$$

The general rule for matching views is thus

$$\{u\,//[\theta]\,\texttt{view}\ f\ p\} = \{f\ u\,//[\theta]\,p\}\ .$$

By defining polar = view cart2polar the multiplication case can be written

$$[r_1,\theta_1]\,\texttt{polar}\,(\hat{r}_1,\hat{\theta}_1) \to [r_2,\theta_2]\,\texttt{polar}\,(\hat{r}_2,\hat{\theta}_2) \to \texttt{polar2cart}(r_1 * r_2, \theta_1+\theta_2))\ .$$

Another application of views is to parametrise *divide-and-conquer* algorithms by their technique for dividing. For example, let divideList $X \to$ List $X *$ List X be a symbol representing a means of splitting a list in two, so that append (divide x) $= x$. The corresponding divide-and-conquer program is then

$$\begin{array}{l}\texttt{divide-and-conquer divide combine conquer} =\\ \quad \texttt{let}\ f =\\ \qquad [x]\ \texttt{singleton}\ \hat{x} \to \texttt{conquer}\ x\\ \quad\ \mid [x,y]\ \texttt{view divide}\ (\hat{x},\hat{y}) \to \texttt{combine}\ (f\ x)\ (f\ y)\ .\end{array}$$

5.9 Notes

Perhaps the earliest exploration of the general issues was in van Oostrom's *generalised λ-calculus* [81] now known as the λ-calculus with patterns [67]. It generalises the usual λ-abstraction $\lambda x.M$ to $\lambda N.M$ so that any term N can be a pattern, but all free symbols of the pattern N are implicitly bound. That is, it is not possible to substitute into a pattern. Also, to ensure confluence, patterns are required to satisfy the *Rigid Pattern Condition* (RPC). This is justified in the original paper above by

> As patterns are meant to be fixed constructs which can not be evaluated, we should allow as patterns only terms which can not be (partially) destroyed by evaluating parts of the term they are in. We give a restriction, the *rigid pattern condition* (RPC), for this to hold.

(emphasis in the original). This excludes nontrivial reduction of patterns, and also patterns such as $x\ y$ in which the variable x appears in an *active position*. Even then, confluence is not easily established. In practice, one appears to be confined to patterns that are headed by a constructor.

This approach to pattern matching has been pursued through the ρ-calculus or *rewriting calculus* [47, 22]. The basic mechanism of the calculus is

$$(\lambda A.B)\ C \longrightarrow \texttt{Solve}(A,C)\ B\ .$$

Its left-hand side is usually as in the generalised pattern calculus but $\texttt{Solve}(A,C)$ is a place-holder for a substitution which is the "solution" to making A match C. The nature of this solution is open-ended, to allow for different solving mechanisms. As well as performing computations through pattern matching, it may be used to search for proofs of theorems. Since a single theorem may have distinct proofs, one does not wish to impose confluence at the outset but this flexibility is not so interesting for programming. Also, at this level of generality there is not much that can be proved. For example, since solutions may be developed modulo some equivalence relation, it is not obligatory to ensure even that $\texttt{Solve}(A,C)A = C$. Even when this equation is assumed, there is not much to be said without adding the Rigid Pattern Condition mentioned above.

Also, it is rare for patterns in ρ-calculus to be allowed free variables. The chief exception is a typed rewriting calculus of [8] where an abstraction $\lambda\mathscr{P}:\mathscr{C}.\mathscr{T}$ binds only the variables in $\mathscr{C}$ allowing other variables in the pattern $\mathscr{P}$ to be available for substitution. However, there is no nontrivial version of the calculus which is confluent [30].

The first attempt to make patterns more dynamic was by the author [56]; it was realised in the first version of the typed programming language **bondi** [10]. The motivation was to support generic searches and updates. Although fundamental to query languages, it seems they had not been considered before in the context of pattern matching. The original **bondi** enforced the requirement that free variables in patterns could only be replaced by *linear* functions, so that reduction could never duplicate or eliminate binding variables. Of course, such an approach will never be able to describe all of the interesting linear functions.

The first account in which any term can be a pattern was developed with Delia Kesner in the *pure pattern calculus* [52]. It represented binding variable occurrences in patterns as free variables (as described in the introduction to this chapter) but struggled with pathological examples. Its proof of confluence using simultaneous reduction provided the template for subsequent calculi, including the dynamic pattern calculus. Our second account avoided the pathology by using context-sensitive information to identify what are now called the matchable symbols. Our third paper [53] provides a systematic and detailed account of all the main calculi for pattern matching, including a proof that the dynamic pattern calculus presented here is equivalent to the context-sensitive pattern calculus mentioned above.

String processing is exemplified by the string processing language SNOBOL [29] introduced in 1964. Later approaches emphasised the use of regular expressions, as in **sed**, a string editor [75] produced in 1973–4 and **awk** in 1979 [2]. Popular today is the **Perl** scripting language, first released in 1987 [104] as a string matching language. String matching can be expressed in the static pattern calculus using operations such as `elim*` defined earlier.

In the same spirit as string matching one can develop patterns corresponding to arbitrary regular expressions or to arbitrary XML paths [48].

Wildcards are probably as old as pattern matching. Usually, a wildcard is just syntactic sugar for a fresh binding symbol. The idea of allowing wildcards as first-class terms, that can be passed as parameters, appears to be new.

Views are commonly used in database theory, but can also be considered as a means to provide more than one interface to an algebraic data type [103]. They may also be referred to as *active patterns* [28, 95]. The mechanism used here to support views appears to be quite different from other approaches, as it exploits the freedom to insert arbitrary functions into patterns.

Chapter 6
Objects

Abstract This chapter considers the relationships between records, tuples and the objects of the *object calculus*, a representative calculus for object-orientation. The main challenge is how to define functions (or methods) that can act on records which have only some fields in common. The object-oriented approach adds the functionality to the record to produce an object. The pattern calculus approach treats methods as pattern-matching functions, adding special cases only when required to do so.

6.1 Records

Many accounts of data are based on records, of the form $\{l_1 = t_1, \ldots l_n = t_n\}$, whose field l_i has value t_i. The field values can be accessed using the "dot" notation and the reduction rule

$$\{l_1 = t_1, \ldots l_n = t_n\}.l_i \longrightarrow t_i\ .$$

A direct translation of records into tuples is given by interpreting such a record as a tuple

$$(t_1, \ldots, t_n)$$

which is shorthand for $\texttt{Pair}\, t_1\, (\texttt{Pair}\, t_2\, (\ldots t_n))$. Then access to the field l_i becomes a case given by

$$(x_1, \ldots, x_n) \rightarrow x_i\ .$$

For clarity, one can add a constructor c to the outside, to get

$$c\ (x_1, \ldots, x_n) \rightarrow x_i\ .$$

The limitation of this approach is that one would like the use of record labels to be stable under the inclusion of additional fields. The solution is to allow a spare label to represent any additional fields, so that the interpretation of the original record above is

$$c\ (\texttt{Un}, t_1, \ldots, t_n)$$

B. Jay, *Pattern Calculus*,
DOI 10.1007/978-3-540-89185-7_6,

where Un is the unit constructor used to indicate the absence of data. Then additional fields can be slotted into the first component of the tuple, in place of Un.

Example 6.1. Employees

For example, an employee given by

$$\{\texttt{number} = 1234, \texttt{name} = \texttt{"John Smith"}, \texttt{salary} = 567\}$$

can be represented by the tuple

$$\texttt{Employee}\ (\texttt{Un}, 1234, \texttt{"John Smith"}, 567)$$

with fields given by

$$\begin{aligned} \texttt{number} &= \texttt{Employee}\ (x_0, x_1, x_2, x_3) \to x_1 \\ \texttt{name} &= \texttt{Employee}\ (x_0, x_1, x_2, x_3) \to x_2 \\ \texttt{salary} &= \texttt{Employee}\ (x_0, x_1, x_2, x_3) \to x_3. \end{aligned}$$

Now, to find the sum of all salaries in an organisation, it is enough to select all employees, and then foldleft with respect to the addition of the function salary across the resulting list. More directly, one can employ a generic fold without creating the intermediate list.

Salary increases can be given by a function

$$\texttt{incrSalary}\ f = \texttt{Employee}(x_0, x_1, x_2, n) \to \texttt{Employee}(x_0, x_1, x_2, f\ n).$$

Suppose now that some employees are managers who get a bonus. Such an employee can be represented by replacing Un by a new constructor Bonus applied to the number representing the bonus, as in

$$\texttt{Employee}(\texttt{Bonus}\ 3, 2345, \texttt{"H. Houdini"}, 6789).$$

Now the function for increasing salaries can be given by

$$\begin{aligned} &\texttt{incrSalary}\ f = \\ &\quad \texttt{Employee}\ (\texttt{Bonus}\ r, x_1, x_2, n) \to \texttt{Employee}(\texttt{Bonus}\ (f\ r), x_1, x_2, (f\ n)) \\ &\mid \texttt{Employee}(x_0, x_1, x_2, n) \to \texttt{Employee}(x_0, x_1, x_2, f\ n) \end{aligned}$$

where bonuses, if any, are also increased.

This example suggests how pattern matching can be used to handle extensible records, since records with additional fields are represented by elaborations of the patterns for basic records.

6.2 Inheritance and Method Specialisation

Some patterns match more terms than others. This natural hierarchy makes it is easy to manage inheritance and method specialisation. For example, suppose people are to be represented by giving their name, a position, a list of their friends (also people) and perhaps some other data (the rest). For this it suffices to have a constructor `Person` so that

$$\texttt{Person}\ r\ (n, p, f)$$

represents a person whose name is n, has position p, has friends f and additional data r. The "method" `get_name` can be given by the case

$$|\ \texttt{Person}\ r\ (n, p, f) \rightarrow n$$

so that $\texttt{homer} = \texttt{Person Un ("Homer"}, 1, \texttt{Nil})$ maps to "Homer". Similarly, `get_position` can be defined by

$$|\ \texttt{Person}\ r\ (n, p, f) \rightarrow p.$$

Now some people may also have a family or proper name. One way of representing such people is `ProperPerson` (pn, n, p, f) in which pn is the proper name. However, this will not support inheritance: if `get_position` is applied to such a representation then matching will fail. A better approach is to represent a proper person by

$$\texttt{Person (ProperPerson}\ r2\ pn)\ (n, p, f)$$

so that a proper person *is* a person, by definition. Now the function `get_position` works uniformly on proper people, too. On the other hand, the function `get_name` is no longer satisfactory, since it ignores the proper name. So add a new case to it, to get

$$\begin{array}{l} \ \ \texttt{Person (ProperPerson}\ r2\ pn)\ (n, p, f) \rightarrow n\ \hat{}\texttt{"\ \ "}\hat{}\ pn) \\ |\ \texttt{Person}\ r\ (n, p, f) \rightarrow n \end{array}$$

so that $\texttt{harry} = \texttt{Person (ProperPerson}\ r2\ \texttt{"Joy") ("Harry"}, 3, \texttt{Nil})$ maps to "Harry Joy". Note that the meaning of `get_name` is determined by the data structure to which it is applied, i.e. by the object that invokes it, For example, given

$$\texttt{honey} = \texttt{Person Un ("Honey"}, 4, [\texttt{homer}, \texttt{harry}])$$

then

$$\begin{array}{l} \texttt{get\_name honey}\ \hat{}\ \texttt{" knows "}\ \hat{}\ \texttt{foldleft}\ (\lambda x.\lambda y.x\ \hat{}\ \texttt{get\_name}\ y\ \hat{}\ \texttt{","})\ \texttt{""} \\ \quad (\texttt{get\_friends honey}) \end{array}$$

yields "Honey knows Homer, Harry Joy,".

6.3 Object Calculus

Continuing on with the example of employees in Section 6.1, an alternative approach to representing the method for updating salaries is to make it part of the employee, which is then a self-contained object, as in

$$\texttt{Employee}\ (\texttt{Un}, 1234, \texttt{"John Smith"}, 567, h)$$

where h is a function that acts on the *whole record*, say,

$$\texttt{Employee}\ (x_0, x_1, x_2, x_3, x_4) \rightarrow \texttt{Employee}\ (x_0, x_1, x_2, (f\ x_3), x_4)\ .$$

By contrast, an example of a manager might be

$$\texttt{Employee}\ (\texttt{Bonus}\ 3, 2345, \texttt{"H. Houdini"}, 6789, k)$$

where k is

$$\texttt{Employee}\ (\texttt{Bonus}\ r, x_1, x_2, y_3, x_4) \rightarrow \texttt{Employee}\ (\texttt{Bonus}\ r, x_1, x_2, (g\ r\ y_3), x_4)\ .$$

Generalising from this, one can consider every attribute to be a method, i.e. a function able to act on the whole object. That is, a method becomes a function of the form

$$l_i = \varsigma(x).b_i$$

where l_i is the method name, x is a variable bound to the object as a whole, the *self parameter*, and b_i is a term, possibly containing x, that describes the method body. For example, the first employee above becomes

$$\texttt{Employee}\ (\varsigma(x).\texttt{Un}, \varsigma(x).1234, \varsigma(x).\texttt{"John Smith"}, \varsigma(x).567), \varsigma(x).b)$$

where $b = \texttt{Employee}\ (x_0, x_1, x_2, x_3, x_4) \rightarrow \texttt{Employee}\ (x_0, x_1, x_2, f\ x_3, x_4)$.

Abadi and Cardelli [1] defined the *pure object calculus* with syntax

$$\begin{array}{lll} a, b ::= & & \text{(object)} \\ & x & \text{(variable)} \\ & [l_i = \varsigma(x).b_i]^{i=1,\ldots,n} & \text{(record)} \\ & a.l & \text{(invocation)} \\ & a.l_i \equiv \varsigma(x).b_i & \text{(update)} \end{array}$$

where l is a meta-variable for a *label* taken from some fixed set $\mathscr{L}$ and x is a variable, as usual. The labels $l_1, \ldots, l_n$ are required to be distinct. The reduction rule for invocation is

$$[l_i = \varsigma(x).b_i]^{i=1,\ldots,n}.l_j \longrightarrow \{[l_i = \varsigma(x).b_i]^{i=1,\ldots,n}/x\}b_j\ .$$

It says that to invoke method l_j of an object $a = [l_i = \varsigma(x).b_i]^{i=1,\ldots,n}$ is to evaluate the body b_j of the method with its self parameter x replaced by a itself. The reduction rule for updating is

$$[l_i = \varsigma(x).b_i]^{i=1,\ldots,n}.l_j \equiv \varsigma(x).b \longrightarrow [l_i = \varsigma(x).b'_i]^{i=1,\ldots,n}$$
$$\text{where } b'_j = b \text{ and } b'_i = b_i \text{ otherwise.}$$

The interpretation of the object calculus into the pattern calculus maps labels to constructors and variables to variables. One way of interpreting records is as pattern-matching functions from labels to terms. That is,

$$\begin{aligned} a = [l_i = \varsigma(x).b_i]^{i=1,\ldots,n} = \\ & l_1\ x \to b_1 \\ & \ldots \\ & \mid l_n\ x \to b_n\ . \end{aligned}$$

Now an invocation $a.l$ is defined to be $a\ (l\ a)$ so that the invocation rule is just an instance of the match rule.

An object update is just an extension, viz

$$a.l_i \equiv \varsigma(x).b_i = l_i\ x \to b_i \mid a$$

since the new description of l_i takes precedence over the old one. Unfortunately, the update rule does not translate directly, since the pattern calculus has no mechanism for removing redundant cases from pattern-matching functions.

The main difficulty with this approach is that it is no longer possible to apply generic queries to records, since generic queries are built to act on data structures, not functions.

An alternative approach is to model records as tuples, just as before. Now

$$a = [l_i = \varsigma(x).b_i]^{i=1,\ldots,n} = (l_1\ (\lambda x.b_1), \ldots, l_n\ (\lambda x.b_n))$$

with

$$a.l_j = \texttt{elim}\ l_j\ (\texttt{head}\ (\texttt{select}\ \texttt{test}_j\ a))\ a$$

where $\texttt{test}_j$ picks out terms constructed by l_j. Similarly,

$$a.l_j \equiv \varsigma(x).b = \texttt{update}\ l_j\ (\lambda y.\lambda x.b)\ a$$

where `update` is defined in Sect. 5.5.

Theorem 6.2. *This translation from pure object calculus to pure static pattern calculus preserves reduction and normal forms, and the distinctness of normal forms.*

Proof. The proof is by straightforward induction on the structure of the reduction. □

6.4 Notes

The use of a placeholder for any additional fields of an object is probably quite old, but it is usually employed in the context of extensible records, rather than mere tuples. The first account of this pattern-matching approach was in [57]. The object calculus is developed in [1].

Part II
Types

Chapter 7
Parametric Polymorphism

Abstract This chapter considers two ways of typing the λ-calculus. *Simple types* are easy to understand, but are not very expressive. Greater power is obtained by introducing type symbols and their quantification, in System **F**. Now the Church encodings of data structures can be typed. Also, reduction is strongly normalising.

7.1 Simply Typed λ-Calculus

The *types* of the *simple type system* are given by the grammar

$$\begin{array}{rll} T ::= & & \text{(types)} \\ & \bullet & \text{(base)} \\ & T \to T & \text{(function type).} \end{array}$$

The base type is used to type numbers, booleans, etc. More such type constants will be added in later calculi but here the focus is on the function types. The arrow is right associative.

A *typed symbol* x^T is given by a term symbol x and a type T. The *term syntax* of the *simply typed* λ*-calculus* is given by the grammar

$$\begin{array}{rll} t ::= & & \text{(term)} \\ & x^T & \text{(variable)} \\ & t\,t & \text{(application)} \\ & \lambda x^T.t & \text{(abstraction).} \end{array}$$

Note that all symbols are typed, both the variables and the binding symbols. This is done to ensure that every expression in this grammar has at most one type, which is independent of the context within which the term is found. Such unique typing is not strictly necessary for λ-calculus, but will be essential later, when types play an active role in reduction.

B. Jay, *Pattern Calculus*,
DOI 10.1007/978-3-540-89185-7_7,

$$\frac{}{\Gamma, x^T \vdash x^T : T} \qquad \frac{\Gamma \vdash r : U \to S \quad \Gamma \vdash u : U}{\Gamma \vdash r\, u : S} \qquad \frac{\Gamma, x^U \vdash s : S}{\Gamma \vdash \lambda x^U.s : U \to S}$$

Fig. 7.1 Simply typed λ-calculus

When constructing well typed terms it is important to ensure that all occurrences of a free variable have the same type, as indicated by the *term context*, which is a set Γ of (typed) term symbols in which no symbol appears twice, e.g. Γ may not contain both x^S and x^T. A term context is sometimes represented as a sequence. In particular, Γ, x^U denotes the disjoint union of the term context Γ with the term context $\{x^U\}$. The *judgement* $\Gamma \vdash t : T$ asserts that t is a term of type T in the term context Γ.

The type derivation rules for the simply typed λ-calculus are in Fig. 7.1. The first rule asserts that if x^T is in the context then x^T has type T. The second rule types an application $r\ u$ by requiring that the type of r be a function type whose argument type is the type of u. The third rule types an abstraction $\lambda x^U.s$ with type $U \to S$ if s has type S when $x : U$ is added to the context.

It is easy to type simple examples such as the identity function on a type T

$$\vdash \lambda x^T.x^T : T \to T\,.$$

Similarly, function composition $\texttt{compose}^{S,T,U}$ for types S, T and U is given by

$$\vdash \lambda g^{T\to U}.\lambda f^{S\to T}.\lambda x^S.g^{T\to U}\ (f^{S\to T}\ x^S) : (T \to U) \to (S \to T) \to S \to U.$$

These examples show how polymorphic functions of the pure λ-calculus, such as the identity function $\lambda x.x$, correspond to families of simply typed functions. Another example is given by the conditional. In the pure λ-calculus, the conditional `if` b `then` r `else` s was given by $b\ r\ s$. Now if r and s have type T then b must have type $T \to T \to T$. That is, there is no one type of booleans here, but rather a family of branching constructions. If such families of functions are to be avoided then the simply typed calculus requires additional types, such as a type `Bool` of booleans, and corresponding term forms, such as conditionals, each with their own type derivation rules.

It is clear from the rule for typing variables that judgements often contain redundant type information, but this simplifies the development: the context ensures that all occurrences of a term variable have the same type, while the explicit typing of variables in terms makes the terms more self-contained, so that we may speak of *the* type of a term, as justified by the following lemma.

Lemma 7.1 (Unique Typing). *Let t be a term of the simply typed λ-calculus. If there are derivations $\Gamma \vdash t : T$ and $\Gamma' \vdash t : T'$ for some types T and T' and term contexts Γ and Γ' then $T = T'$.*

Proof. The proof is by a straightforward induction on the structure of the derivation. □

Most of the typed calculi to be developed will have the unique typing property. Throughout the book, the unique type T of a term t may be denoted t^T. This will indicate that there exists a term context Γ with a derivation of $\Gamma \vdash t : T$. Also, it will prove convenient to elide the types from symbols when these are specified elsewhere. In this way, the identity function on T is written $\lambda x^T.x : T \to T$.

Fundamental to reduction is the β*-reduction rule*

$$(\lambda x^U.s)\ u \longrightarrow \{u/x\}s \quad (\beta)$$

just as in the pure λ-calculus, except that symbols are now decorated with types. As in Fig. 2.1, the reduction rule is used to define a *rewriting relation* and then *general reduction*, as in Fig. 2.2.

In a typed calculus, it is crucial that reduction should *preserve typing*. For the (β)-rule above, the key point is that substitution of a term of type U for a symbol of type U in a term s preserves the type of s. Throughout the book, each typed calculus will require a Substitution Lemma such as the one that follows.

Lemma 7.2 (Substitution Lemma). *Suppose that there are derivations of* $\Gamma, x^U \vdash s : S$ *and of* $\Gamma \vdash u : U$ *for some term context* Γ, x^U *and terms* s *and* u. *Then there is a derivation of* $\Gamma \vdash \{u/x\}s : S$.

Proof. The proof is by induction on the structure of the term s. If s is x^U then S is U and $\{u/x\}s = u : U$ as required. If s is an application $s_1\ s_2$ then examining the derivation of the type of s shows that there is a type S_2 such that $s_1 : S_2 \to S$ and $s_2 : S_2$. Hence $\{u/x\}s_1 : S_2 \to S$ and $\{u/x\}s_2 : S_2$ by induction and so $\{u/x\}(s_1\ s_2) = \{u/x\}s_1\ \{u/x\}s_2 : S$ as required. If s is an abstraction $\lambda y^V.r$ (for some y not free in u) then S is of the form $V \to R$ for some type R. Hence $\{u/x\}r : R$ by induction and so $\{u/x\}(\lambda y^V.r) = \lambda y^V.\{u/x\}r : S$. □

Theorem 7.3 (Type Preservation). *If* $\Gamma \vdash t_1 : T$ *and there is a reduction* $t_1 \longrightarrow t_2$ *then there is a derivation of* $\Gamma \vdash t_2 : T$.

Proof. The proof is by induction on the structure of the rewriting step. This reduces the problem to consideration of the reduction relation and then to the reduction rule, in which case apply the Substitution Lemma. □

There is a type-erasing translation $|-|$ from the simply typed λ-calculus to the pure λ-calculus given by

$$\begin{aligned} |x^T| &= x \\ |r\ u| &= |r|\ |u| \\ |\lambda x^U.s| &= \lambda x.|s|\ . \end{aligned}$$

Theorem 7.4 (Type Erasure). *Type erasure preserves the general reduction relation. That is, if* $t \longrightarrow t'$ *in the simply typed* λ*-calculus then* $|t| \longrightarrow |t'|$ *in the pure* λ*-calculus. Further, if* $|t| \longrightarrow t''$ *then there is a term* t' *such that* $t \longrightarrow t'$ *in the simply typed* λ*-calculus and* $|t'| = |t''|$.

Proof. The type erasure of (β) is the β-rule for pure λ-calculus. □

Theorem 7.5 (Confluence). *Reduction is confluent in the simply typed λ-calculus.*

Proof. Suppose that t is a term that reduces to both t' and t''. Then $|t|$ reduces to both $|t'|$ and $|t''|$. Now confluence of the pure λ-calculus shows $|t'|$ and $|t''|$ have a common reduct u which must be the erasure of some common reduct t''' of t' and t'' by the Type Erasure Theorem. □

7.2 Data Structures as Typed Abstractions

The Church encoding of data structures in the pure λ-calculus does not work with simple types. A representative example is given by pairing. The Church encoding of pairs can be given a typed form as

$$\lambda x^R.\lambda y^S.\lambda f^{R\to S\to T}.f\,x\,y : R\to S\to (R\to S\to T)\to T\,.$$

Here, the desired product type $R*S$ is supplanted by the type $(R\to S\to T)\to T$ in which an extraneous type T has appeared. The direct solution is to introduce a new type form, for *product types* $R*S$ and to add constructors for pairing. Further, these must be parametrised by the types R and S to get the constructors

$$\mathtt{Pair}^{R,S} : R\to S\to R*S\,.$$

In the same spirit, one must add operators for the projections, namely $\mathtt{fst}^{R,S} : R*S\to R$ and $\mathtt{snd}^{R,S} : R*S\to S$ with associated parametrised families of reduction rules $\mathtt{fst}^{R,S}\ (\mathtt{Pair}^{R,S}\ r\ s) \longrightarrow r$ and $\mathtt{snd}^{R,S}\ (\mathtt{Pair}^{R,S}\ r\ s) \longrightarrow s$. Of course, the process must be repeated for lists, binary trees, etc.

This approach is easy to understand but relatively inexpressive compared to the pure λ-calculus. Since the difficulties arose from the need for extraneous type parameters, a better solution is to control the parameters by introducing type variables and their quantification.

For example, to type typing pairing, replace the type T above by a type variable Z to get

$$R\to S\to (R\to S\to Z)\to Z\,.$$

Finally, since Z is independent of R and S it may be *quantified*, to produce a term of type

$$R\to S\to \forall Z.(R\to S\to Z)\to Z$$

in which the original type parameter T is replaced by a bound variable Z. So, *define* the product type $R*S$ to be $\forall Z.(R\to S\to Z)\to Z$ so that pairing has type

$$R\to S\to R*S\,.$$

Indeed, R and S are themselves parameters which may be replaced by bound type variables X and Y so that it is enough to define a term

$$\texttt{pair} : \forall X.\forall Y.X \to Y \to X * Y\ .$$

In this manner, data types can be represented as quantified function types, whose constructors and eliminators have typed encodings.

These are central ideas of Jean-Yves Girard's System **F** of variable types, and their use in computation, as presented by John Reynolds. It is able to support all of the usual inductive data types without requiring any special constants or reduction rules, and all in a strongly normalising calculus. These data types are defined using type parameters to represent the types of the data. Such *parametric polymorphism* will underpin several other sorts of program reuse, too.

7.3 Quantified Types

Throughout the book, there is a collection of *type symbols* (meta-variables F,G,H and W,X,Y and Z). A *type context* (meta-variables Δ, Φ, Ψ) is a sequence of distinct type symbols (not a context that provides types for term symbols). If $X \in \Delta$ and $Y \notin \Delta$ then define $\{Y/X\}\Delta$ to be the result of replacing X by Y in Δ.

The syntax of the *quantified types* is given by the grammar

$$\begin{array}{lll} T ::= & & \text{(type)} \\ & X & \text{(variable)} \\ & T \to T & \text{(function)} \\ & \forall X.T & \text{(quantified).} \end{array}$$

Each type symbol is also a type variable. Function types are as before. A quantified type $\forall X.S$ binds the symbol X in S, much as a λ-abstraction binds a term symbol. Note the absence of type constants or product types, etc. It will emerge that these are not necessary for fundamental examples, which can now be interpreted using just these forms.

The machinery for manipulating type symbols (free variables, substitutions, α-equivalence, etc.) is similar to that for handling term symbols.

The *free type variables* $\mathsf{FV}(T)$ of a type T are given by

$$\begin{aligned} \mathsf{FV}(X) &= \{X\} \\ \mathsf{FV}(U \to S) &= \mathsf{FV}(U) \cup \mathsf{FV}(S) \\ \mathsf{FV}(\forall X.S) &= \mathsf{FV}(S) \setminus X\ . \end{aligned}$$

Throughout the book, a *type substitution* (meta-variables ρ, υ) is a function from type symbols to types, following the same conventions as the term substitutions in Chap. 2. For example, a type substitution ρ *avoids* a set of symbols if these symbols are neither in the domain nor the range of ρ.

The *union* $\rho_1 \cup \rho_2$ of type substitutions ρ_1 and ρ_2 is defined to be their union as relations, if this is a function. That is

$$
\begin{array}{ll}
(\rho_1 \cup \rho_2)X = \rho_1 X & \text{if } \rho_1 X = \rho_2 X \\
(\rho_1 \cup \rho_2)X = \rho_1 X & \text{if } X \in \mathsf{dom}(\rho_1) \setminus \mathsf{dom}(\rho_2) \\
(\rho_1 \cup \rho_2)X = \rho_2 X & \text{if } X \in \mathsf{dom}(\rho_2) \setminus \mathsf{dom}(\rho_1) \\
(\rho_1 \cup \rho_2)X = \text{undefined otherwise.} &
\end{array}
$$

A type substitution is *applied* to a type using the following rules:

$$
\begin{array}{rll}
\rho X &= \rho X & \text{if } X \in \mathsf{dom}(\rho) \\
\rho X &= X & \text{if } X \notin \mathsf{dom}(\rho) \\
\rho(U \to S) &= \rho U \to \rho S & \\
\rho(\forall X.S) &= \forall X.\rho S & \text{if } \rho \text{ avoids } X.
\end{array}
$$

The *α-equivalence* of types is the congruence generated by the following relation

$$\forall X.S =_\alpha \forall Y.\{Y/X\}S$$

provided that $Y \notin \mathsf{FV}(S)$. The *types* are equivalence classes of type syntax under α-equivalence.

7.4 System F

Now let us consider the corresponding terms. These will support abstraction and application with respect to both types and terms. The *term syntax* of System **F** is given by

$$
\begin{array}{lll}
t ::= & & \text{(term)} \\
& x^T & \text{(variable)} \\
& t\ t & \text{(application)} \\
& \lambda x^T.t & \text{(abstraction)} \\
& t\ T & \text{(type application)} \\
& \Lambda X.t & \text{(type abstraction)}\ .
\end{array}
$$

Note that a type application is here the application of a term *to* a type, not of a type to something. Now terms have free type and term variables, and can be affected by both type and term substitutions, etc.

The set of *free type variables* $\mathsf{FV}(t)$ of a term t is defined in the obvious manner, in the appendix. Similarly, the set of free type variables $\mathsf{FV}(\Gamma)$ of a term context Γ is given by the union of the sets of the free type variables of the types of all the term variables in Γ.

Throughout the book, a typed term t is *closed* if $\mathsf{FV}(t) = \{\}$ and $\mathsf{fv}(t) = \{\}$.

The *α-equivalence* of terms is the congruence relation generated by the renaming of binding type and term symbols by fresh symbols as follows:

$$
\begin{array}{l}
\lambda x^U.s =_\alpha \lambda y^U.\{y^U/x\}s \text{ if } y \notin \mathsf{fv}(s) \\
\Lambda X.s =_\alpha \Lambda Y.\{Y/X\}s \text{ if } Y \notin \mathsf{FV}(s).
\end{array}
$$

$$\frac{}{\Gamma, x^T \vdash x^T : T} \qquad \frac{\Gamma \vdash r : U \to S \quad \Gamma \vdash u : U}{\Gamma \vdash r\, u : S} \qquad \frac{\Gamma, x^U \vdash s : S}{\Gamma \vdash \lambda x^U.s : U \to S}$$

$$\frac{\Gamma \vdash t : \forall X.S}{\Gamma \vdash t\, U : \{U/X\}S} \qquad \frac{\Gamma \vdash t : T}{\Gamma \vdash \Lambda X.t : \forall X.T}\ X \notin \mathsf{FV}(\Gamma)$$

Fig. 7.2 System **F**

Define a *term* to be an equivalence class of the term syntax under α-equivalence.

The type derivation rules are given in Fig. 7.2. The first three are as for the simply typed λ-calculus. Type application triggers a type substitution in the type of the term itself. Type abstraction comes with a side condition which is designed to avoid binding of type symbols before binding the free term variables that use them. A typical binding arises in the example

$$\Lambda X.\lambda x^X.x^X : \forall X.X \to X$$

of the polymorphic identity function whose derivation first binds x^X and then X. A typical example of an illegal binding is $\Lambda X.x^X$ in which the free term variable x no longer has a meaningful type. Once again, terms have unique typing.

Lemma 7.6 (Substitution).

1. *If there is a derivation of $\Gamma \vdash t : T$ and ρ is a type substitution then there is a derivation of $\rho\Gamma \vdash \rho t : \rho T$.*
2. *If $\Gamma, x : U \vdash s : S$ is a term and $\Gamma \vdash u : U$ then $\Gamma \vdash \{u/x\}s : S$.*

Proof. The proofs are by straightforward induction on the structure of the terms. □

7.5 Reduction of Type Applications

The *reduction rules* of System **F** are given by two forms of β-reduction, for terms and types:

$$\begin{array}{lll} (\lambda x^U.s)\, u & \longrightarrow \{u/x\}s & (\beta 1) \\ (\Lambda X.s)\, U & \longrightarrow \{U/X\}s & (\beta 2). \end{array}$$

Theorem 7.7 (Type Preservation). *In System* **F**, *if there is a derivation of $\Gamma \vdash t : T$ and $t \longrightarrow t'$ then there is a derivation of $\Gamma \vdash t' : T$.*

Proof. Without loss of generality the reduction is given by a rule and now the Substitution Lemma applies. □

There is a natural translation from System **F** to the pure λ-calculus given by erasing types where the *type erasure* $|t|$ of a term t is defined by

$$\begin{aligned}
|x^T| &= x \\
|r\,u| &= |r|\,|u| \\
|\lambda x^U.s| &= \lambda x.|s| \\
|r\,U| &= |r| \\
|\Lambda X.s| &= |s|\,.
\end{aligned}$$

Theorem 7.8 (Type Erasure). *Type erasure in System* **F** *preserves the general reduction relation. That is, if $t \longrightarrow^* t'$ in System* **F** *then $|t| \longrightarrow^* |t'|$ in the pure λ-calculus.*

Proof. The type erasure of $(\beta 1)$ is the β-rule for pure λ-calculus while the type erasure of $(\beta 2)$ is the identity. Now apply induction. □

Theorem 7.9 (Confluence). *Reduction in System* **F** *is confluent.*

Proof. The proof is by simultaneous reduction. □

7.6 Lists as Functions

Here are some examples in System **F**.

Example 7.10. Functions

The *polymorphic identity* is

$$\mathtt{identity} = \Lambda X.\lambda x^X.x : \forall X.X \to X\,.$$

The identity can be applied to its type and itself to get

$$\mathtt{identity}\ (\forall X.X \to X)\ \mathtt{identity} : \forall X.X \to X$$

and reduces to `identity` in two steps. This shows that self-application can sometimes be typed.

Polymorphic *application* is given by

$$\mathtt{apply} = \Lambda X.\Lambda Y.\lambda x^{Y \to X}.\lambda y^Y.x\,y : \forall X.\forall Y.(Y \to X) \to Y \to X.$$

Composition is given by

$$\begin{aligned}
\mathtt{compose} &= \Lambda X.\Lambda Y.\Lambda Z.\lambda g^{(Y \to Z)}.\lambda f^{X \to Y}.\lambda x^X.g\ (f\ x) \\
&: \forall X.\forall Y.\forall Z.(Y \to Z) \to (X \to Y) \to (X \to Z).
\end{aligned}$$

Example 7.11. Pairs

Pairing is given by the term

$$\mathtt{pair} = \Lambda X.\Lambda Y.\lambda x^X.\lambda y^Y.\Lambda Z.\lambda f^{(X\to Y\to Z)}.f\,x\,y : \\ \forall X.\forall Y.X \to Y \to \forall Z.(X \to Y \to Z) \to Z\,.$$

For example, if $r : R$ and $s : S$ are terms then $\mathtt{pair}\ R\ S\ r\ s$ reduces to the term $\Lambda Z.\lambda f^{R\to S\to Z}.f\,r\,s : \forall Z.(R \to S \to Z) \to Z$ so that $R*S$ is just $\forall Z.(R \to S \to Z) \to Z$. The projections are given by

$$\begin{aligned} \mathtt{fst} &= \Lambda X.\Lambda Y.\lambda f^{X*Y}.f\ X\ (\lambda x^X.\lambda y^Y.x) : \forall X.\forall Y.X*Y \to X \\ \mathtt{snd} &= \Lambda X.\Lambda Y.\lambda f^{X*Y}.f\ Y\ (\lambda x^X.\lambda y^Y.y) : \forall X.\forall Y.X*Y \to Y \end{aligned}$$

so that

$$\begin{aligned} \mathtt{fst}\,R\,S\,(\mathtt{pair}\,R\,S\,r\,s) &\longrightarrow r \\ \mathtt{snd}\,R\,S\,(\mathtt{pair}\,R\,S\,r\,s) &\longrightarrow s\,. \end{aligned}$$

Example 7.12. Booleans and Conditionals

The type `bool` of booleans is given by

$$\mathtt{bool} = \forall Z.Z \to Z \to Z$$

with truth values

$$\begin{aligned} \mathtt{true} &= \Lambda Z.\lambda x^Z.\lambda y^Z.x \\ \mathtt{false} &= \Lambda Z.\lambda x^Z.\lambda y^Z.y \end{aligned}$$

and conditionals given by

$$\mathtt{if}\ b\ \mathtt{then}\ r^T\ \mathtt{else}\ s^T = b\ T\ r\ s\,.$$

For example, the conjunction of booleans is given by

$$\mathtt{conjunction} = \lambda x^{\mathtt{bool}}.\lambda y^{\mathtt{bool}}.\mathtt{if}\ x\ \mathtt{then}\ y\ \mathtt{else}\ \mathtt{false}.$$

Example 7.13. Alternatives

More generally, the *coproduct type* of types R and S is defined by

$$R+S = \forall Z.(R \to Z) \to (S \to Z) \to Z\,.$$

The left inclusion is given by

$$\mathtt{inl} = \Lambda X.\Lambda Y.\lambda x^X.\Lambda Z.\lambda f^{(X\to Z)}.\lambda g^{(Y\to Z)}.f\,x : \forall X.\forall Y.X \to X+Y\,.$$

Similarly, the right inclusion and the case analysis term are given by

$$\begin{aligned} \mathtt{inr} &= \Lambda X.\Lambda Y.\lambda y^Y.\Lambda Z.\lambda f^{(X\to Z)}.\lambda g^{(Y\to Z)}.g\,y : \forall X.\forall Y.Y \to X+Y \\ \mathtt{alt} &= \Lambda X.\Lambda Y.\Lambda Z.\lambda f^{X\to Z}.\lambda g^{Y\to Z}.\lambda z^{X+Y}.z\,Z\,f\,g \\ &: \forall X.\forall Y.\forall Z.(X \to Z) \to (Y \to Z) \to (X+Y \to Z)\,. \end{aligned}$$

For example, when `alt Bool (Bool * Bool) Bool identity fst` of type `Bool` + `Bool` * `Bool` → `Bool` is applied to `inr (pair false true)` it reduces to `false`.

Example 7.14. Natural Numbers

The *natural numbers* are given by the type

$$\texttt{nat} = \forall X.(X \to X) \to X \to X$$

with *zero* and *successor* given by

$$\begin{aligned}\texttt{zero} &= \Lambda X.\lambda f^{X\to X}.\lambda x^X.x\\ \texttt{succ} &= \lambda n^{\texttt{nat}}.\Lambda X.\lambda f^{X\to X}.\lambda x^X.f\ (n\,X\,x\,f)\,.\end{aligned}$$

For example, the number one is given by

$$\texttt{one} = \texttt{succ}\ \texttt{zero}$$

and addition of natural numbers is given by

$$\texttt{plusnat} = \lambda x^{\texttt{nat}}.\lambda y^{\texttt{nat}}.y\ \texttt{nat}\ x\ \texttt{succ}\,.$$

Example 7.15. Lists

Parametrised data types can also be handled. For example, given a type T define the type of *lists of* T by

$$\texttt{list}\ T = \forall Z.Z \to (T \to Z \to Z) \to Z$$

with the empty list given by

$$\texttt{nil} = \Lambda X.\Lambda Z.\lambda z^Z.\lambda f^{X\to Z\to Z}.z : \forall X.\texttt{list}\ X$$

and the operation of adding a new entry to the head of a list is given by

$$\begin{aligned}\texttt{cons} &= \Lambda X.\lambda x^X.\lambda y^{\texttt{list}\ X}.\Lambda Z.\lambda z^Z.\lambda f^{X\to Z\to Z}.f\ x\ (y\ f\ z)\\ &: \forall X.X \to \texttt{list}\ X \to \texttt{list}\ X\,.\end{aligned}$$

For example, the append of lists is given by

$$\texttt{append} = \Lambda X.\lambda x^{\texttt{list}\ X}.\lambda y^{\texttt{list}\ X}.x\ (\texttt{list}\ X)\ (\texttt{cons}\ X)\ y.$$

Case analysis on lists of X is given by

$$\texttt{foldright} = \Lambda X.\Lambda Z.\lambda z^Z.\lambda f^{X\to Z\to Z}.\lambda x^{\texttt{list}\ X}.x\ Z\ f\ z\,.$$

For example, to map a function across all the entries of a list is given by the function

$$\begin{aligned}\texttt{maplist} = {}& \Lambda X.\Lambda Y.\lambda f^{X\to Y}.\\ & \quad \texttt{foldright}\ X\ Y\ (\texttt{nil}\ Y)\ (\lambda x^X.\lambda z^{\texttt{list}\ Y}.\texttt{cons}\ Y\ (f\ x)\ z)\\ : {}& \forall X.\forall Y.(X \to Y) \to \texttt{list}\ X \to \texttt{list}\ Y\,.\end{aligned}$$

Example 7.16. Existential Types

The *existential type* $\exists X.T$ can be defined by

$$\exists X.T = \forall Z.(\forall X.T \to Z) \to Z\,.$$

If U is a type and $t : \{U/X\}T$ then the *package* $\langle U,t\rangle : \exists X.T$ is given by

$$\Lambda Z.\lambda f^{\forall X.T\to Z}.f\;U\;t\,.$$

7.7 Strong Normalisation

The strong normalisation theorem here uses Girard's technique of reducibility candidates inspired by Tait's reducibility predicates. Although all the proofs are by structural induction, the delicacy of the argument is in the interplay between induction on the type structure, induction on the term structure, and induction on the length of the reduction sequence. In particular, substitution may expand the structure of a type or term, so that the constructions employed in the argument must be parametrised by substitutions.

A term is *neutral* if it is not an abstraction.

A *reducibility candidate* of type U is a set $\mathscr{R}$ of terms of type U such that:

(CR1) If $t \in \mathscr{R}$ then t is strongly normalisable.
(CR2) If $t \in \mathscr{R}$ and $t \longrightarrow t_0$ then $t_0 \in \mathscr{R}$.
(CR3) If t is neutral, and every one-step reduct of t is in $\mathscr{R}$ then $t \in \mathscr{R}$.

Observe that if $t : U$ is neutral and normal then it is in $\mathscr{R}$. In particular, every term variable of type U is in $\mathscr{R}$.

A *reducibility substitution* is given by a type substitution ρ and a reducibility candidate $\mathscr{R}_i$ of type $\rho(X_i)$ for each symbol X_i in its domain. If T is a type whose free variables are in the domain of ρ then define the reducibility candidate $RED_T[\rho]$ for ρT by induction on the structure of T, as follows.

- If T is X_i then $RED_T[\rho] = \mathscr{R}_i$.
- If T is $U \to S$ then a term t is in $RED_T[\rho]$ if $u \in RED_U[\rho]$ implies $t\;u \in RED_S[\rho]$.
- If T is $\forall X.S$ then a term t is in $RED_T[\rho]$ if for every type U and reducibility candidate $\mathscr{S}$ for U then $t\;U \in RED_S[\rho, U/X]$.

Lemma 7.17. *$RED_T[\rho]$ is a reducibility candidate for ρT.*

Proof. The proof is by induction on the structure of T. If T is a variable then the result is immediate. Suppose that T is of the form $U \to S$.

(CR1) If $t \in RED_T[\rho]$ then $t\;x^U \in RED_S[\rho]$ for any term variable x. Hence $t\;x^U$ is strongly normalising by induction and (CR1), which implies that t is too.

(CR2) If $t \in RED_T[\rho]$ and $t \longrightarrow t'$ then consider some $u \in RED_U[\rho]$. Now $t\;u \in RED_S[\rho]$ and $t\;u \longrightarrow t'\;u$ which implies that $t'\;u \in RED_S[\rho]$ by induction and (CR2). Hence $t' \in RED_T[\rho]$.

(CR3) Suppose that t is neutral and $t \longrightarrow t'$ implies that $t' \in RED_T[\rho]$. Given $u \in RED_U[\rho]$ then $t\ u$ is neutral. Hence, by induction and (CR3) it suffices to prove that every reduct of it is in $RED_S[\rho]$ by induction on the reduction rank of u. Since t is neutral, a reduction of $t\ u$ is either by a reduction of t to some t' (in which case $t'\ u \in RED_S[\rho]$ by assumption) or of u in which case the rank is decreased.

Finally, suppose that T is of the form $\forall X.S$.

(CR1) If $t \in RED_T[\rho]$ then $t\ X \in RED_S[\rho, X/X]$ for any choice of reducibility candidate for X, e.g. its strongly normalising terms. Hence $t\ X$ is strongly normalising, and so t is too.
(CR2) If $t \in RED_T[\rho]$ and $t \longrightarrow t'$ then for all types U and reducibility candidates $\mathscr{S}$ for U we have $t\ U \in RED_S[\rho, U/X]$ and so its reduct $t'\ U \in RED_S[\rho, U/X]$ by induction and (CR2). Hence $t' \in RED_T[\rho]$.
(CR3) Let t be neutral and suppose all the t' one step from t are in $RED_T[\rho]$. For each type U with reducibility candidate $\mathscr{S}$ it suffices to prove that all one-step reducts of the neutral term $t\ U$ are in $RED_S[\rho, U/X]$ (by induction and (CR3)). Since t is neutral such reducts are given by reduction of t to some $t' \in RED_T[\rho]$ and so $t'\ U \in RED_{\{U/X\}S}[\rho]$ as required.

□

Lemma 7.18. *For all types T and V and type symbol X and reducibility substitution ρ it holds that*

$$RED_{\{U/X\}S}[\rho] = RED_S[\rho, \rho U/X]$$

where ρU has reducibility candidate $RED_U[\rho]$.

Proof. The proof is by straightforward induction on the structure of S. □

Lemma 7.19. *Let $t : T$ be a term and ρ be a reducibility substitution whose domain includes* $\mathsf{FV}(T)$ *let and σ be a term substitution with domain* $\mathsf{fv}(t)$ *such that $\sigma\rho x \in RED_U[\rho]$ for each x^U free in t. Then $\sigma\rho t \in RED_T[\rho]$.*

Proof. The proof is by induction on the structure of t. If t is a symbol then $\sigma\rho x$ is reducible by assumption. If t is an application $r\ u$ then $\sigma\rho r$ and $\sigma\rho u$ are reducible by induction and so $\sigma\rho(r\ u)$ is reducible by the definition of $RED_T[\rho]$. If t is an abstraction $\lambda x^U.s$ then it suffices to show that $\sigma\rho(\lambda x^U.s)\ u$ is reducible for each $u \in RED_U[\rho]$. Since it is neutral, it suffices to prove that all of its reducts are reducible. Now s and u are reducible and hence strongly normalising. The proof is by induction on the sum of the ranks of s and u. Now consider a reduction of $t\ u$. If it is of s or u then apply induction on the sum of ranks. If it is the β-reduction rule then apply induction on s and $\sigma' = \sigma \cup \{u/x\}$.

If t is a type application $r\ U$ then $\sigma\rho(r\ U) = \sigma\rho r\ \rho U$ which is reducible since $\sigma\rho r$ is. If t is a type abstraction $\Lambda X.s$ then it suffices to show that for each type U with reducibility candidate $\mathscr{S}$ the term $\sigma\rho t\ U$ is in $RED_S[\rho, U/X]$. Since $t\ U$ is neutral, it suffices to prove that all reducts of $\sigma\rho t\ U)$ are in $RED_{\{U/X\}S}[\rho]$. By Lemma 7.18, this set is also $RED_S[\rho, U/X]$. Since $\sigma\rho s$ is reducible and hence strongly normalising, the proof can proceed by induction on its reduction rank. Now consider a reduction of $\sigma\rho t\ U$. If it is of $\sigma\rho s$ then apply induction on the rank. If it is the β-reduction rule then let ρ' be the substitution $\rho, U/X$. Now $\{U/X\}\sigma\rho s$ is $\sigma\rho' s$ and induction implies that this is in $RED_S[\rho, U/X]$ as required. □

Theorem 7.20. *All terms in System* **F** *are strongly normalising.*

Proof. Apply the lemma above to the identity type and term substitutions on the free variables of t with reducibility candidates consisting of all strongly normalising terms of the required types. □

7.8 Notes

Alonzo Church introduced the simply typed λ-calculus in 1940 [20] to avoid paradoxical uses of the untyped λ-calculus. In 1967, Tait [96] showed that its β-reduction is strongly normalising. There is an extensive literature on simply typed λ-calculus and related issues, but they are not central to the concerns of this book.

System **F** was introduced by Jean-Yves Girard in his 1972 thesis [34] which proved strong normalisation. The standard reference is now [35]. John Reynolds independently discovered this use of quantified types for parametrically polymorphic programming [89]. System **F** appears within programming languages such as HASKELL [84] and **F#** [31] and supports the typing of theorem provers such as Coq [97].

An overview of typed λ-calculi is given by [7].

Chapter 8
Functor Polymorphism

Abstract Functorially polymorphic terms such as map (defined in Chap. 4) require additional type machinery to support them. Type matching is used to choose the correct term for the type of the argument, while the overall type of map requires a type application $F\ X$ to describe an arbitrary structure (or functor) F containing data of type X.

8.1 Ad Hoc Polymorphism

The earliest discussions of polymorphism distinguished the parametric polymorphism of append and other functions in System **F** from the *ad hoc* polymorphism of operations such as $+$ which employs different algorithms for integers or floats or booleans, etc. A common view, as proposed by Strachey, is that ad hoc polymorphism is rather superficial, in that it is resolved statically, e.g. during type inference, before the real computation begins. However, this viewpoint does not allow for any dynamic choice between the algorithms being driven by the values of types.

Consider a function toString which converts its argument into a string, suitable for printing. It may have special cases of type nat $\rightarrow$ string and bool $\rightarrow$ string as well as a default that yields an error message, of type $X \rightarrow$ string that is parametrically polymorphic in X. Suppose that toString is applied to some term variable $y : Y$ where Y is a type variable. Until the value of Y is known, it is impossible to determine whether to use the special case for natural numbers, or booleans, or the default. Hence it is necessary to be able to combine the various cases as a term, and use type information to choose between them, so that toString nat reduces to the special case for nat and toString (nat $*$ nat) reduces to the default case. Note that toString Y will not reduce at all, until the value of the type variable Y is known.

Although these intentions are fairly clear, they are not so easy to realise. Suppose that the default case of toString has type $\forall X.X \rightarrow$ string. When toString is applied to nat $*$ nat then X is instantiated to nat $*$ nat and the resulting term has

B. Jay, *Pattern Calculus*,
DOI 10.1007/978-3-540-89185-7_8, © Springer-Verlag Berlin Heidelberg 2009

type `nat*nat` $\rightarrow$ `string` as expected. However, now suppose that there is a special case for products, of type $\forall X.\forall Y.X * Y \rightarrow$ `String`. Now it is necessary to *match* the type $X * Y$ against `nat*nat` to find values for the type symbols X and Y.

The first step in the solution is to generalise System **F** so that type symbol instantiation is handled by *type matching* in System **FM**. Then it is a simple matter to add machinery for choosing between such typecases in the *typecase calculus*. Note the inversion of the order of development, in that this chapter will add pattern matching to the type system, even though terms do not yet contain patterns.

8.2 Typecases

The types of System **FM** are given by the grammar

$$\begin{array}{lll} T ::= & & \text{(type)} \\ & X & \text{(variable)} \\ & T \rightarrow T & \text{(function)} \\ & \forall_T[\Delta].T & \text{(typecase).} \end{array}$$

Type variables and function types are as in System **F**. The *typecase* $\forall_P[\Delta].S$ quantifies the type S by the type symbols in the sequence Δ under the restriction that instantiation of symbols in Δ will be achieved by matching of P, in the sense to be explained later in this section. The usual quantified type $\forall X.S$ can be defined as $\forall_X[X].S$ since the variable X will match any type. Similarly, if $\Delta = X_1,\ldots,X_n$ then $\forall\Delta.S$ is defined to be $\forall X_1.\ldots.\forall X_n.S$.

The *free type variables* of a typecase are given by

$$\mathsf{FV}(\forall_P[\Delta].S) = (\mathsf{FV}(P) \cup \mathsf{FV}(S)) \setminus \Delta.$$

A typecase $\forall_P[\Delta].S$ is *well-formed* if $\Delta \cap \mathsf{FV}(S) \subseteq \mathsf{FV}(P)$. More generally, a type T is *well-formed* if every typecase within it is. The restriction on well-formed types will be necessary to ensure that bound variables do not become free after type matching.

The *α-equivalence* of types is the congruence generated by

$$\forall_P[\Delta].S =_\alpha \forall_{\{Y/X\}P}[\{Y/X\}\Delta].\{Y/X\}S \text{ if } X \in \Delta \text{ and } Y \text{ fresh.}$$

The *types* are α-equivalence classes of well-formed type syntax.

A *unifier* for types S and T is a type substitution ρ such that $\rho S = \rho T$ i.e. that solves the equation $S = T$. A *most general unifier* for them is a unifier υ of S and T through which any other such unifier *factors*. That is, for any unifier ρ there is a type substitution σ such that $\sigma \circ \upsilon = \rho$. For example, the types X and $Y \rightarrow Y$ are unified by the substitution $\{U \rightarrow U/X, U/Y\}$ for any type U, and have most general unifier $\{Y \rightarrow Y/X\}$.

$$\begin{aligned}
\{X = X\} &= \{\} \\
\{S = X\} &= \{S/X\} \text{ if } X \notin \mathsf{FV}(S) \\
\{X = T\} &= \{T/X\} \text{ if } X \notin \mathsf{FV}(T) \\
\{P \to S = Q \to T\} &= \text{let } \upsilon_1 = \{P = Q\} \text{ in} \\
&\quad\ \text{let } \upsilon_2 = \{\upsilon_1 S = \upsilon_1 T\} \text{ in} \\
&\quad\ \upsilon_2 \circ \upsilon_1 \\
\{\forall_P[\Delta].S = \forall_Q[\Delta].T\} &= \text{let } \upsilon_1 = \{P = Q\} \text{ in} \\
&\quad\ \text{let } \upsilon_2 = \{\upsilon_1 S = \upsilon_1 T\} \text{ in} \\
&\quad\ \upsilon_2 \circ \upsilon_1 \quad \text{if this avoids } \Delta \\
\{S = T\} &= \text{undefined otherwise}
\end{aligned}$$

Fig. 8.1 Type unification

Define the substitution $\{S = T\}$ by applying the rules in Fig. 8.1 in order. Some care is required to apply the rule for typecases so here are some examples:

$$\begin{aligned}
\{\forall_X[X].Y = \forall_X[X].Z \to Z\} &= \{Z \to Z/Y\} \\
\{\forall_X[X].Y = \forall_{Z\to Z}[X].Y &= \text{undefined} \\
\{\forall_X[X].Y = \forall_X[X].X\} &= \text{undefined} \\
\{\forall_X[X].X = Z \to Y\} &= \text{undefined.}
\end{aligned}$$

The three undefined substitutions arise because substitutions cannot: eliminate bound symbols; introduce bound symbols; or eliminate quantifiers. In general, to unify types given by the syntax $\forall_P[\Delta_1].S$ and $\forall_Q[\Delta_2].T$ it is necessary to first rename bound variables so that both bind the same type context Δ.

Theorem 8.1. *Two types S and T have a unifier if and only if $\{S = T\}$ exists, in which case it is their most general unifier.*

Proof. The proof is by straightforward induction on the type structure. □

It is also useful to have a one-sided form of unification called type matching. A *type match* is either a *successful match*, of the form some ρ where ρ is a type substitution, or a *failure*, denoted by none. A failed match is distinct from an undefined match, which may evolve to a success or failure.

The three possible outcomes of the process of type matching will be some type substitution, representing success, or none, representing definite failure, or undefined, where the result depends on the values of free type variables not currently available for substitution. When deriving types, being undefined will be akin to failure. This is captured by defining the application of none to a type to be undefined. However, matching will also be used during reduction, in which case match failure triggers default behaviour, while undefined matches will block reduction until the type match has a definite value.

Operations on substitutions are extended to matches of the form some ρ in the obvious manner. Indeed, the distinction between the match and the substitution will

$$\begin{aligned}
\{U/[\Delta]\,X\} &= \mathsf{some}\ \{U/X\} \text{ if } X \in \Delta \\
\{X/[\Delta]\,X\} &= \mathsf{some}\ \{\} \text{ if } X \notin \Delta \\
\{U/[\Delta]\,X\} &= \text{undefined, otherwise} \\
\{X/[\Delta]\,P\} &= \text{undefined, otherwise} \\
\{P \to S/[\Delta]\,Q \to T\} &= \{P/[\Delta]\,Q\} \cup \{S/[\Delta]\,T\} \\
\{\forall_P[\Phi].S/[\Delta]\,\forall_Q[\Phi].T\} &= \{P/[\Delta]\,Q\} \cup \{S/[\Delta]\,T\} \text{ if this avoids } \Phi \\
\{U/[\Delta]\,P\} &= \mathsf{none}\ \text{otherwise}
\end{aligned}$$

Fig. 8.2 Type matching

typically be suppressed when there is no risk of ambiguity. Operations involving undefined matches are undefined; otherwise, operations involving none produce none. Also, none *avoids* all type symbols.

Given a type context Δ and types P and U a *match of P against U with respect to Δ* is some type substitution ρ whose domain is within Δ such that $\rho P = U$. It is *most general* if any other such factors through it. The algorithm for the most general match $\{U/[\Delta]\ P\}$ of a type P against a type U with respect to a type context Δ is given in Fig. 8.2.

Theorem 8.2. *Let Δ be a type context and let P and U be types. There is a match of P against U with respect to Δ if and only if $\{U/[\Delta]\ P\}$ is some substitution, in which case it is their most general such.*

Proof. The proof is a routine induction on the structure of P, given the care already taken with typecases. For example, suppose that $\rho(\forall_P[\Phi].S) = \forall_Q[\Phi].T$ where ρ has domain within Δ. Then, without loss of generality, ρ avoids Φ, too. □

Lemma 8.3. *Let $\{U/[\Delta]P\}$ exist for some type context Δ and types U and P. If ρ is a type substitution which avoids Δ then $\{\rho U/[\Delta]\rho P\}$ exists and*

$$\{\rho U/[\Delta]\rho P\} \circ \rho = \rho \circ \{U/[\Delta]P\}\,.$$

Proof. The proof is by induction on the structure of P. If P is a variable X in Δ then $\rho P = X$ and $\{\rho U/[\Delta]\rho P\} \circ \rho = \{\rho U/X\} \circ \rho = \rho \circ \{U/X\}$. If P is any other variable then U is P and so both sides are ρ. If P is a function type or typecase then so is U so apply induction twice. □

8.3 System FM

The *term syntax* of System **FM** is given by the grammar

$$\frac{}{\Gamma, x^T \vdash x^T : T} \qquad \frac{\Gamma \vdash r : U \to S \quad \Gamma \vdash u : U}{\Gamma \vdash r\, u : S} \qquad \frac{\Gamma, x^U \vdash s : S}{\Gamma \vdash \lambda x^U.s : U \to S}$$

$$\frac{\Gamma \vdash r : \forall_P[\Delta].S}{\Gamma \vdash r\, U : \{U/[\Delta]\, P\}S} \qquad \frac{\Gamma \vdash s : S}{\Gamma \vdash [\Delta]\, P \to s : \forall_P[\Delta].S}\ \Delta \cap \mathsf{FV}(\Gamma) = \{\}$$

Fig. 8.3 System **FM**

$$\begin{array}{lll} t ::= & & \text{(term)} \\ & x^T & \text{(variable)} \\ & t\ t & \text{(application)} \\ & \lambda x^T.t & \text{(abstraction)} \\ & t\ T & \text{(type application)} \\ & [\Delta]\ T \to t & \text{(typecase)}\,. \end{array}$$

This is almost the same as that of System **F**, the only difference being the replacement of type abstractions by typecases. A typecase $[\Delta]\, P \to s$ abstracts s with respect to the type symbols in Δ with P representing a constraint upon how the type symbols may be instantiated. It is *well-formed* if $\Delta \cap \mathsf{FV}(s) \subseteq \mathsf{FV}(P)$. More generally, a term t is *well-formed* if all typecases within it are.

The *free type variables* of a typecase are given by

$$\mathsf{FV}([\Delta]\, P \to s) = (\mathsf{FV}(P) \cup \mathsf{FV}(s)) \setminus \Delta\,.$$

Then the definitions of free type and term variables, substitutions and α-conversion are as expected.

The type derivation rules for System **FM** are given in Fig. 8.3. The first three rules are the same as those of the simply typed λ-calculus but the rules for type applications and match abstractions are new. A term $r : \forall_P[\Delta].S$ may be applied to a type U only if $\{U/[\Delta]\ P\}S$ is some substitution. That is, the type P provides a constraint upon how the type variables in Δ may be instantiated. Note that since all variables in Δ are free in P, the domain of the resulting substitution contains all of Δ. The rule for typecases is the natural generalisation of the rule for type abstractions in System **F**.

The *reduction rules* of System **FM** are given by the β-reduction of terms plus a rule for typecases, namely

$$\begin{array}{rcll} (\lambda x^U.s)\ u & \longrightarrow & \{u/x\}s & (\beta 1) \\ ([\Delta]\, P \to s)\ U & \longrightarrow & \{U/[\Delta]\ P\}s & \text{(match2)}. \end{array}$$

Note that if the redex is well-typed then the type match $\{U/[\Delta]\ P\}$ is some substitution.

Theorem 8.4 (Type Preservation). *In System* **FM***, if there is a derivation of* $\Gamma \vdash t : T$ *and* $t \longrightarrow t'$ *then there is a derivation of* $\Gamma \vdash t' : T$.

Proof. Without loss of generality the reduction is given by a rule. For ($\beta 1$) the Substitution Lemma applies. For ($\beta 2$) above let $\rho = \{U/[\Delta]\ P\}$ and suppose that $\Gamma \vdash s : S$. Now $\Delta \cap \mathsf{FV}(\Gamma) = \{\}$ implies that $\rho\Gamma = \Gamma$ and so $\Gamma \vdash \rho s : \rho S$ as required, by the Substitution Lemma. □

Theorem 8.5 (Confluence). *Reduction in System* **FM** *is confluent.*

Proof. The proof is by simultaneous reduction. □

There is a natural embedding of System **F** to System **FM** given by identifying $\forall X.S$ with $\forall_X [X].S$ and identifying $\Lambda X.s$ with $[X]\ X \to s$. It preserves reduction since the β-rule for types becomes an instance of the rule for typecases.

$$([X]\ X \to s)\ U \longrightarrow \{U/[X]\ X\}s = \{U/X\}s\ .$$

Conversely, there is a translation $[\![-]\!]$ of System **FM** to System **F**. Let Δ be some $X_1, \ldots X_n$. In System **F** define $\forall\Delta.T$ to be $\forall X_1 . \ldots . \forall X_n.T$ and $\Lambda\Delta.t$ to be $\Lambda X_1 . \ldots . \Lambda X_n.t$. Then the translation is given by

$$\begin{aligned}
[\![X]\!] &= X \\
[\![U \to S]\!] &= [\![U]\!] \to [\![S]\!] \\
[\![\forall_P [\Delta].S]\!] &= \forall\Delta.[\![S]\!] \\
[\![x^T]\!] &= x^T \\
[\![r\ u]\!] &= [\![r]\!]\ [\![u]\!] \\
[\![r^{\forall_P[\Delta].S}\ U]\!] &= [\![r]\!]\ U_1\ \ldots\ U_n \text{ where } U_i = [\![\{U/[\Delta]\ P\}X_i]\!] \\
[\![[\Delta]\ P \to s]\!] &= \Lambda\Delta.[\![s]\!]\ .
\end{aligned}$$

Note how the constraints embodied by the type P are captured in the translation of type applications, not of match abstractions. Reduction of a type application translates to a sequence of reductions of System **F** whose length is the number of bound type symbols

$$(\Lambda\Delta.s)\ U_1\ \ldots\ U_n \longrightarrow^* [\![\{U/[\Delta]\ P\}]\!]s$$

where the translation of the type substitution is defined in the obvious manner. This coarser granularity will prove useful later when the nature of Δ is determined dynamically.

Theorem 8.6. *The translation from System* **FM** *to System* **F** *maps terms from System* **F** *to themselves, and preserves type erasure.*

Proof. The proof is by a straightforward induction on the syntax of types and terms. □

The most common use of typecases arises when the type to be matched is the argument type of a function, so that it is convenient to introduce some special notation. Define the *quantified function type*

$$[\Delta]\ P \to S$$

to be $\forall_P [\Delta].P \to S$ and the *quantified abstraction* $\lambda[\Delta]\ x^P.s$ to be $[\Delta]\ P \to \lambda x^P.s$.

$$\frac{\Gamma \vdash s : S \quad \Gamma \vdash r : R \quad S \approx R}{\Gamma \vdash s \,\#\, r : R}$$

Fig. 8.4 Choices

8.4 Typecase Calculus

It is a simple matter to add choices between typecases to System **FM**. The basic idea is that when such a choice $s \# r$ is applied to some type U it reduces to either $s\ U$ or $r\ U$ according to the success or failure of some type matching. When creating a choice it is essential that any potential type ambiguity be harmless. That is, if both terms can apply to arguments of the same type then they must produce results of the same type. This will be guaranteed by requiring that the types of the two alternatives be *similar*.

Consider two typecases $\forall_P[\Delta].S$ and $\forall_Q[\Phi].T$ where Δ and Φ are assumed disjoint. These types are *similar* (written $\forall_P[\Delta].S \approx \forall_Q[\Phi].T$) if any solution of $P = Q$ is also a solution of $S = T$. That is, if $\upsilon = \{P = Q\}$ exists then $\upsilon S = \upsilon T$.Note that if P and Q do not have a unifier then the typecases are automatically similar, since there is no ambiguity to be concerned about. For example, $[]\ \texttt{nat} \rightarrow \texttt{nat} \approx []\ \texttt{bool} \rightarrow \texttt{bool} \rightarrow \texttt{bool}$. The more common situation is represented by $[]\ \texttt{nat} \rightarrow \texttt{nat} \approx [X]\ X \rightarrow X$ while $[]\ \texttt{nat} \rightarrow \texttt{nat}$ is not similar to $[X]\ X \rightarrow \texttt{bool}$.

Lemma 8.7. *If $S \approx R$ and ρ is a type substitution then $\rho S \approx \rho R$.*

Proof. Let S be $\forall_P[\Delta].S_1$ and R be $\forall_Q[\Phi].R_1$. Without loss of generality, ρ avoids Δ and Φ. If ρP and ρQ can't be unified then there is nothing to prove, so suppose that $\upsilon = \{\rho P = \rho Q\}$ exists. Then $\upsilon \circ \rho$ factors through $\{P = Q\}$ by some substitution σ and so $\upsilon \rho S = \sigma\{P = Q\}S = \sigma\{P = Q\}T = \upsilon \rho T$. □

The type derivation rules for the typecase calculus are given by those of System **FM** plus the rule for choices in Fig. 8.4. In a choice $s \# r$ the term s is its *special case* while r is its *default*. Note that although similarity is a symmetrical relation, the type of a choice is the type of its default.

The reduction rules for choices are given by

$$\begin{array}{llll} (s^{\forall_P[\Delta].S} \,\#\, r)\ U & \longrightarrow s\ U & \text{if } \{U/[\Delta]\ P\} = \mathsf{some}\ \rho & \text{(left)} \\ (s^{\forall_P[\Delta].S} \,\#\, r)\ U & \longrightarrow r\ U & \text{if } \{U/[\Delta]\ P\} = \mathsf{none} & \text{(right).} \end{array}$$

Of course, if $\{U/[\Delta]\ P\}$ is undefined then the left-hand side above does not reduce.

Theorem 8.8 (Type Preservation). *In typecase calculus, if there is a derivation of $\Gamma \vdash t : T$ and $t \longrightarrow t'$ then there is a derivation of $\Gamma \vdash t' : T$.*

Proof. Without loss of generality the reduction is given by a rule. For the rules of System **FM** proceed as before. To show that type substitutions preserve typing, note that type substitutions preserve similarity of types, by Lemma 8.7, and preserve type matching, by Lemma 8.3. For the reduction of a choice to its left branch, exploit similarity. For the reduction of a choice to its right branch, the result is immediate. □

Example 8.9. Addition
A simple example of a choice is to define $\mathtt{plus} : \forall_X[X].X \to X \to X$ by

$$\begin{array}{l} [\,]\ \mathtt{nat} \to \mathtt{plusnat} \\ \#\ [\,]\ \mathtt{bool} \to \mathtt{conjunction} \\ \#\ [X]\ X \to \lambda x^X.\lambda y^X.x. \end{array}$$

When applied to nat or bool then it reduces to plusnat or conjunction. On other types it defaults to the first projection (though one can use some error term if preferred).

8.5 Combinatory Types

Till now, types of lists and trees, such as list nat and btree X have been defined as function types. In particular, the expression list is not a type. At best, it is a meta-function for constructing types from type arguments. However, the syntax is suggestive, since it reinforces the view that the list structure is separate from the nature of its entries. To some extent, this is already captured by parametric polymorphism, but the latter concerns only the type of the list entries, without allowing for any polymorphism in the choice of the structure.

This section introduces type constants and type applications as primitives. For example, given type constants List and Int one can create the type List Int of lists of integers. Types so constructed will be loosely referred to as *data types*. To be sure, the type List does not have any associated closed terms. Rather, its applications to types has values. If desired, this distinction can be reflected in a system of *kinds* for classifying types, but it is not essential. Again, if inhabited types such as Int correspond to objects in a *category* then types such as List correspond to functors between categories. This approach allows for the creation of types such as $F\ X$ where F is a type variable as well as X. The ability to instantiate F by different functors, such as List or Btree leads to *functor polymorphism*. The canonical example of functor polymorphism is

$$\mathtt{map} : \forall X,Y.(X \to Y) \to \forall F.F\ X \to F\ Y$$

where F is a type variable representing an unknown structure, or functor. Other examples will be given for folding or zipping.

Such data types will have several other uses in the chapters ahead, in establishing strong normalisation, and in typing object-orientation. Hence they may be included in any subsequent type systems, even though they are not essential to typing of pattern calculus.

The *combinatory types* are given by the grammar

$$\begin{array}{lll} T ::= & & \text{(type)} \\ & X & \text{(variable)} \\ & T \to T & \text{(function)} \\ & \forall_T[\Delta].T & \text{(match)} \\ & C & \text{(constant)} \\ & T\,T & \text{(application).} \end{array}$$

It is obtained by adding *type constants* (meta-variable C) and type applications $S\,T$ to the types of System **FM**. The type constants and applications can be used to represent datum types, such as `Int` and `Float` of integers and floats, or a unit type `Unit` or `List` or `Product`. For example, we may write $S*T$ for `Product` $S\,T$. Since type applications do not bind any type symbols, the definitions of type unification and matching are extended in the obvious manner.

8.6 Functorial Mapping

To create terms whose type is a constant or application requires some associated term constants. Constructors are enough when pattern matching is available, but till then some operators are required too. For example, suppose the following boolean and list constants are given :

$$\begin{array}{rl} \texttt{True} : & \texttt{Bool} \\ \texttt{False} : & \texttt{Bool} \\ \texttt{cond} : & \forall X.\texttt{Bool} \to X \to X \to X \\ \texttt{fix} : & \forall X.(X \to X) \to X \\ \texttt{Nil} : & \forall X.\texttt{List}\; X \\ \texttt{Cons} : & \forall X.X \to \texttt{List}\; X \to \texttt{List}\; X \\ \texttt{isNil} : & \forall X.\texttt{List}\; X \to \texttt{Bool} \\ \texttt{head} : & \forall X.\texttt{List}\; X \to X \\ \texttt{tail} : & \forall X.\texttt{List}\; X \to \texttt{List}\; X \end{array}$$

with reduction rules

$$\begin{array}{rcl} \texttt{cond}\;\texttt{True} & \longrightarrow & \lambda x.\lambda y.x \\ \texttt{cond}\;\texttt{False} & \longrightarrow & \lambda x.\lambda y.y \\ \texttt{fix}\;T\;f & \longrightarrow & f\;(\texttt{fix}\;T\;f) \\ \texttt{isNil}\;T\;(\texttt{Nil}\;T) & \longrightarrow & \texttt{True} \\ \texttt{isNil}\;T\;(\texttt{Cons}\;T\;h\;t) & \longrightarrow & \texttt{False} \\ \texttt{head}\;T\;(\texttt{Cons}\;T\;h\;t) & \longrightarrow & h \\ \texttt{tail}\;T\;(\texttt{Cons}\;T\;h\;t) & \longrightarrow & t\,. \end{array}$$

Now the usual list operations, for appending, mapping and folding, in Sect. 4.4 can be defined to be polymorphic in the choice of list entry type. More generally, one can use choices between typecases to define generic mapping so that it is polymorphic in the choice of "functor" as well as the choice of "data" type. That said, the details are far too tedious to be illuminating. Rather, this generic mapping will be defined in **bondi** in Sect. 14.4.

8.7 Notes

Branching on the value of a type is an idea almost as old as typed programming and occurs in various guises. For example, *intentional type analysis* [39] uses dynamic analysis of type structure to generate specialised code for unboxed data. Also, [80] considers type-indexed functions as a design pattern. However, the use of type matching (substitution), rather than equality, may be new, especially at the level of a calculus, rather than a programming language. In particular, System **FM** appears to be new. Other variants of System **F** have been developed recently [51].

Robinson's original unification algorithm [90] is here generalised to handle quantified symbols, by introducing the concept of a substitution avoiding a symbol.

Chapter 9
Path Polymorphism

Abstract Typing terms that act uniformly on all data structures is challenging because the type of a compound does not determine the types of its components, so that direct attempts to type `car` or `cdr` produce ill formed types. The query calculus can be seen as a typed version of the compound calculus, in which the operators `car` and `cdr` are replaced by folds built from functions that are polymorphic enough to handle whatever components may arise. Such folds are expressive enough to represent many path polymorphic functions including the usual generic queries. Further, by constraining the types of constructors to avoid higher types, reduction becomes strongly normalising. When typing the static pattern calculus, the challenges are met by careful characterisation of the local type symbols that are implicitly bound in a case.

9.1 Typing Components

The types of System **F** (or System **FM**) are expressive enough to type the generic queries of Chap. 4. For example, the query `size` that counts the number of atoms in its argument has type

$$\texttt{size} : \forall X.X \rightarrow \texttt{nat} \,.$$

Nevertheless, there are some challenges to be addressed.

Consider the problem of typing `cdr` of some compound $u\ v$. Its type is that of v but there is no general mechanism for determining this from the type of $u\ v$. For example, if the compound is a tree then v could be a leaf or a subtree. In a simply typed setting, `cdr` could be given by a family of operators $\texttt{cdr}^{U,V}$ with the reduction rule

$$\texttt{cdr}^{U,V}\ (u\ v) \longrightarrow v \text{ if } v : V$$

that checks the type of the components during evaluation. However, it is not appropriate to give `cdr` the type $\forall X.\forall Y.X \rightarrow Y$ since the choice of Y cannot be determined by the environment. Slightly better is the type

B. Jay, *Pattern Calculus*,
DOI 10.1007/978-3-540-89185-7_9,

$$\texttt{cdr} : \forall X.X \rightarrow \exists Y.Y$$

where the unknown type of the second component is represented by an existential type, as defined in Sect. 7.6. While correct, the existential type is rather unhelpful, since it provides no detailed type information. In particular, if `car` is given type

$$\texttt{car} : \forall X.X \rightarrow \exists Y.Y \rightarrow X$$

then the relationship between the types of the components is lost. A better solution is to combine `car` and `cdr` into a single term

$$\forall X.X \rightarrow \exists Y.(Y \rightarrow X) * Y$$

in which the sharing is recorded. To exploit such existentials requires a function of type $\forall Y.(Y \rightarrow X) * Y \rightarrow S$.

Rather than proceed directly, this suggests a way to type the folds introduced at the end of Sect. 4.6. If $d\ v$ is a compound then a term $\texttt{fold}(d\ v, s, r)$ reduces to apply r to the result of folding on d and v. For example, when defining `size` then r is addition of natural numbers while when defining `apply2all` then r is application, of type $\forall X.\forall Y.(Y \rightarrow X) \rightarrow Y \rightarrow X$. These possibilities can be generalised by requiring that r have type

$$r : \forall X.\forall Y.\{Y \rightarrow X/Z\}T \rightarrow \{Y/Z\}T \rightarrow \{X/Z\}T$$

for some type T. The examples above are handled by setting T to be `nat` or Z. Similarly, the type of s above must be

$$s : \forall Z.Z \rightarrow T\ .$$

Given $u : U$ then

$$\texttt{fold}(u, s, r) : \{U/Z\}T$$

has reduction rules

$$\begin{array}{rll} \texttt{fold}(u^U, s, r) & \longrightarrow s\ U\ u & \text{if } u \text{ is an atom} \\ \texttt{fold}(u^{V \rightarrow U}\ v, s, r) & \longrightarrow r\ U\ V\ \texttt{fold}(u, s, r)\ \texttt{fold}(v, s, r) & \text{if } u\ v \text{ is a compound.} \end{array}$$

In this manner, one can add folds to System **F** and use them to define generic queries such as `size`, `apply2all` and `select`. Since `size` cannot be defined in System **F** itself, this shows the potential for additional expressive power in the terms without changing the type system. That said, to gain significant expressive power requires choice terms, so typecase calculus will provide the foundation.

$$\frac{c:T}{\Gamma \vdash c:T} \qquad \frac{c:T \quad \Gamma \vdash u:U}{\Gamma \vdash c \;\texttt{eqa}\; u:\texttt{bool}}$$

$$\frac{\Gamma \vdash u:U \qquad \Gamma \vdash s:\forall Z.Z \to T \qquad \Gamma \vdash r:\forall X.\forall Y.\{Y \to X/Z\}T \to \{Y/Z\}T \to \{X/Z\}T}{\Gamma \vdash \texttt{fold}(u,s,r):\{U/Z\}T}\; X,Y \notin \mathsf{FV}(T)$$

Fig. 9.1 Novel typing rules of the query calculus

9.2 Query Calculus

The *query calculus* adds constructors, constructor equality and folds to typecase calculus with combinatory types. The terms of the query calculus are given by the grammar

$t ::=$	(term)
x^T	(variable)
$t\ t$	(application)
$\lambda x^T.t$	(abstraction)
$t\ T$	(type application)
$[\Delta]\ T \to t$	(typecase)
$t \# t$	(choice)
c^T	(constructor)
$c\ \texttt{eqa}\ t$	(constructor equality)
$\texttt{fold}(t,t,t)$	(fold).

The constructors and constructor equality are as in the compound calculus. Folds are as described above.

The type derivation rules are given by those of the typecase calculus in Figs. 8.3 and 8.4 plus the new rules in Fig. 9.1. The rules for constructors and their equality are straightforward. Note that constructor equality does not require the constructor and term to have the same type. Note too that the type `bool` of System **F** is used rather than a type constant `Bool` but this is more for convenience than anything else. The rule for a fold $\texttt{fold}(u,s,r)$ produces something of type $\{U/Z\}T$ for some type T parametrised by Z. The function s must be able to act on an arbitrary atom and produce something of type T, so its type is $\forall Z.Z \to T$. The function r must be able to act on the results of folding the components of u. These will have types $\{Y \to X/Z\}T$ and $\{Y/Z\}T$ for some types X and Y and so r must have type $\forall X.\forall Y.\{Y \to X/Z\}T \to \{Y/Z\}T \to \{X/Z\}T$. The use of substitution in the rule prevents T itself being replaced by a type parameter.

The *data structures* are the terms headed by a constructor, as before. The *explicit functions* are the abstractions, typecases and choices. The *compounds* are the matchable forms which are term applications, while all other matchable forms, including type applications, are *atoms*.

The *reduction rules* for the query calculus are given by those of the typecase calculus plus the novel rules in Fig. 9.2.

$$
\begin{array}{rcll}
c^T\ \texttt{eqa}\ c^T & \longrightarrow & \texttt{true} & \text{(same)}\\
c^T\ \texttt{eqa}\ u\ U & \longrightarrow & c\ \texttt{eqa}\ u \quad \text{if } u\ U \text{ is matchable} & \text{(strip)}\\
c\ \texttt{eqa}\ u & \longrightarrow & \texttt{false} \quad \text{otherwise, if } u \text{ is matchable} & \text{(different)}\\
\texttt{fold}(u^U,s,r) & \longrightarrow & s\ U\ u \quad \text{if } u \text{ is an atom} & \text{(atom)}\\
\texttt{fold}(u^{V\to U}\ v,s,r) & \longrightarrow & r\ U\ V\ \texttt{fold}(u,s,r) & \\
 & & \texttt{fold}(v,s,r) \quad \text{if } u\ v \text{ is a compound} & \text{(compound).}
\end{array}
$$

Fig. 9.2 Novel reduction rules of the query calculus

Theorem 9.1 (Type Preservation). *Reduction preserves typing in the query calculus.*

Proof. Without loss of generality the reduction is a rule. The proofs for the novel rules are routine. □

Theorem 9.2 (Progress). *The closed irreducible terms of the query calculus are matchable forms.*

Proof. The proof is by straightforward induction on the structure of the term. □

Theorem 9.3 (Confluence). *The reduction relation of the query calculus is confluent.*

Proof. Use simultaneous reduction techniques once again. □

9.3 Selecting

Here are some generic queries and other examples in the style of Sect. 7.6.

Example 9.4. Size

The *size* of a data structure can be given by

$$\texttt{size} : \forall Z.Z \to \texttt{nat} = \Lambda Z.\lambda z^Z.\texttt{fold}(z, \Lambda Z.\lambda z^Z.\texttt{one}, \Lambda X.\Lambda Y.\texttt{plusnat})\,.$$

A variant on the size function is to count occurrences of some constructor c. Define $\texttt{is\_}c = \Lambda X.\lambda x^X.\texttt{if}\ c\ \texttt{eqa}\ x\ \texttt{then one else zero}$ and then

$$\texttt{count\_}c : \forall Z.Z \to \texttt{nat} = \Lambda Z.\lambda z^Z.\texttt{fold}(z, \texttt{is\_}c, \Lambda X.\Lambda Y.\texttt{plusnat})$$

where one and zero take the obvious meanings.

Example 9.5. Applying to All

The function apply2all is given by

$$\begin{array}{l}\texttt{apply2all} : (\forall X.X \to X) \to (\forall Z.Z \to Z) = \\ \quad \lambda f^{\forall X.X \to X}.\Lambda Z.\lambda z^Z.(\texttt{fold}(z, f, \Lambda X.\Lambda Y.\lambda x^{Y \to X}.\lambda y^Y.f\ X\ (x\, y)))\end{array}$$

with applications proceeding as before.

Example 9.6. Selecting

The generic selector is defined by

$$\begin{array}{l}\texttt{select} : \forall X.(\forall Y.Y \to \texttt{list}\ X) \to \forall Z.Z \to \texttt{list}\ X = \\ \quad \Lambda X.\lambda f^{\forall Y.Y \to \texttt{list}\ X}.\Lambda Z.\lambda z^Z.\texttt{fold}(z, \forall Z.\lambda z^Z.\texttt{nil}, \texttt{append})\end{array}$$

where `nil` and `append` are the familiar list operations.

Example 9.7. Operations of the Compound Calculus

The operation `pair?` : $\forall Z.Z \to \texttt{bool}$ is easily defined as the function

$$\Lambda Z.\lambda z^Z.\texttt{fold}(z, \Lambda Z.\lambda z^Z.\texttt{false}, \Lambda X.\Lambda Y.\lambda x^{\texttt{bool}}.\lambda y^{\texttt{bool}}.\texttt{true}).$$

The operations `car` and `cdr` are not so easily expressed since the types of components are not determined by that of the compound, as discussed in Sect. 9.1. Even the simply typed versions are not so easy to express. For example, suppose types U and V are given and consider how to define $\texttt{car}^{U,V}$ and $\texttt{cdr}^{U,V}$ using a fold. For atoms some error term is required. For compounds, with first component of type $Y \to X$ it is necessary to test that $Y \to X$ is $V \to U$ and then return something of type $(V \to U) * V$. Since both $Y \to X$ and $V \to U$ are required in the result, the required fold must have type $\forall Z.Z \to Z * (V \to U) * V$ given by

$$\Lambda Z.\lambda z^Z.\texttt{fold}(z, \texttt{error}, r)$$

where

$$\begin{aligned} W &= (V \to U) * V \\ r &= \Lambda X.\Lambda Y.\lambda x^{(Y \to X) * W}.\lambda y^{Y * W}.\texttt{pair}\ X\ W\ r_1\ ((r_2 \,\#\, r_3)\ (V \to U)) \\ r_1 &= (\texttt{fst}\ (Y \to X)\ W\ x)\ (\texttt{fst}\ Y\ W\ y) \\ r_2 &= [\,]\ (Y \to X) \to \texttt{pair}\ (Y \to X)\ Y\ (\texttt{fst}\ (Y \to X)\ W\ x)\ (\texttt{fst}\ Y\ W\ y)) \\ r_3 &= [\,]\ (V \to U) \to \texttt{pair}\ (V \to U)\ V\ \texttt{error}\ \texttt{error}\,. \end{aligned}$$

That is, r_1 recreates the original structure, while r_2 produces the components of type $Y \to X$ and Y and r_3 produces the error terms of type $(V \to U) * V$. If $Y \to X$ is $V \to U$ then the pair of components is produced, else an error term results. Now $\texttt{car}^{U,V}$ and $\texttt{cdr}^{U,V}$ are defined by projecting from the pair produced by the fold above.

A polymorphic version of this fold can be created by introducing an existential quantifier to produce

$$\texttt{cleave} : \forall X.X \to \exists Y.(Y \to X) * Y\,.$$

In brief, given a compound $u\ v$ it first produces two pairs, of u and its components, and v and its components. Then it returns the pair of $u\ v$ and the package of pair $u\ v$, discarding the components of u and of v. This elaborate machinery is analogous to that for defining the predecessor of a natural number by primitive recursion.

Example 9.8. Fixpoints

Fixpoints can be defined in a manner similar to Sect. 4.4 Suppose a constructor Rec of type $(T \to T) \to T$ is given (though one of type $\forall X.(X \to X) \to X$ would also do). Define

$$
\begin{aligned}
&\mathtt{fix1} : \forall_{(T\to T)\to T}[].((T \to T) \to T) \to (T \to T) \to T \\
&\quad = [\,]\ ((T \to T) \to T) \to \lambda x^{(T\to T)\to T}.\lambda f^{T\to T}.\ f\ (x\ f) \\
&\mathtt{fix2} : \forall_{Y\to X}[X,Y].(Y \to X) \to Y \to X \\
&\quad = [X,Y]\ (Y \to X) \to \lambda x^{Y\to X}.\lambda y^{Y}.x\ y \\
&\mathtt{fix3} : \forall X.Y.(Y \to X) \to Y \to X \\
&\quad = \Lambda X.\Lambda Y.(\mathtt{fix1}\ \#\ \mathtt{fix2})\ (Y \to X) \\
&\mathtt{fix0} : T \to T \\
&\quad = \lambda y^{T}.\mathtt{fold}(y, \mathtt{identity}, \mathtt{fix3}) \\
&\mathtt{fix} : (T \to T) \to T = \\
&\quad \lambda f^{T\to T}.\mathtt{fix0}\ (\mathtt{Rec}\ (\lambda x^{T}.f\ (\mathtt{fix0}\ x)))\ .
\end{aligned}
$$

The function fix1 embodies the recursion by mapping x and f to $x\ (f\ x)$ as usual. This can only be applied to a compound $x\ f$ if the types are appropriate; otherwise, fix2 must be applied, to reconstitute the original compound. In fix3, these two possibilities are combined using a choice, whose type must be restored to one appropriate for folding to produce $\mathtt{fix0} : T \to T$. Then fix is defined as in Sect. 2.5.

9.4 Terminating Queries

The existence of fixpoints means that query calculus is not strongly normalising. This can be distracting in practice, since typical query languages guarantee that their queries on databases will terminate. However, one can constrain the types of constructors to obtain strong normalisation.

The source of the difficulties is constructors with higher-order types, such as

$$\mathtt{Rec} : (T \to T) \to T\ .$$

Constructors with such types cannot be avoided if one is to represent data types as function types, but with type applications available, it is possible to restrict the types of constructors to exclude those such as Rec. The required restrictions are more subtle than a direct comparison of type structures. For example, it is useful to support a tree type whose nodes take any finite number of branches, as expressed by a constructor of type

$$\mathtt{List\ Tree} \to \mathtt{Tree}\ .$$

That is, the restrictions should ignore type constants and applications. These restrictions are used to define the *ranked constructors*. If all constructors are ranked then reduction is strongly normalising.

Summarising, the *ranked query calculus* generalises the typecase calculus to support path polymorphic queries while maintaining good properties such as strong normalisation found in System **F**.

Define the *atoms* $\mathscr{A}(T)$ of a type T to be a set of types defined by induction on the structure of T as follows

$$\begin{aligned} \mathscr{A}(X) &= \{X\} \\ \mathscr{A}(C) &= \{\} \\ \mathscr{A}(T_1\ T_2) &= \mathscr{A}(T_1) \cup \mathscr{A}(T_2) \\ \mathscr{A}(T) &= \{T\} \text{ (otherwise)} . \end{aligned}$$

The *atomic order* on types is given by $S \leq T$ if each type A in $\mathscr{A}(S)$ is a subexpression of a type B in $\mathscr{A}(T)$. Write $S \sim T$ if $S \leq T \leq S$.

A constructor c is *ranked* if its given type is of the form

$$\forall \Delta . D_1 \to \ldots \to D_i \to \ldots \to D_n \to D$$

where $\mathscr{A}(D_i) \subseteq \Delta$ for each i and $\mathscr{A}(D) = \Delta$ and D is not a variable. The *arity* of c is n.

For example, all of the constructors familiar from data type declarations are ranked but $\texttt{Rec} : \forall X.(X \to X) \to X$ is not. The restriction that D not be a variable is necessary to avoid simulating Rec. For example, if $\texttt{Error} : \forall X.X$ were ranked then it could be used to define fixpoints.

A *ranked query calculus* is a query calculus in which all constructors are ranked. Assume this for the rest of the chapter.

Lemma 9.9. *If $u : U$ is a component of a data structure $d : D$ then $U \leq D$.*

Proof. Let $d = c\ V_1\ \ldots\ V_m\ u_1\ \ldots\ u_k$. If u is d then the result is immediate. Otherwise, u is a component of some $u_i : U_i$. If k is the arity of c then $U_i \leq D$ by the definition of ranked constructors. Otherwise U_i is a subexpression of D and so $U_i \leq D$. Now apply induction with respect to u and u_i. □

The proof that every term of the ranked query calculus is strongly normalising adapts the reducibility candidates technique of Sect. 7.7 in two ways. First, the *neutral terms* were defined to be those which are not abstractions but here they are all terms that are not explicit functions, i.e. neither abstractions nor typecases nor choices. The second change is that induction with respect to types will use the atomic order on types rather than the type structure.

A *reducibility candidate* of type U is a set $\mathscr{R}$ of terms of type U such that:

(CR1) If $t \in \mathscr{R}$ then t is strongly normalisable.
(CR2) If $t \in \mathscr{R}$ and $t \longrightarrow t_0$ then $t_0 \in \mathscr{R}$.
(CR3) If t is neutral, and every one-step reduct of t is in $\mathscr{R}$ then $t \in \mathscr{R}$.

From (CR3) we have in particular that if $t : U$ is neutral and normal then $t \in \mathscr{R}$. Hence $\mathscr{R}$ must contain all the variables of type U, and all the data structures in normal form.

A *reducibility substitution* is given by a type substitution ρ and a reducibility candidate $\mathscr{R}_X$ for ρX for each type symbol $X \in \mathsf{dom}(\rho)$.

If T is a type whose free variables are in the domain of ρ then the reducibility candidate $RED_T[\rho]$ for ρT will be defined by induction on the atomic ordering. More precisely, $RED_S[\rho]$ will be defined simultaneously for all types $S \sim T$. Within the definition below, a term $t : \rho T$ is a *data reducible term* if it is of the form ρd for some data structure d each of whose components $u : U$ satisfies $\rho u \in RED_U[\rho]$. Note that Lemma 9.9 implies that $U \leq T$ so this definition will be well founded.

- If T has no atoms (e.g. is a type constant) then $t \in RED_T[\rho]$ if t is data reducible.
- If T has a unique atom which is a type symbol X then $t : \rho T$ is in $RED_T[\rho]$ if either t is data reducible or $t \in \mathscr{R}_X$.
- If T has a unique atom which is a function type $U \to S$ then $t : \rho T \in RED_T[\rho]$ if either t is data reducible or $t : \rho(U \to S)$ and $u \in RED_U[\rho]$ implies $t\ u \in RED_S[\rho]$.
- If T has a unique atom which is of the form $\forall_P.[\Delta]S$ then $t \in RED_T[\rho]$ if either t is data reducible or $t : \rho(\forall_P.[\Delta]S)$ and the following condition holds: for all types U such that $\{U/[\Delta]\ P\}$ is some substitution υ with $\mathscr{S}_Y$ being a reducibility candidate for ρY for each symbol $Y \in \Delta$ it follows that $t\ \rho U \in RED_S[\rho \cup \upsilon]$.
- If T has two or more atoms then $t \in RED_T[\rho]$ if it is data reducible.

Lemma 9.10. *If ρ is a reducibility substitution with respect to $\mathscr{R}$ then $RED_T[\rho]$ is a reducibility candidate for T.*

Proof. The proof is by induction on the atomic order, and secondarily on the structure of the terms involved. If $t \in RED_T[\rho]$ is data reducible then its reductions must be of components, so apply induction. The other possibilities are handled just as in Lemma 7.17 for System **F**. □

Lemma 9.11. *If $d \in RED_T[\rho]$ is a data structure then it is data reducible.*

Proof. Apply d to term variables (which are necessarily reducible) to produce a reducible term $t : T$ where T is not a function type. Now T cannot be a variable or typecase since all constructors are ranked. Hence t is data reducible, whence d is too. □

Lemma 9.12. *Let ρ be a reducible type substitution whose domain includes all free type variables of some type T and let $t : T$ be a term and let σ be a term substitution whose domain is the free variables of t such that $\sigma\rho x \in RED_U[\rho]$ for each x^U free in t. Then $\sigma\rho t \in RED_T[\rho]$.*

Proof. The proof is by induction on the structure of t.

If t is a variable x then $\sigma\rho x$ is reducible by assumption. If t is an application $r\ u$ then $\sigma\rho r$ and $\sigma\rho u$ are reducible by induction and so $\sigma\rho(r\ u)$ is reducible by the definition of $RED_T[\rho]$.

If t is an abstraction $\lambda x^U.s$ then it suffices to show that for all reducible $u \in RED_U[\rho]$, the term $\sigma\rho(\lambda x^U.s)\ u$ is reducible. Since this term is neutral, it suffices to show that all one-step reducts of it are reducible. Now $\rho\sigma s$ and u are reducible and hence strongly normalising. The proof is by induction on the sum of the ranks of $\rho\sigma s$ and u. Now consider a reduction of $\sigma\rho t\ u$. If it is of s or u then apply induction on the sum of ranks. If it is the β-rule then apply induction to s and ρ and $\{u/x\} \circ \sigma$.

If t is a type application $r\ U$ then $\sigma\rho r$ is reducible by induction and so $\sigma\rho t$ is reducible by definition.

If t is a typecase $[\Delta]\ P \to s$ then it suffices to show that for all types U such that $\{U/[\Delta]\ P\}$ is some substitution υ then $t\ U$ is reducible. Since this term is neutral, it suffices to show that all one-step reducts of it are reducible. Now $\rho\sigma s$ is reducible and hence strongly normalising. The proof is by induction on the rank of $\rho\sigma s$. Now consider a reduction of $\sigma\rho t\ U$. If it is of s then apply induction. If it is the β-rule then apply induction to s and $\rho \cup \upsilon$ and σ.

If t is a choice $s\ \#\ r$ then it suffices to show that $t\ U$ is reducible for all types U such that $r\ U$ is well-typed. Since $t\ U$ is neutral, it suffices to show that all one-step reducts of it are reducible. Now $\rho\sigma s$ and $\rho\sigma r$ are reducible and hence strongly normalising. The proof is by induction on the sum of their ranks. Now consider a reduction of $\sigma\rho t\ U$. If it is of s or r then apply induction. If it produces $s\ U$ or $r\ U$ then these are reducible by induction.

If t is a constructor c then $\sigma\rho t = c$ is data reducible.

If t is a constructor equality c `eqa` u then it is neutral and $\sigma\rho u$ is reducible by induction, and so proceed by induction on its rank.

If t is a fold $\texttt{fold}(u,s,r)$ then it is neutral, so it suffices to show that all one-step reductions of $\sigma\rho t$ are reducible by induction on the sum of the reduction ranks of $\sigma\rho u, \sigma\rho s$ and $\sigma\rho r$ (and then the complexity of u). The interesting cases are when a rule is applied. If $\sigma\rho u : U$ is an atom then $\sigma\rho t$ reduces to $\sigma\rho(s\ U\ u)$ which is reducible since $\sigma\rho s$ and $\sigma\rho u$ are. If $\sigma\rho u : U$ is a compound $d\ v$ for some d and $v : V$ then $\sigma\rho t$ reduces to $\sigma\rho r\ U\ V\ \texttt{fold}(d,\sigma\rho s,\sigma\rho r)\ \texttt{fold}(v,\sigma\rho s,\sigma\rho r)$. Now d and v are reducible by Lemma 9.11 and so their folds are reducible by induction. Now reducibility of $\sigma\rho r$ yields the result.

□

Theorem 9.13 (Strong Normalisation). *All terms in the ranked query calculus are strongly normalising.*

Proof. Apply the lemma above to the identity type substitution with each type variable taking the reducibility candidate of strongly normalising terms and the identity term substitution. Hence t is strongly normalising. □

9.5 Typed Static Pattern Calculus

The query calculus shows how path polymorphism can be supported by adding constructors and operations such as folding to the λ-calculus, albeit with some awkwardness. This section will show how to explicitly type the static pattern calculus, to achieve similar functionality. The types are as for the query calculus.

The *patterns* (meta-variables, p,q) of the typed static pattern calculus are given by the grammar

$$\begin{array}{lll} p ::= & & \text{(pattern)} \\ & x^T & \text{(variable)} \\ & c^T & \text{(constructor)} \\ & p\ p & \text{(application)} \\ & p\ T & \text{(type application).} \end{array}$$

Define the *local type symbols* $\mathsf{LV}(p)$ of a pattern p of type P to be

$$\mathsf{LV}(p^P) = \mathsf{FV}(p) \setminus \mathsf{FV}(P)\ .$$

In a case $p \to s$ the local type symbols of p will be implicitly bound, just as its free term symbols are.

The *terms* are given by the grammar

$$\begin{array}{lll} t ::= & & \text{(term)} \\ & x^T & \text{(variable)} \\ & c^T & \text{(constructor)} \\ & t\ t & \text{(application)} \\ & p \to t & \text{(case)} \\ & t\ T & \text{(type application)} \\ & [\Delta]\ T \to t & \text{(typecase)} \\ & t \# t & \text{(choice).} \end{array}$$

It can be obtained from that of the query calculus by generalising term abstractions to cases, and deleting the constructor equality and folds. A case $p \to s$ will implicitly bind the free term symbols of p and its local type symbols, so that matching must find values for all of them.

The *free type symbols* $\mathsf{FV}(t)$ of a case are given by

$$\mathsf{FV}(p^P \to s) = (\mathsf{FV}(s) \setminus \mathsf{FV}(p)) \cup \mathsf{FV}(P)\ .$$

Note how the free type variables of a case $p \to s$ depends upon the type P of its pattern.

The *application* of a type substitution ρ to a case is defined by

$$\rho(p \to s) = \rho p \to \rho s \text{ (if } \rho \text{ avoids } \mathsf{LV}(p)).$$

The judgement $\Gamma \vdash t : T$ asserts that t is a term of type T in term context Γ, as usual. The derivation rules for (patterns and) terms are given in Fig. 9.3.

Lemma 9.14. *Type derivations are stable under type substitution.*

Proof. The proof is by induction on the structure of the derivation, using the stability of type matching (Lemma 8.3) and of type similarity (Lemma 8.7). □

$$\frac{}{\Gamma, x:T \vdash x^T : T} \qquad \frac{}{\Gamma \vdash c^T : T}$$

$$\frac{\Gamma \vdash r : U \to S \quad \Gamma \vdash u : U}{\Gamma \vdash r\,u : S} \qquad \frac{B \vdash p : P \quad \Gamma, B \vdash s : S}{\Gamma \vdash p \to s : P \to S}\ \begin{array}{l}\mathsf{FV}(p) \cap \mathsf{FV}(S) \\ \subseteq \mathsf{FV}(P)\end{array}$$

$$\frac{\Gamma \vdash r : \forall_P[\Delta].S}{\Gamma \vdash r\,U : \{U/[\Delta]\,P\}S} \qquad \frac{\Gamma \vdash s : S}{\Gamma \vdash [\Delta]\,P \to s : \forall_P[\Delta].S}\ \mathsf{FV}(\Gamma) \cap \Delta = \{\}$$

$$\frac{\Gamma \vdash s : S \quad \Gamma \vdash r : R \quad S \approx R}{\Gamma \vdash s \# r : R}$$

Fig. 9.3 Typed static pattern calculus

The definition of *matchable forms* is as usual, consisting of the data structures (terms headed by a constructor) and the explicit functions (cases, typecases and choices).

Matching must be adapted to consider local type symbols as well as term symbols. That is, a *typed match* μ is a pair of a term match and type match. The *union* of typed matches is given by

$$(\mathsf{some}\ \sigma_1, \mathsf{some}\ \rho_1) \cup (\mathsf{some}\ \sigma_2, \mathsf{some}\ \rho_2) = (\mathsf{some}\ (\sigma_1 \uplus \sigma_2), \mathsf{some}\ (\rho_1 \cup \rho_2))$$

if this is defined, and is $(\mathsf{none}, \mathsf{none})$ otherwise, e.g. if σ_1 and σ_2 are not disjoint.

Match *failure* is given by the constructor $\mathtt{Nomatch} : \forall X.X$. The application of a typed match μ to a term t is defined by

$$\begin{aligned} (\mathsf{some}\ \sigma, \mathsf{some}\ \rho)\ t &= \sigma(\rho t) \\ \mu\ t^T &= \mathtt{Nomatch}\ T \quad \text{otherwise.} \end{aligned}$$

The *basic typed match* $\{u\,//[\Delta]\,p\}$ of a static pattern p against an argument u relative to a type context Δ is defined in Fig. 9.4. Define $\{u\,/\,p\}$ to be $\{u\,//[\mathsf{LV}(p)]\ p\}$ if this is of the form $(\mathsf{some}\ \sigma, \mathsf{some}\ \rho)$ where $\mathsf{dom}(\sigma) = \mathsf{fv}(p)$ and $\mathsf{dom}(\rho) = \mathsf{LV}(p)$, and to be $(\mathsf{none}, \mathsf{none})$ otherwise. The *reduction rules* for the types static pattern calculus are in the same figure.

Lemma 9.15. *Let $B \vdash p : P$ be a pattern and $\Gamma \vdash u : U$ be a term in some context Γ where Γ, B is well formed and $\Delta \cap \mathsf{FV}(\Gamma) = \{\}$. If $\{u/p\}$ is a pair of some substitutions σ and ρ then for each free term symbol x^V in p then $\Gamma \vdash \sigma x : \rho V$.*

Proof. The proof is by straightforward induction on the typing of p. □

Theorem 9.16 (Type Preservation). *In the typed static pattern calculus, reduction preserves typing.*

Proof. Without loss of generality the reduction is a rule. If the reduction is a successful term match then apply Lemma 9.15. If the reduction is a term match failure

$$\begin{array}{rcll}
\{u^U \mathbin{//} [\Delta] x^P\} &=& (\mathsf{some}\ \{u/x\}, \{U/[\Delta]P\}) & \\
\{c^T \mathbin{//} [\Delta] c^T\} &=& (\mathsf{some}\ \{\}, \mathsf{some}\ \{\}) & \\
\{u\, v \mathbin{//} [\Delta]\, p\, q\} &=& \{u \mathbin{//} [\Delta]\, p\} \cup \{v \mathbin{//} [\Delta]\, q\} & \text{if } u\,v \text{ is matchable} \\
\{u\, U \mathbin{//} [\Delta]\, p\, P\} &=& \{u \mathbin{//} [\Delta]\, p\} \cup (\mathsf{some}\ \{\}, \{U/[\Delta]\, P\}) & \text{if } u\,U \text{ is matchable} \\
\{u \mathbin{//} [\Delta]\, p\} &=& (\mathsf{none}, \mathsf{none}) & \text{otherwise, if } u \text{ is matchable} \\
\{u \mathbin{//} [\Delta]\, p\} &=& \text{undefined} & \text{otherwise.}
\end{array}$$

$$\begin{array}{rcll}
(p \to s)\ u &\longrightarrow& \{u/p\}s. & \text{(match1)} \\
([\Delta]\ P \to s)\ U &\longrightarrow& \{U/[\Delta]\ P\}s & \text{(match2).} \\
(s^{\forall_P[\Delta].S} \,\#\, r)\ U &\longrightarrow& s\ U \quad \text{if } \{U/[\Delta]\ P\} = \mathsf{some}\ \rho & \text{(left).} \\
(s^{\forall_P[\Delta].S} \,\#\, r)\ U &\longrightarrow& r\ U \quad \text{if } \{U/[\Delta]\ P\} = \mathsf{none}. & \text{(right).}
\end{array}$$

Fig. 9.4 Basic matching and reduction rules for typed static pattern calculus

then the correct typing is immediate. If the reduction is a type match then apply the Substitution Lemma. The rules for choices are straightforward. □

9.6 Selectors by Patterns

This section reworks some of the examples of Sect. 9.3 using static patterns.

Example 9.17. Fixpoints
Given $\mathtt{Rec} : (T \to T) \to T$ define

$$\begin{array}{r}
\mathtt{fix0} : T \to T = x^{(T\to T)\to T}\ f^{T\to T} \to f\ (x\ f) \\
\mathtt{fix} : (T \to T) \to T = \lambda f.\mathtt{fix0}\ (\mathtt{Rec}\ (\lambda y^{T\to T}.f\ (\mathtt{fix0}\ y)))\ .
\end{array}$$

This is much simpler than the previous definition since the pattern matching checks types as well as terms, so `fix0` can be given by a single case.

Recursion in the examples below will be implicit.

Example 9.18. Extensions
If $p : P$ and $s : S$ and $r : P \to S$ then the extension $p \to s \mid r : P \to S$ is defined by

$$p \to s \mid r = x^P \to (\mathtt{Nomatch}\ S\ y^S \to y)\ ((p \to z^S \to \mathtt{Nomatch}\ S\ s)\ x\ (r\ x))\ .$$

Note that the special case and the default are here required to have the same type.

Example 9.19. Size
The *size* of a data structure can be given by

$$\begin{array}{l}
\mathtt{size} : \forall Z.Z \to \mathtt{nat} = \Lambda Z. \\
\quad x^{Y\to X}\ y^Y \to \mathtt{plusnat}\ \ (\mathtt{size}\ (Y \to X)\ x)\ \ (\mathtt{size}\ Y\ y) \\
\mid z^Z \to \mathtt{one}\ .
\end{array}$$

Example 9.20. Applying to all

The function apply2all is given by

$$\begin{aligned}
&(\texttt{apply2all} : (\forall X.X \to X) \to (\forall Z.Z \to Z))\ f\ Z = \\
&\quad x^{Y \to Z}\ y^{Y} \to f\ Z\ ((\texttt{apply2all}\ f\ (Y \to Z)\ x)\ (\texttt{apply2all}\ f\ Y\ y)) \\
&\mid z^{Z} \to f\ Z\ z\,.
\end{aligned}$$

Example 9.21. Selecting

The generic selector is defined by

$$\begin{aligned}
&(\texttt{select} : \forall X.(\forall Y.Y \to \texttt{list}\ X) \to \forall Z.Z \to \texttt{list}\ X)\ f\ Z = \\
&\quad x^{Y \to Z}\ y^{Y} \to \texttt{append}\ X\ (\texttt{select}\ f\ (Y \to Z)\ x)\ (\texttt{select}\ f\ Y\ y) \\
&\mid z^{Z} \to f\ Z\ z\,.
\end{aligned}$$

9.7 Notes

The folding of the query calculus can be seen as the computational analogue of structural induction. If this can be formalised then it will strengthen the correspondence between proofs and programs.

The ranked constructors are related to ideas in the Calculus of Constructions [87], except that constructors there are only introduced in the context of type declarations, whereas the constructors here are freestanding. Their combination with the generic fold, as opposed to ad hoc operators, is new, as is the proof that reducibility candidates can be employed in the presence of data structures. For example, the strong normalisation result is not an immediate consequence of the techniques based on higher-order recursive path orderings of Jean-Pierre Jouannaud and Albert Rubio in [64].

The Curry–Howard Correspondence motivated some early work on typed pattern calculus by Val Breazu-Tannen, Delia Kesner and Laurence Puel [11].

Chapter 10
Pattern Polymorphism

Abstract This chapter types dynamic patterns. Cases bind both type and term symbols, any of which may appear as either variables or matchables. Once this machinery is all in place, the development is quite routine.

10.1 Matchable Type Symbols

The syntax of the *matchable types* is given by the grammar

$$\begin{array}{lll} T ::= & & \text{(type)} \\ & X & \text{(variable)} \\ & \hat{X} & \text{(matchable)} \\ & T \to T & \text{(function)} \\ & \forall_T[\Delta].T & \text{(typecase).} \end{array}$$

This adds matchable type symbols to the types of System **FM**. One could equally add type constants and applications but these are not essential to the development.

The *free variable type symbols* $\mathsf{FV}(T)$ of a type T are defined as before, with $\mathsf{FV}(\hat{X}) = \{\}$. The *free matchable type symbols* $\mathsf{FM}(T)$ of a type T are given by

$$\begin{aligned} \mathsf{FM}(X) &= \{\} \\ \mathsf{FM}(\hat{X}) &= \{X\} \\ \mathsf{FM}(P \to S) &= \mathsf{FM}(P) \cup \mathsf{FM}(S) \\ \mathsf{FM}(\forall_P[\Delta].S) &= \mathsf{FM}(P) \cup \mathsf{FM}(S)\,. \end{aligned}$$

Note that typecases do *not* bind matchable symbols. Rather, these behave like type constants within types, being bound only within case terms introduced in Sect. 10.2.

The type syntax $\forall_P[\Delta].S$ is *well-formed* if $\Delta \cap \mathsf{FV}(S) \subseteq \mathsf{FV}(P)$ as before. Type substitutions are defined as usual. A substitution *avoids* a symbol X if X is not in the domain of ρ and is not a free variable *or* free matchable of its range. A type substitution is *applied* to a type using the following rules:

B. Jay, *Pattern Calculus*,
DOI 10.1007/978-3-540-89185-7_10,

$$
\begin{array}{rcl}
\{U/[\Delta]\hat{X}\} &=& \mathsf{some}\ \{U/X\}\ \text{if}\ X \in \Delta \\
\{\hat{X}/[\Delta]\hat{X}\} &=& \mathsf{some}\ \{\}\ \text{if}\ X \notin \Delta \\
\{X/[\Delta]X\} &=& \mathsf{some}\ \{\} \\
\{U/[\Delta]X\} &=& \text{undefined, otherwise} \\
\{X/[\Delta]P\} &=& \text{undefined, otherwise} \\
\{P \to S/[\Delta]\ Q \to T\} &=& \{P/[\Delta]Q\} \cup \{S/[\Delta]T\} \\
\{\forall_P[\Phi].S/[\Delta]\ \forall_Q[\Phi].T\} &=& \{P/[\Delta]Q\} \cup \{\hat{S}/[\Delta]\hat{T}\} \text{if it avoids } \Phi \text{ and } \Delta \cap \Phi = \{\} \\
\{U/[\Delta]P\} &=& \text{none otherwise.}
\end{array}
$$

Fig. 10.1 Type matching with matchable symbols

$$
\begin{array}{rcll}
\rho(X) &=& \rho X & \text{if } X \in \mathsf{dom}(\rho) \\
\rho(X) &=& X & \text{if } X \notin \mathsf{dom}(\rho) \\
\rho(\hat{X}) &=& \hat{X} & \\
\rho(P \to S) &=& \rho P \to \rho S & \\
\rho(\forall_P[\Delta].S) &=& \forall_{\rho P}[\Delta].\rho S & \text{if } \rho \text{ avoids } \Delta.
\end{array}
$$

Similarly, $\hat{\rho}$ is applied using the following rules:

$$
\begin{array}{rcll}
\hat{\rho}(X) &=& X & \\
\hat{\rho}(\hat{X}) &=& \rho X & \text{if } X \in \mathsf{dom}(\rho) \\
\hat{\rho}(\hat{X}) &=& \hat{X} & \text{if } X \notin \mathsf{dom}(\rho) \\
\hat{\rho}(P \to S) &=& \hat{\rho} P \to \hat{\rho} S & \\
\hat{\rho}(\forall_P[\Delta].S) &=& \forall_{\hat{\rho} P}[\Delta].\hat{\rho} S & \text{if } \rho \text{ avoids } \Delta.
\end{array}
$$

Given a type context Δ define $\{\hat{\Delta}/\Delta\}$ to be the type substitution that substitutes $\hat{X}$ for X for each symbol X in Δ. Conversely, define $\{\Delta/\hat{\Delta}\}$ to be $\hat{\rho}$ where ρ maps each $X \in \Delta$ to itself. When Δ is understood from the context, the notation $\hat{S}$ denotes $\{\hat{\Delta}/\Delta\}S$ and the notation $\check{P}$ denotes $\{\Delta/\hat{\Delta}\}P$. For example, given a quantified function type $[\Delta]\ P \to S = [X]\mathtt{list}\ \hat{X} \to X$ then $\check{P}$ is $\mathtt{list}\ X$ and $\hat{S}$ is $\hat{X}$.

Theorem 10.1. *Two matchable types S and T have a unifier if and only if they have a most general unifier.*

Proof. The most general unifier $\{S = T\}$ of types S and T can be defined much as in System **FM**, by adding a clause for matchable symbols to the rules in Fig. 8.1. Then the proof is by straightforward induction on the type structure. □

The rules for type matching require more care, since now the binding symbols are represented by matchable symbols in the type P being matched, not variables. A *match of a matchable type P against a type U with respect to a type context* Δ is a type match some ρ such that $\hat{\rho}P = U$. It is the most general such if any other such match factors through it.

The algorithm for the most general match $\{U/[\Delta]P\}$ is given in Fig. 10.1. Note that when matching quantified function types, the bound symbols Φ are replaced by matchable symbols in the result types S and T to ensure that match failures are not confused with undefined matches.

Theorem 10.2. *Let Δ be a type context and let P and U be types. There is a match of P against U with respect to Δ if and only if $\{U/[\Delta]P\}$ is some substitution, in which case it is their most general such.*

Proof. The proof is a routine induction on the structure of P. □

Lemma 10.3. *Let $\{U/[\Delta]P\}$ be some substitution for some type context Δ and types U and P. If ρ is a type substitution which avoids Δ then $\{\rho U/[\Delta]\rho P\}$ exists and*

$$\{\rho U/[\Delta]\rho P\} \circ \rho = \rho \circ \{U/[\Delta]P\} .$$

Proof. The proof is by induction on the structure of P. □

10.2 Typed Pattern Calculus

A *context* θ is given by a pair $\Delta;B$ where Δ is a type context and B is a term context. The application to it of a type substitution ρ is given by $\Delta;\rho B$ if ρ avoids Δ and is undefined otherwise. Operations that are common to all sequences and sets, such as concatenation and union, will be applied to contexts point-wise. For example, $(\Delta;B_1),(\Phi;B_2) = (\Delta,\Phi;B_1,B_2)$. Given Δ, the term context $\hat{B}$ is obtained as follows. Each symbol x^U in B is replaced by $\hat{x}^{\hat{U}}$ where $\hat{U} = \{\hat{\Delta}/\Delta\}U$. For example, if $\Delta;B$ is $X;x^{X*Y}$ then $\hat{B}$ is $x^{\hat{X}*Y}$.

The *term syntax* of the typed pattern calculus is given by the grammar

$$\begin{array}{lll} t ::= & x^T & \text{(variable)} \\ & \hat{x}^T & \text{(matchable)} \\ & t\ t & \text{(application)} \\ & [\theta]t \to t & \text{(case)} \\ & t\ T & \text{(type application)} \\ & [\Delta]\ T \to t & \text{(typecase)} \\ & t \# t & \text{(choice).} \end{array}$$

Now $\lambda x^U.s$ is given by $[\ ;x^U]\hat{x}^U \to s$. The *explicit functions* are given by cases, typecases and choices. As before, `Nomatch` is a constructor, now of type $\forall X.X$, that does not appear in well-formed contexts.

The *free type variables* and *free type matchables* of a case are defined by

$$\begin{aligned} \mathsf{FV}([\Delta;B]p \to s) &= \mathsf{FV}(p) \cup ((\mathsf{FV}(B) \cup \mathsf{FV}(s)) \setminus \Delta) \\ \mathsf{FM}([\Delta;B]p \to s) &= (\mathsf{FM}(p) \setminus \Delta) \cup \mathsf{FM}(B) \cup \mathsf{FM}(s) \\ \mathsf{fv}([\Delta;B]p \to s) &= \mathsf{fv}(p) \cup (\mathsf{fv}(s) \setminus B) \\ \mathsf{fm}([\Delta;B]p \to s) &= (\mathsf{fm}(p) \setminus B) \cup \mathsf{fm}(s) . \end{aligned}$$

$$\frac{}{\Gamma, x:T \vdash x^T : T} \qquad \frac{}{\Gamma, \hat{x}^T \vdash \hat{x}^T : T}$$

$$\frac{\Gamma \vdash r : U \to S \quad \Gamma \vdash u : U}{\Gamma \vdash r\,u : S} \qquad \frac{\Gamma, \hat{B} \vdash p : P \quad \Gamma, B \vdash s : S}{\Gamma \vdash [\Delta; B]\, p \to s : P \to S}\ (\mathsf{FV}(P \to S) \cup \mathsf{FV}(\Gamma)) \cap \Delta = \{\}$$

$$\frac{\Gamma \vdash r : \forall_P[\Delta].S}{\Gamma \vdash r\,U : \{U/[\Delta]\,P\}S} \qquad \frac{\Gamma \vdash s : S}{\Gamma \vdash [\Delta]\,P \to s : \forall_P[\Delta].S}\ \mathsf{FV}(\Gamma) \cap \Delta = \{\}$$

$$\frac{\Gamma \vdash s : S \quad \Gamma \vdash r : R \quad S \approx R}{\Gamma \vdash s \# r : R}$$

Fig. 10.2 Typed dynamic pattern calculus

The type derivation rules of the typed dynamic pattern calculus are given in Fig. 10.2. The rules for cases combine several elements. The pattern is typed using the binders as matchable type and term symbols. The body is typed using the binders as variables. The bound type symbols must be local to the case, in the sense that they are not free in the context, or the overall type of the case. For example, the naive term syntax $[Y; x^{Y \to X}, y^Y]\ \hat{x}\ \hat{y} \to y$ for `cdr` has no type since the type symbol Y is free in the result type of the function type $X \to Y$.

10.3 Matching Typed Patterns

The definition of *matchable forms* is as usual, consisting of the data structures (terms headed by a matchable symbol) and the explicit functions (cases, typecases and choices).

Let $\theta = \Delta; B$ be a context of *binding symbols*. Let p and u be terms. The *basic matching* $\{u /\!/ [\theta]\, p\}$ is the match defined by applying the rules in Fig. 10.3, in order. These rules mimic those of the dynamic pattern calculus, except that they perform type matching as well as term matching. The *match* $\{u / [\theta]\, p\}$ *of p against u relative to binding symbols* θ is defined as follows. If $\{u /\!/ [\theta]\, p\} = (\mathsf{some}\ \sigma, \mathsf{some}\ \rho)$ where $\mathsf{dom}(\sigma) = B$ and $\mathsf{dom}(\rho) = \Delta$ then it is the desired match. Otherwise, the match is $(\mathsf{none}, \mathsf{none})$. The *reduction rules* for the types dynamic pattern calculus are given in the same figure. They are identical with the rules for the static calculus, except for the rule (match1), which now has explicit binding symbols.

Lemma 10.4. *Let* $[\theta]\, p \to s : U \to S$ *and* $u : U$ *be terms in some context* Γ*. If* $\{u/[\theta]\, p\}$ *is of the form* $\mathsf{some}\ (\sigma, \rho)$ *then there is a derivation of* $\sigma\rho s : S$*.*

Proof. First note that there is a derivation of $\Gamma \vdash [\,;\rho B]\ \rho p \to \rho s : P \to S$ so without loss of generality the type context in Δ is empty. The proof is by induction on the typing of p. If p is a matchable $\hat{x}^P$ in B then apply the Substitution Lemma. If p is

$$
\begin{array}{rcll}
\{u^U \,//[\theta]\hat{x}^P\} &=& (\mathsf{some}\ \{u/x\},\{U/[\Delta]P\}) & \text{if } x^P \in B \\
\{\hat{x}^T \,//[\theta]\hat{x}^T\} &=& (\mathsf{some}\ \{\},\mathsf{some}\ \{\}) & \text{if } x^T \notin B \\
\{u\,v //[\theta]\,p\,q\} &=& \{u//[\theta]\,p\} \cup \{v//[\theta]\,q\} & \text{if } p\,q \text{ and } u\,v \text{ are matchable} \\
\{u\,U //[\theta]\,p\,P\} &=& \{u//[\theta]\,p\} \cup (\mathsf{some}\ \{\},\{U/[\Delta]\,P\}) & \text{if } p\,P \text{ and } u\,U \text{ are matchable} \\
\{u//[\theta]\,p\} &=& (\mathsf{none},\mathsf{none}) \text{ otherwise} & \text{if } p \text{ and } u \text{ are matchable} \\
\{u//[\theta]\,p\} &=& \text{undefined otherwise.} &
\end{array}
$$

$$
\begin{array}{rcllr}
([\theta]\ p \to s)\ u &\longrightarrow& \{u/[\theta]\ p\}s. & & \text{(match1)} \\
([\Delta]\ P \to s)\ U &\longrightarrow& \{U/[\Delta]\ P\}s & & \text{(match2).} \\
(s^{\forall_P[\Delta].S}\ \#\ r)\ U &\longrightarrow& s\,U & \text{if } \{U/[\Delta]\ P\} = \mathsf{some}\ \rho & \text{(left).} \\
(s^{\forall_P[\Delta].S}\ \#\ r)\ U &\longrightarrow& r\,U & \text{if } \{U/[\Delta]\ P\} = \mathsf{none}. & \text{(right).}
\end{array}
$$

Fig. 10.3 Basic matching and reduction rules for typed pattern calculus

any other matchable then u is p and all substitutions are identities. If p and u are applications then divide B in two and apply induction twice. □

Theorem 10.5 (Type Preservation). *Reduction in the typed pattern calculus preserves typing.*

Proof. Without loss of generality the reduction is the match rule. If the reduction is a successful term match then apply Lemma 10.4. If the reduction is a match failure then the correct typing is immediate. The other cases are routine. □

Theorem 10.6 (Progress). *The closed irreducible terms of the typed pattern calculus are matchable forms.*

Proof. The proof is by straightforward induction on the structure of the term. For example, suppose t is some application $([\theta]\,p \to s)\ u$. Then p is a closed irreducible term (since the symbols in θ are all matchables in p) and so is a matchable form. Similarly, u is a matchable form. Hence $\{u//[\theta]\,p\}$ is defined and (match1) can be applied. □

Theorem 10.7 (Confluence). *Reduction in the typed pattern calculus is confluent.*

Proof. The proof is by simultaneous reduction. □

10.4 Generic Equality

This section presents some examples.

Example 10.8. Applying to all

The generic `apply2all` is given by

$$\begin{array}{l}(\texttt{apply2all} : (\forall X.X \to X) \to (\forall Z.Z \to Z) = \lambda f.\Lambda Z.\\ \quad [Y;z^{Y\to Z},y^{Y}]\,\hat{z}\,\hat{y} \to f\,Z\,(\texttt{apply2all}\ f\ (Y \to Z)\ z\ (\texttt{apply2all}\ f\ Y\ y))\\ \quad \mid f\,Z\,.\end{array}$$

It requires a local type symbol Y to type the second component y of the unknown compound $\hat{z}\,\hat{y}$. Note how Y is free in the body of the case, but not in its type Z.

Example 10.9. Generic Eliminator

The generic eliminator is typed by

$$(\texttt{elim} : \forall X.\forall Y.(Y \to X) \to X \to Y) = \Lambda X.\Lambda Y.\lambda x^{Y\to X}.[\,;y^{Y}]\,x\,\hat{y} \to y.$$

Also

$$\begin{array}{l}(\texttt{elim*} : \forall X.(X \to X) \to X = \Lambda X.\lambda x^{X\to X}.\\ \quad [\,;y^{X}]\,x\,\hat{y} \to \texttt{elim*}\ y\\ \quad \mid [\,;y^{X}]\,y \to y\,.\end{array}$$

Example 10.10. Equality

The generic equality of the dynamic pattern calculus can now be typed by

$$\begin{array}{l}(\texttt{equal} : \forall X.X \to X \to \texttt{bool}) = \Lambda X.\lambda x^{X}.\\ \quad [\,;\,]\,x \to \texttt{true}\\ \quad \mid [\,;y^{X}]\,y \to \texttt{false}\,.\end{array}$$

As before, it uses its first argument x as the pattern to match against its second argument.

Example 10.11. Updating

Define the typed update by

$$\begin{array}{l}(\texttt{update} : \forall X.\forall Y.(X \to Y) \to (X \to X) \to \forall Z.Z \to Z) = \Lambda X.\Lambda Y.\lambda g^{X\to Y}.\lambda f^{X\to X}.\\ \quad (\,[] \to [\,;x^{X}]\,g\,\hat{x} \to g\,(f\,x)\\ \quad \mid [\,;y^{Y}]\,\hat{y} \to y)\\ \#\\ \Lambda Z.([W;x^{W\to Z},y^{W}]\,\hat{x}\,\hat{y} \to (\texttt{update}\,X\ Y\ g\ f\ (W \to Z)\ x)\ (\texttt{update}\,X\ Y\ g\ f\ W\ y)\\ \quad \mid [\,;x^{Z}]\,\hat{x} \to x).\end{array}$$

It is a choice between a case for the type Y and a case for all other types Z. Each case is given by an extension: that for Y has a special case for the "constructor" c while that for Z has a special case for a compound.

As before, the salary update problem can be handled using a variable to denote the unknown pattern for salaries.

Example 10.12. Wildcards

Now let us consider how to type wildcards, as described in Sect. 5.7. Let the wildcard have type

$$\_ : \forall X.X$$

and add the match rule

$$\{u^U \,//[\Delta;B]\,\_\,P\} = (\mathsf{some}\ \{\}, \{U/[\Delta]P\})\ .$$

Example 10.13. Views

Views are created by an operator `view` as in Sect. 5.8. Given a term $f : T \to S$ and a term $p : S$ then

$$\texttt{view}(f,p) : T\ .$$

10.5 Notes

A variant of the system presented in this chapter appeared in a workshop paper [59]. Earlier presentations combined cases and typecases into a single construction. Although possible, it mixes the construction of function types and quantified types (i.e. typecases) by mixing the implicit and explicit binding of type symbols.

Chapter 11
Inclusion Polymorphism

Abstract Subtyping provides an alternative to type variables as a means of supporting polymorphism: together they generate type inequalities. These do not always have most general solutions, so some care is required to solve those of interest. Indeed, this is difficult, if not impossible, if functions are central to the development, but the issues become tractable when subtyping is seen as a property of data types, and function types are invariant under subtyping. The approach is developed through three calculi that add methods to a simply typed λ-calculus, a parametrically polymorphic λ-calculus, and the pattern calculus.

11.1 Methods Without Objects

Subtyping allows a single term to have more than one type. If t is of some type S and S is a subtype of some type T (written $S < T$) then t is also of type T. For example, if the type `colourpoint` is a subtype of the type `point` of points, then a coloured point has all the attributes of any point, and also those that are special to coloured points. This is particularly useful when handling a collection containing a mix of coloured points and mere points since each point in the collection may behave differently, according to its nature. For example, coloured points may display in colour, while mere points display in black and white. This phenomenon is known as *dynamic dispatch*: a point whose known or static type is `point` may evaluate to a coloured point, which then determines how it is to be displayed.

A natural way of thinking about this is to represent the display method as a function with several cases, including a default case that works for any point, and a special case for coloured points. This is much as in the typecase calculus of Chap. 8.4 but now with subtyping.

For example, let the default display method be m : `point` $\rightarrow$ `Unit` where `Unit` is used as a type of commands. Then the special case is some n : `colourpoint` $\rightarrow$ `Unit`. These cases can be combined as the *method choice term*

B. Jay, *Pattern Calculus*,
DOI 10.1007/978-3-540-89185-7_11,

$$n \,\&\, m : \texttt{colourpoint} \rightarrow \texttt{Unit} \,\&\, \texttt{point} \rightarrow \texttt{Unit}$$

whose type is a *choice type*. Now let $u : \texttt{point}$ be a point and consider the *invocation* $u.(n \,\&\, m)$ of $n \,\&\, m$ by u. If u is (or reduces to) a coloured point v then the invocation should reduce to $v.n$ but if u reduces to a mere point w then the invocation should reduce to $w.m$. It is relatively easy to identify the coloured points, so the central question is how to determine of a point that it cannot reduce to a coloured point. The standard approach is to insist that u be fully evaluated before tackling the invocation but this severely limits any reduction strategy. The approach adopted here is to require that the type U of u be *minimal* in the sense that the only subtype of U is U itself, and use this type to reduce the invocation. Then $u.(n \,\&\, m)$ reduces to $u.n$ if the latter is well-typed, and to $u.m$ otherwise. Of course, this approach requires a plentiful supply of minimal types.

In particular, the type `point` of all points is not minimal, so that it requires a subtype `merepoint` to represent the *mere* points, that have no auxiliary attributes. Rather than add several type constants for points, it is easier to introduce a new type constant, the *top type* `Top` and the subtyping rules

$$\frac{}{T < \texttt{Top}} \qquad\qquad \frac{S < T}{F\,S < F\,T}$$

which assert that `Top` is a supertype of every type, and relate type applications. That `merepoint` is a subtype of `point` can be captured by

$$\texttt{Point Unit} < \texttt{Point Top}\,.$$

Similarly, the type `colourpoint` is of the form `Point` T for some type T that involves the colour. The simplest choice for T is some type constant `Colour` of colours, but a type of the form `ColourPoint Top` allows for different sorts of coloured points.

When subtyping the λ-calculus, the natural approach is to make function types *covariant* in their result types but *contravariant* in their arguments, so that $P \rightarrow S < Q \rightarrow T$ if $Q < P$ and $S < T$. However, this would imply that $\texttt{point} \rightarrow \texttt{point}$ is not minimal, since it would have subtype $\texttt{Top} \rightarrow \texttt{point}$. That is, no interesting function type would ever be minimal and ordinary functions would not be allowed to invoke methods. To stop this, function argument types must be *invariant*, so that $P \rightarrow S < Q \rightarrow T$ only if $P = Q$.

Less clear is how to handle result types. To make them covariant would not actually help much, since attaining the minimum type of an abstraction would require reduction of its body, which is not very practical. Even if this is done, the minimum type of a closed irreducible term could be $\texttt{Bool} \rightarrow \texttt{point}$ which would not be minimal in the subtype order. Thus, for the reduction systems of this chapter, the simplest approach is to make function result types invariant, too. In Chap. 12, various simplification will eliminate these concerns, and a more generous, and convenient, subtyping will be admitted.

In the simply typed setting the approach taken here is easily understood. For example, the invocation by a term of type U of a method whose special case has type $P \to S$ has type S if $U < P$. Although quite simple, it is not as expressive as desired. For example, if is useful to be able to define a method for points whose result has exactly the same type as the invoking point, i.e. that maps a coloured point to a coloured point, a mere point to a mere point, etc. The obvious solution is to introduce type symbols, and give such a method the type

$$\forall X.\texttt{Point}\ X \to \texttt{Point}\ X$$

which was defined to be $\forall_X[X].\texttt{Point}\ X \to \texttt{Point}\ X$ in Sect. 8.3. Slightly betters is that a simple method has type $\forall_P[\Delta].P \to S$. It can be invoked by a term of type U if the inequality $U < P$ can be solved by substituting for symbols in Δ, i.e. if there is a *submatch* of P against U with respect to Δ.

submatching is relatively straightforward but the situation is even more delicate when specialising a method of type $[\Phi]\ Q \to T$ by a special case of type $[\Delta]\ P \to S$. Ambiguity arises if such a method is invoked by a term of type U where both $U < P$ and $U < Q$ can be solved. The resulting substitutions relate P and Q so the goal is to define their *most general relator.*

For these to exist imposes further constraints upon the subtyping relation. For example, suppose that P is $F\ X\ Y$ and Q is $F\ Z\ Z$ where F is some type and X,Y and Z are type symbols in Δ and Φ. The obvious rule for relating type applications reduces the problem to two inequalities, namely $X < Z$ and $Y < Z$ but these can be solved in two unrelated ways, either by identifying X,Y and Z or by mapping Z to Top. Using this approach, there is no most general relator. Note, however, that this approach does *not* follow from the displayed subtyping rules above, since there the left-hand side of a type application is invariant. Thus, original inequality reduces to the *equation* $F\ X = F\ Z$ and the relation of Y and Z. These have a most general solution that identifies all three symbols.

One way of appreciating the success of these rules is to observe that the supertypes of a type always form a linear order, so that if types P and Q have a lower bound U then either $P < Q$ or $Q < P$ holds. Without this property, there is a tendency for problems to reduce to sets of inequalities, such as $S < X < T$, for which there is no general solution. As it stands, a general inequality $P < Q$ can be *simplified* to a substitution plus a single constraint of the form $R < X$. This constraint is not very appealing, but it is manageable in practice.

Since the whole approach is unfamiliar, it will be developed by adding to three existing calculi, of increasing complexity: the simply typed λ-calculus; System **FM**; and pattern calculus. Then examples follow in Sect. 11.7.

$$\frac{}{T < \mathtt{Top}} \qquad \frac{S < T}{F\,S < F\,T} \qquad \frac{}{T < T}$$

Fig. 11.1 Subtyping

11.2 Subtyping

The subtyping rules are given in Fig. 11.1. Every type is a subtype of Top. Type applications are invariant on the left and covariant on the right. Every type is a subtype of itself. Although several type systems will be considered in this chapter, the same subtyping rules will apply throughout. Types P and Q are *related* (written $P \sim Q$) if $P < Q$ or $Q < P$. A type T is *minimal* if it has no subtypes other than itself.

Lemma 11.1. *The subtyping relation is a partial order. The supertypes of a type form a finite linear order. Hence, if two types P and Q have a lower bound then they are related.*

Proof. The proofs of antisymmetry and transitivity, etc. are by straightforward induction. Finally, note that proper supertypes of a type are always smaller expressions, of which there are finitely many. □

The *simple combinatory types* are given by the grammar

$$\begin{array}{lll} T ::= & & \text{(type)} \\ & C & \text{(constant)} \\ & T\,T & \text{(application)} \\ & T \to T & \text{(function)}\,. \end{array}$$

The constants include the top type Top and the constant & (written infix) for building *choice types* of the form $N\ \&\ M$.

In general, the type of a method will be a choice between those of its various cases, from which the type of a method invocation will be created. Given simple combinatory types U and M define the *type invocation* $U.M$ by

$$\begin{array}{rcll} U.(P \to S) &=& S & \text{if } U < P \\ U.(N\ \&\ M) &=& U.M & \text{if defined} \\ U.(N\ \&\ M) &=& U.N & \text{otherwise} \\ U.M &=& \text{undefined} & \text{otherwise}\,. \end{array}$$

In general, type invocation is not stable under subtyping. For example, if M is some $P \to S\ \&\ Q \to T$ where $P < Q$ then there is no reason why $P.M = S$ should be a subtype of $Q.M = T$. Ratehr, this will be ensured if $P \to S$ is a *specialisation* of $Q \to T$, as defined in Fig. 11.2. From now on, choice types $N\ \&\ M$ will be required to satisfy $N \ll M$.

Lemma 11.2. *Let $V < U$ be types and let M be a type. If $U.M$ is defined then $V.M$ is defined and is a subtype of $U.M$.*

$$\frac{S < T}{P \to S \ll Q \to T} \qquad \frac{P \not< Q}{P \to S \ll Q \to T} \qquad \frac{T \ll N \quad T \ll M}{T \ll N \,\&\, M}$$

Fig. 11.2 Type specialisation for simple types

Proof. The proof is by routine induction on the structure of M, given the restriction on choice types above. □

11.3 Simply Typed Method Calculus

The simply typed method calculus adds invocations and method choices to a variant of the simply typed λ-calculus of Chap. 7.1.

The terms of the *simply typed method calculus* are given by the grammar

$$\begin{array}{lll} t ::= & & \text{(term)} \\ & x^T & \text{(variable)} \\ & t\ t & \text{(application)} \\ & (\lambda x.t)^T & \text{(abstraction)} \\ & t.t & \text{(invocation)} \\ & t \,\&\, t & \text{(method choice)}\ . \end{array}$$

The term variables, applications and abstractions are just as in the simply typed λ-calculus except that abstractions now carry their type as an explicit superscript, just like term variables. The invocation $u.m$ of m (the *method*) by u is a generalisation of function application used when m is a method choice. A method choice n & m combines a *special case* n with a *default* m. The type derivation rules are given in Fig. 11.3. Term invocations are typed by type invocations. Method choices are typed by type choices if the specialisation relation holds. The subsumption rule is standard.

A *minimum type* for a term t is a type T such that there is a derivation of the form $\Gamma \vdash t : T$ and any derivation of the form $\Gamma \vdash t : S$ has the property that $T < S$. Note that the minimum type U of a term need not be minimal as a type, as in $x^{\mathtt{Top}}$. That t has minimum type T may be denoted by t^T.

Lemma 11.3. *Every well-typed term of the simply typed method calculus has a minimum type.*

Proof. The proof is by induction on the structure of t. Consider an invocation $u.m : U.M$. The minimum type of U is some subtype V of U. Now $V.M$ is a subtype of $U.M$ by Lemma 11.2, and so is minimum for $u.m$. The other cases are routine. □

The reduction rules for the simply typed method calculus are in Fig. 11.4.

$$\frac{}{\Gamma, x^T \vdash x^T : T} \qquad \frac{\Gamma \vdash r : U \to S \quad \Gamma \vdash u : U}{\Gamma \vdash r\, u : S} \qquad \frac{\Gamma, x^P \vdash s : S}{\Gamma \vdash (\lambda x.s)^{P \to S} : P \to S}$$

$$\frac{\Gamma \vdash u : U \quad \Gamma \vdash m : M}{\Gamma \vdash u.m : U.M} \qquad \frac{\Gamma \vdash n : N \quad \Gamma \vdash m : M \quad N \ll M}{\Gamma \vdash n \,\&\, m : N \,\&\, M} \qquad \frac{\Gamma \vdash t : S \quad S < T}{\Gamma \vdash t : T}$$

Fig. 11.3 Simply typed method calculus

Theorem 11.4 (Type Preservation). *If there is a derivation of the form $\Gamma \vdash t : T$ in the simply typed method calculus and t reduces to some term t' then there is a derivation of $\Gamma \vdash t' : T$.*

Proof. The proof is by routine induction on the nature of reduction. □

Theorem 11.5 (Progress). *The closed irreducible terms of the simply typed method calculus are abstractions and method choices. Also, their minimum types are minimal as types.*

Proof. The proof is by induction on the structure of the term. Suppose that there is an irreducible, closed invocation $u.m$. By induction, m is an abstraction or method choice and the minimum type of u is minimal, so a reduction can be performed. The other clauses of the induction are routine. □

Theorem 11.6 (Confluence). *Reduction of the simply typed method calculus is confluent.*

Proof. The proof is by simultaneous reduction. □

11.4 Method Types

Now consider the combinatory types of Chap. 8.5 equipped with the subtyping rules of Fig. 11.1.

Lemma 11.7. *If $V < U$ are types and ρ is a type substitution then $\rho V < \rho U$.*

Proof. The proof is by a straightforward induction on the structure of U. □

In this setting, the type of a method m is a quantified type $M = \forall_P[\Delta]\, P \to S$ such as $\forall_{\texttt{Point}\ X}[X]$ `Point` $X \to$ `Unit` so that its invocation by some $u : U$ must solve the inequality $U < P$ by a substitution on Δ.

Let U and P be types and let Δ be a type context. A *submatch* of P against U with respect to Δ is some type substitution ρ whose domain is within Δ such that $U < \rho P$. A substitution υ is a *general* such if $\upsilon P < \rho P$ for any other such submatch ρ. If υ_1 and υ_2 are both general then $\upsilon_1 P = \upsilon_2 P$ but this does not necessarily imply that υ_1 and υ_2 are equal since they may differ on symbols in Δ that are not free in

$$\begin{array}{rcll}
(\lambda x.s)^T\, u & \longrightarrow & \{u/x\}\, s & & (\beta)\\
u^U.r^{P\to S} & \longrightarrow & r\, u & & \text{(invoke)}\\
u^U.(n^N \,\&\, m) & \longrightarrow & u.n & \text{if } U \text{ is minimal and } U.N \text{ defined} & \text{(special)}\\
u^U.(n^N \,\&\, m) & \longrightarrow & u.m & \text{if } U \text{ is minimal and } U.N \text{ undefined} & \text{(default)}\,.
\end{array}$$

Fig. 11.4 Reduction rules for simply typed method calculus

P. A submatch υ is *most general* if it is the unique general submatch. Uniqueness follows if Δ consists of free variables of P that are not free in U. An algorithm for a general submatch $\{U < [\Delta]P\}$ of P against U with respect to Δ is given in Fig. 11.5.

Theorem 11.8. *Let U and P be types and let Δ be a type context. Then U and P have a submatch relative to Δ if and only if $\{U < [\Delta]P\}$ is some substitution υ, in which case it is a general submatch. If P is minimal then $U = \upsilon P$.*

Proof. Suppose that there is a submatch ρ. The proof that $\{U < [\Delta]P\}$ exists and is general is by induction on the structure of P. If P is Top then $\upsilon P = \rho P$. If P is a type application $G\ Q$ then U must be a type application $F\ V$. Now $\rho G = F$ and so factors through $\{F/[\Delta]G\}$. Hence, without loss of generality, F is G and now apply induction. Otherwise, ρ must be a match.

The proofs of the rest are routine. □

Lemma 11.9. *Let U and P be types and let Δ be a type context such that $\{U < [\Delta]\ P\}$ exists. If ρ is a type substitution which avoids Δ then $\{\rho U < [\Delta]\ \rho P\}$ exists and*

$$\{\rho U < [\Delta]\ \rho P\} \circ \rho = \rho \circ \{U < [\Delta]\ P\}\,.$$

Proof. The proof is by straightforward induction on the structure of P. □

Type invocation will be defined so that, if it exists, $U.([\Delta]\ P \to S)$ is $\{U < [\Delta]\ P\}S$. However, it is not enough that the submatch exist, since type invocation must be stable with respect to subtyping, so that if $U.M$ is defined and V is a subtype of U then $V.M$ is defined and a subtype of $U.M$. For example, taking Δ to be some symbol X and letting P be X, this implies that $\{V/X\}S$ is a subtype of $\{U/X\}S$. However, this is not true in general, as S may contain invariant occurrences of X. For example, $V * V$ is not a subtype of $U * U$. To restore order requires some additional concepts and constraints.

Define the *covariant variables* $\mathsf{CV}(T)$ of a type T by

$$\begin{aligned}
\mathsf{CV}(X) &= \{X\}\\
\mathsf{CV}(F\ U) &= \mathsf{CV}(U) \setminus \mathsf{FV}(F)\\
\mathsf{CV}(U) &= \{\}\ \text{otherwise}\,.
\end{aligned}$$

For example, X is a covariant variable of `Point` X and `Point` (`ColourPoint` X) and `List` X but not of $X *$ `Point` X. Define the *invariant variables* of a type T to be $\mathsf{IV}(T) = \mathsf{FV}(T) \setminus \mathsf{CV}(T)$.

$$\begin{aligned}
\{U < [\Delta]\texttt{Top}\} &= \{\} \\
\{F\,U < [\Delta]\;G\,P\} &= \text{let } \upsilon_1 = \{F/[\Delta]G\} \text{ in} \\
&\quad\ \text{let } \upsilon_2 = \{U < [\Delta]\upsilon_1 P\} \text{ in} \\
&\quad\ \upsilon_2 \circ \upsilon_1 \\
\{U < [\Delta]P\} &= \{U/[\Delta]\;P\} \text{ otherwise}
\end{aligned}$$

Fig. 11.5 Submatching

Lemma 11.10. *Let $V < U$ and $S < T$ be types. If a type variable X is covariant in S then $\{V/X\}S < \{U/X\}T$.*

Proof. The proof is by induction on the structure of T. If T is an application $F\ T_1$ then S is an application $F\ S_1$ where $S_1 < T_1$. Now X is not free in F so apply induction to V, U, S_1, T_1 and X. The other nontrivial cases are similar. □

A *simple method type*

$$P \Rightarrow S$$

is a match type of the form $\forall_P[\mathsf{CV}(P)]\ P \rightarrow S$ where any covariant variable of P that is free in S is a covariant variable of S, i.e. $\mathsf{CV}(P) \cap \mathsf{FV}(S) \subseteq \mathsf{CV}(S)$. Examples of simple method types include:

$$\begin{aligned}
&\texttt{Int} \Rightarrow \texttt{Float}\ ; \\
&\texttt{point} \Rightarrow \texttt{point}\ ; \\
&X \Rightarrow \texttt{Float}\ ; \\
&X \Rightarrow X\ ; \\
&\texttt{Point}\ X \Rightarrow \texttt{Point}\ X\ ; \text{ and} \\
&\texttt{Point}\ X \Rightarrow \texttt{List}\ X\ .
\end{aligned}$$

Counter examples include:

$$\begin{aligned}
\forall_{\texttt{Point}\ X}\ [\Delta]\ \texttt{Point}\ X \rightarrow \texttt{Point}\ X \quad & (\text{if } \Delta \neq X)\ ; \\
\texttt{point} \rightarrow \texttt{point} \quad & (\text{no quantification}) \\
\forall_X[X]\ X \rightarrow X * X \quad & (X \text{ invariant in } X * X)\ .
\end{aligned}$$

It is convenient to define $\{U \lhd P\}$ to be $\{U < [\mathsf{CV}(P)]P\}$ for types U and P. For example $U.(P \Rightarrow S)$ will be defined to be $\{U \lhd P\}S$.

Lemma 11.11. *Let $V < U$ be types and let P be a type. If $\{U \lhd P\}$ exists then $\{V \lhd P\}$ exists. Further, if X is a covariant variable of P then $\{V \lhd P\}X < \{U \lhd P\}X$.*

Proof. The proof is by routine induction on the structure of P.

The second challenge is to define type specialisation. If a term of type U is choosing between a special case of type $P \Rightarrow S$ and a default of type $Q \Rightarrow T$ then ambiguity arises if $\upsilon_1 = \{U \lhd P\}$ and $\upsilon_2 = \{U \lhd Q\}$ are both defined. Assume henceforth that

$$
\begin{aligned}
\{P \sim \mathtt{Top}\} &= \{\} \\
\{\mathtt{Top} \sim Q\} &= \{\} \\
\{F\ U \sim X\} &= \{U \sim Y\} \circ \{F\ Y/X\} \quad (Y \text{ fresh}) \\
\{X \sim F\ U\} &= \{Y \sim U\} \circ \{F\ Y/X\} \quad (Y \text{ fresh}) \\
\{F\ P \sim G\ Q\} &= \text{let } \upsilon_1 = \{F = G\} \text{ in} \\
&\quad\ \text{let } \upsilon_2 = \{\upsilon_1 P \sim \upsilon_1 Q\} \text{ in} \\
&\quad\ \upsilon_2 \circ \upsilon_1 \\
\{P \sim Q\} &= \{P = Q\} \text{ otherwise}
\end{aligned}
$$

Fig. 11.6 Relating

P and Q are *separated*, in the sense that the covariant type symbols of one are not free in the other, i.e.

$$\mathsf{CV}(P) \cap \mathsf{FV}(Q) = \{\} \quad \text{and} \quad \mathsf{CV}(Q) \cap \mathsf{FV}(P) = \{\}\,.$$

To maintain type safety, it is necessary that $\upsilon_1 S < \upsilon_2 T$ holds. The challenge is to find a substitution υ such that υP and υQ share a lower bound that can serve in place of all possible such U. Since sharing a lower bound is equivalent to being related in the subtype order, the goal is to find a *relator* υ. Further, it should have the property that for all types U, if $\{U \lhd P\} \cup \{U \lhd Q\}$ exists then it factors through υ.

That is, a *most general relator* for separated types P and Q is a relator υ for them, such that for all types U if $\{U \lhd P\} \cup \{U \lhd Q\}$ exists then it factors through υ.

The algorithm for the most general relator $\{P \sim Q\}$ of separated types P and Q is given in Fig. 11.6, whose rules must be applied in order. Some care must be taken with type variables. For example, when relating C Top and X it is important to map X to $C\ Y$ for some fresh variable Y and not to C Top.

Theorem 11.12. *Let P and Q be separated types. They have a relator if and only if they have a most general relator, given by $\{P \sim Q\}$. If P and Q are both minimal then $\{P \sim Q\}$ unifies P and Q.*

Proof. The proofs are by straightforward induction on the structure of Q and P. □

Lemma 11.13. *Let P and Q be separated types such that $\{P \sim Q\}$ exists. If ρ is a type substitution which avoids $\mathsf{CV}(P) \cup \mathsf{CV}(Q)$ then $\{\rho P \sim \rho Q\}$ exists and*

$$\{\rho P \sim \rho Q\} \circ \rho = \rho \circ \{P \sim Q\}\,.$$

Proof. The proof is by straightforward induction on the structure of Q. □

Now *type specialisation* is defined in Fig. 11.7. Implicit in the definition is the assumption that P and Q are separated. From now on, all choice types N & M are required to satisfy $N \ll M$.

Now define *type invocation* by

$$\frac{\{P \sim Q\}S < \{P \sim Q\}T}{P \Rightarrow S \ll Q \Rightarrow T} \qquad \frac{\{P \sim Q\} \text{ undefined}}{P \Rightarrow S \ll Q \Rightarrow T} \qquad \frac{T \ll N \quad T \ll M}{T \ll N \,\&\, M}$$

Fig. 11.7 Type specialisation

$$\begin{aligned} U.(P \Rightarrow S) &= \{U \lhd P\}S & \\ U.(N \,\&\, M) &= U.N & \text{if defined} \\ U.(N \,\&\, M) &= U.M & \text{otherwise} \\ U.M &= \text{undefined} & \text{otherwise.} \end{aligned}$$

Lemma 11.14. *Let M and U be types such that $U.M$ exists and let ρ be a type substitution. Then $\rho U.\rho M < \rho(U.M)$.*

Proof. The proof is by induction on the structure of M. The only nontrivial situation is when M is of the form $P \Rightarrow S \,\&\, N$ and $U.M = U.N$ but $\rho U.\rho M = \rho U.\rho(P \Rightarrow S)$. Without loss of generality, N is of the form $Q \Rightarrow T$ where P and Q are separated and ρ avoids their covariant variables. Then $\rho U.\rho M = \{\rho U \lhd \rho P\}\rho S = \rho\{U \lhd P\}S < \rho\{U \lhd Q\}T = \rho(U.M)$ by Lemma 11.9. □

Lemma 11.15. *Let $V < U$ be types and let M be a method type. If $U.M$ is defined then $V.M$ is defined and is a subtype of $U.M$.*

Proof. The proof is by induction on the structure of M. If it is a simple method type $P \Rightarrow S$ then proceed by induction on the structure of P. If P is a variable X then apply Lemma 11.10. The rest is routine.

Now suppose that M is of the form $P \Rightarrow S \,\&\, N$. If $U.M$ is $U.(P \Rightarrow S)$ then $V.N$ is $V.(P \Rightarrow S)$, by induction, and the result follows by induction. Alternatively, suppose that $U.M$ is $U.N$. If $V.M$ is $V.N$ then apply induction, so assume that $V.M$ is $V.(P \Rightarrow S)$. Without loss of generality, N is of the form $Q \Rightarrow T$ where P and Q are separated.

That $\{U \lhd Q\}$ exists implies that $\{V \lhd Q\}$ exists by Lemma 11.11. Now $\rho = \{V \lhd P\} \cup \{V \lhd Q\}$ relates P and Q and so factors through $\{P \sim Q\}$. Hence $V.M = \{V \lhd P\}S = \rho S < \rho T = \{V \lhd Q\}T$. This last is a subtype of $\{U \lhd Q\}T = U.M$ by Lemmas 11.11 and 11.7. □

Lemma 11.16. *If $P \Rightarrow S \ll M$ and ρ is a type substitution then $\rho(P \Rightarrow S) \ll \rho M$.*

Proof. The proof is by induction on the structure of M. If M is a simple method type $Q \Rightarrow T$ then without loss of generality, P and Q are separated. If ρP and ρQ cannot be related then there is nothing to prove, so suppose that they can. Then $\{\rho P = \rho Q\} \circ \rho = \rho \circ \{P \sim Q\}$ by Lemma 11.13. Hence

$$\{\rho P \sim \rho Q\}\rho S = \rho\{P \sim Q\}S < \rho\{P \sim Q\}T = \{\rho P \sim \rho Q\}\rho T\,.$$

If M is a method choice then apply induction twice. □

$$\frac{}{\Gamma, x^T \vdash x^T : T} \qquad \frac{\Gamma \vdash r : U \to S \quad \Gamma \vdash u : U}{\Gamma \vdash r\,u : S} \qquad \frac{\Gamma, x^U \vdash s : S}{\Gamma \vdash (\lambda x.s)^{U \to S} : U \to S}$$

$$\frac{\Gamma \vdash r : \forall_P[\Delta].S}{\Gamma \vdash r\,U : \{U/[\Delta]\,P\}S} \qquad \frac{\Gamma \vdash s : S}{\Gamma \vdash ([\Delta]\,P \to s)^{\forall_P[\Delta].S} : \forall_P[\Delta].S}\ \Delta \cap \mathsf{FV}(\Gamma) = \{\}$$

$$\frac{\Gamma \vdash n : N \quad \Gamma \vdash m : M \quad N \ll M}{\Gamma \vdash n \,\&\, m : N \,\&\, M} \qquad \frac{\Gamma \vdash u : U \quad \Gamma \vdash m : M}{\Gamma \vdash u.m : U.M} \qquad \frac{\Gamma \vdash s : S \quad S < T}{\Gamma \vdash s : T}$$

Fig. 11.8 Parametric method calculus

11.5 Parametric Method Calculus

The terms of the parametric method calculus are obtained by adding invocations and method choices to those of System **FM**, and giving abstractions and typecases explicit types. The type derivation rules are given in Fig. 11.8.

Lemma 11.17. *Every well-typed term of the parametric method calculus has a minimum type.*

Proof. The proof is by a routine induction on the structure of t. Note that the explicit types of abstractions are necessary to ensure minimality. □

Lemma 11.18. *If there is a derivation of $\Gamma \vdash t : T$ and ρ is a type substitution then there is a derivation of $\rho\Gamma \vdash \rho t : \rho T$.*

Proof. The proof is by straightforward induction on the structure of the derivation of $\Gamma \vdash t : T$ since all of the type constructions are preserved (or become smaller) under type substitution. For type applications, use Lemma 8.3. For method choices, use Lemma 11.16. For invocations, use Lemma 11.14. For subsumption, use Lemma 11.7. □

The reduction rules for the parametric method calculus are given in Fig. 11.9. They combine the rules of System **FM** with those of the simply typed method calculus, except that the rule (invoke) now introduces a type application as well as a term application. This type application employs the minimum type U of the invoking term, which must be minimal. To ensure minimality under substitution U must also be closed.

Theorem 11.19 (Type Preservation). *If there is a derivation of $t : T$ in the parametric method calculus and t reduces to some term t' then there is a derivation of $t' : T$.*

Proof. The proof is routine. □

Theorem 11.20 (Progress). *The closed irreducible terms of the parametric method calculus are abstractions, typecases and method choices whose minimum types are closed and minimal.*

$(\lambda x.s)^T\ u \longrightarrow \{u/x\}s$			$(\beta 1)$
$([\Delta]\ P \to s)^T\ U \longrightarrow \{U/[\Delta]\ P\}s$			(match2)
$u^U.m^{P \Rightarrow S} \longrightarrow m\ U\ u$	if U is closed, minimal		(invoke)
$u^U.(n^N\ \&\ m) \longrightarrow u.n$	if U is closed, minimal and $U.N$ defined		(specialise)
$u^U.(n^N\ \&\ m) \longrightarrow u.m$	if U is closed, minimal and $U.N$ undefined		(default)

Fig. 11.9 Reduction rules for method calculus

Proof. The proof is by a straightforward induction on the structure of the term. □

Theorem 11.21 (Confluence). *Reduction of the parametric pattern calculus is confluent.*

Proof. The proof is by simultaneous reduction. Note that all of the reduction rules are stable under the application of type or term substitutions. □

11.6 Subtyped Pattern Calculus

The subtyped pattern calculus adds invocations and method choices to the typed pattern calculus. Most things develop as expected. The only subtlety is that during pattern matching, types must be handled by submatching. For example, if a λ-abstraction of the form $[;x^{\mathtt{Top}}]\ \hat{x}^{\mathtt{Top}} \to s$ is applied to some integer $u : \mathtt{Int}$ then type matching should proceed since $\mathtt{Int} < \mathtt{Top}$.

The terms of the subtyped pattern calculus are given by the grammar

$$t ::= x^T \mid \hat{x}^T \mid t\,t \mid ([\theta]\ t \to t)^T \mid t\ T \mid ([\Delta]\ T \to t)^T \mid t \# t \mid t.t \mid t \,\&\, t\,.$$

The type derivation rules are given in Fig. 11.10.

Lemma 11.22. *Every well-typed term of the subtyped pattern calculus has a minimum type.*

Proof. The proof is by a routine induction on the structure of t. □

Lemma 11.23. *If there is a derivation of $\Gamma \vdash t : T$ and ρ is a type substitution then there is a derivation of $\rho\Gamma \vdash \rho t : \rho T$.*

Proof. The proof is by straightforward induction on the structure of the type derivation. □

Let $\theta = \Delta; B$ be a context of *binding symbols*. Let p and u be terms. The *basic submatching* $\{u \,//\, [\theta]\ p\}$ is the match defined by applying the rules in Fig. 11.11 in order. This is just as in typed pattern calculus, except that the first clause has been modified to employ submatching instead of matching.

$$\frac{}{\Gamma, x^T \vdash x^T : T} \qquad \frac{}{\Gamma, \hat{x}^T \vdash \hat{x}^T : T}$$

$$\frac{\Gamma \vdash r : U \to S \quad \Gamma \vdash u : U}{\Gamma \vdash r\, u : S} \qquad \frac{\Gamma, \hat{B} \vdash p : P \quad \Gamma, B \vdash s : S}{\Gamma \vdash ([\Delta; B]\, p \to s)^{P \to S} : P \to S}\ (\mathsf{FV}(P \to S) \cup \mathsf{FV}(\Gamma)) \cap \Delta = \{\}$$

$$\frac{\Gamma \vdash r : \forall_P[\Delta].S}{\Gamma \vdash r\, U : \{U/[\Delta]\, P\}S} \qquad \frac{\Gamma \vdash s : S}{\Gamma \vdash ([\Delta]\, P \to s)^{\forall_P[\Delta].S} : \forall_P[\Delta].S}\ \mathsf{FV}(\Gamma) \cap \Delta = \{\}$$

$$\frac{\Gamma \vdash s : S \quad \Gamma \vdash r : R}{\Gamma \vdash s \# r : R}\ S \approx R \qquad \frac{\Gamma \vdash s : S \quad S < T}{\Gamma \vdash s : T}$$

$$\frac{\Gamma \vdash u : U \quad \Gamma \vdash m : M}{\Gamma \vdash u.m : U.M} \qquad \frac{\Gamma \vdash m : M \quad \Gamma \vdash n : N \quad M \ll N}{\Gamma \vdash m \,\&\, n : M \,\&\, N}$$

Fig. 11.10 Subtyped pattern calculus

The *submatch* $\{u < [\theta]\, p\}$ *of p against u relative to binding symbols* θ and *result type* T is defined as follows. If $\{u // [\theta]\, p\}$ is of the form $(\mathsf{some}\ \sigma, \mathsf{some}\ \rho)$ whose domain is θ then the submatch is the same. Otherwise, the match is $(\mathsf{none}, \mathsf{none})$. When $(\mathsf{none}, \mathsf{none})$ is applied to a term s^S then it yields `Nomatch` S as before, except that now S is the minimum type of s.

Lemma 11.24. *Let* $u : U$ *and* $([\theta]\ p \to s)^{U \to S}$ *be terms. If* $\{u < [\theta]\, p\}$ *is some pair of substitutions* (σ, ρ) *then there is a derivation of* $\sigma\rho s : S$.

Proof. Without loss of generality, ρ is the identity and $\theta = \ ; B$ does not bind any type symbols. The proof is by induction on the structure of p. If it is a binding symbol $\hat{x}$ then U is a subtype of P so $u : P$ and the Substitution Lemma applies. If p is any other matchable then u is p and σ is the identity. If p and u are applications then divide θ in two and apply induction twice. □

The reduction rules for the method calculus are given in Fig. 11.12, where the *matchable forms* are the data structures, cases, typecases, choices and method choices.

Lemma 11.25 (Substitution). *If* $t \longrightarrow t'$ *is a reduction of terms and* ρ *is a type substitution then* $\rho t \longrightarrow \rho t'$.

Proof. Without loss of generality, the reduction is a rule. For most rules, the result follows since type substitution preserves type matching and submatching. For term invocations, observe that the minimal type of a data structure is stable under type substitutions. □

Theorem 11.26 (Type Preservation). *If there is a derivation of* $t : T$ *and* t *reduces to some term* t' *then there is a derivation of* $t' : T$.

$$\begin{array}{rcll}
\{u^U /\!/ [\theta]\hat{x}^{\hat{P}}\} & = & (\mathsf{some}\ \{u/x\}, \{U < [\Delta]P\}) & \text{if } x^P \in B \\
\{\hat{x}^T /\!/ [\theta]\hat{x}^T\} & = & (\mathsf{some}\ \{\}, \mathsf{some}\ \{\}) & \text{if } x^T \notin B \\
\{u\, v /\!/ [\theta]\, p\, q\} & = & \{u /\!/ [\theta]\, p\} \cup \{v /\!/ [\theta]\, q\} & \text{if } p\,q \text{ and } u\,v \text{ are matchable} \\
\{u\, U /\!/ [\theta]\, p\, \hat{P}\} & = & \{u /\!/ [\theta]\, p\} \cup (\mathsf{some}\ \{\}, \{U / [\Delta]\, P\}) & \text{if } p\,P \text{ and } u\,U \text{ are matchable} \\
\{u /\!/ [\theta]\, p\} & = & \mathsf{none\ otherwise} & \text{if } p \text{ and } u \text{ are matchable} \\
\{u /\!/ [\theta]\, p\} & = & \mathsf{undefined} & \text{otherwise.}
\end{array}$$

Fig. 11.11 Basic matching for subtyped pattern calculus

Proof. Without loss of generality the reduction is a rule. If the rule is a match then apply Lemma 11.24. The other cases are straightforward. □

Theorem 11.27 (Progress). *The closed irreducible terms of the method calculus are matchable forms.*

Proof. The proof is by a straightforward induction on the structure of the term. □

Theorem 11.28 (Confluence). *Reduction of the subtyped pattern calculus is confluent.*

Proof. The proof is by simultaneous reduction. Note that all of the rules are stable under the application of type or term substitutions. □

11.7 Coloured Circles

Here are some examples.

Example 11.29. Names and Proper Names

The different ways of naming a person can be used to illustrate dynamic dispatch. Suppose there are constructors

$$\begin{array}{rl}
\texttt{Person} : & X \Rightarrow \texttt{String} * \texttt{Int} * \texttt{List}\ (\texttt{Person Top}) \rightarrow \texttt{Person}\ X \\
\texttt{ProperPerson} : & Z \Rightarrow \texttt{String} \rightarrow \texttt{ProperPerson}\ Z
\end{array}$$

where $\texttt{Person}\ x\ (n,p,f)$ denotes a person with name n and position p and friends f and additional fields x and,

$$\texttt{Person}\ (\texttt{ProperPerson}\ z\ n\texttt{1})\ (n,p,f)$$

is such a person with a proper name $n1$ as well as name n. The use of `Top` allows various classes of friends to mix.

Define $\texttt{friends} : \texttt{Person}\ X \Rightarrow \texttt{List}\ (\texttt{Person}[\![\texttt{Top}]\!])$ by

$$
\begin{array}{rcll}
([\theta]p \to s)^T\, u & \longrightarrow & \{u < [\theta]\, p\}\, s & & \text{(match1)}\\
([\Delta]\, P \to s)\, U & \longrightarrow & \{U < [\Delta]\, P\} s & & \text{(match2)}\\
(s^{\forall_P[\Delta].S} \,\#\, r)\, U & \longrightarrow & s\, U & \text{if } \{U < [\Delta]\, P\} = \mathsf{some}\ \rho & \text{(left)}\\
(s^{\forall_P[\Delta].S} \,\#\, r)\, U & \longrightarrow & r\, U & \text{if } \{U < [\Delta]\, P\} = \mathsf{none} & \text{(right)}\\
u^U.m^{P \Rightarrow S} & \longrightarrow & m\, U\, u & \text{if } U \text{ is closed, minimal} & \text{(invoke)}\\
u^U.(n^N \,\&\, m) & \longrightarrow & u.n & \text{if } U \text{ is closed, minimal and } U.N \text{ defined} & \text{(specialise)}\\
u^U.(n^N \,\&\, m) & \longrightarrow & u.m & \text{if } U \text{ is closed, minimal and } U.N \text{ undefined} & \text{(default)}\,.
\end{array}
$$

Fig. 11.12 Reduction rules for subtyped pattern calculus

$$\mathtt{Person}\, x^X\, (n^{\mathtt{String}}, p^{\mathtt{Int}}, f^{\mathtt{List}\ (\mathtt{Person\ Top})}) \to f$$

(using static pattern notation). It works equally well for both a person and a proper person. Now define the pattern-matching function name by

$$
\begin{array}{l}
(\mathtt{name} : \mathtt{Person\ ProperPerson}\, Y \Rightarrow \mathtt{String} \,\&\, \mathtt{Person}\, X \Rightarrow \mathtt{String}) = \\
\quad \mathtt{Person}\ (\mathtt{ProperPerson}\, y\, n1)\ (n,p,f) \to n\hat{\ }n1 \\
\ \&\ \mathtt{Person}\, x\ (n,p,f) \to n
\end{array}
$$

where ^ concatenates strings. It is well-typed since both cases have the same return type. The type of the special case can be hidden by abstraction, using

$$\mathtt{name1} = [\,; x^{\mathtt{Person}\ X}]\ \hat{x} \to \mathtt{name}\ x : \mathtt{Person}\ X \to \mathtt{String}\,.$$

When name1 is mapped across some list of friends, it will produce a list of strings that includes proper names as well as names.

Example 11.30. Circles and Coloured Circles

The previous example did not stretch the typing since name will always produce a string. Here is an example in which the specialised method uses subtyping.

Suppose there are constructors

$$
\begin{array}{rl}
\mathtt{Point} : & (\mathtt{Float} * \mathtt{Float}) * X \Rightarrow \mathtt{Point}\ X\\
\mathtt{CPoint} : & \mathtt{Int} * Y \Rightarrow \mathtt{CPoint}\ Y\\
\mathtt{Circle} : & (\mathtt{Point\ Top} * \mathtt{Float}) * X \Rightarrow \mathtt{Circle}\ X\\
\mathtt{CCircle} : & \mathtt{Int} * Z \Rightarrow \mathtt{CCircle}\ Z
\end{array}
$$

where Int is used to represent colours. As with names, coloured points and circles are built using combinations of constructors. As with the friends above, the point argument of Circle has type Point Top so that the centre can be any sort of point.

Now consider a method get_centre which is to get the "centre" of a circle. In default, this is just the centre field, defined in the usual manner, but for coloured circles, it will return a coloured point, built from the position of the centre field and the colour of the circle. It is defined by a method choice

$$
\begin{aligned}
&\texttt{get\_centre}:\\
&\quad \texttt{Circle}\ (\texttt{CCircle}\ Y) \Rightarrow \texttt{Point Int}\\
&\ \&\ \texttt{Circle}\ X \Rightarrow \texttt{Point Top} =\\
&\quad [Y]\ \texttt{Circle}\ (\texttt{CCircle}\ Y) \rightarrow\\
&\qquad \texttt{Circle}\ (\texttt{CCircle}\ y\ c)\ (\texttt{Point}\ ((x1,y1),x) \rightarrow \texttt{Point}\ ((x1,y1),\texttt{CPoint Un}\ c)\\
&\ \&\ [X]\ \texttt{Circle}\ X \rightarrow \texttt{Circle}\ ((p,r),x) \rightarrow p\,.
\end{aligned}
$$

This is well-typed since

$$\texttt{Circle}\ (\texttt{CCircle}\ Y) \Rightarrow \texttt{Point Int} \ll \texttt{Circle}\ X \Rightarrow \texttt{Point Top}.$$

11.8 Notes

There is a huge literature on subtyping which cannot be given justice here. However, most of it is informed by the functional viewpoint, in which the types of objects are either type constants or are represented as quantified function types. The latter require nontrivial subtyping on function argument types which blocks consideration of minimal types for controlling method specialisation. Further, in such a setting, type inequalities quickly become unmanageable, so that type variables must be severely constrained, either to avoid subtyping altogether, or by introducing complex machinery involving self types. By contrast, the treatment of subtyping here is closely aligned with that of popular object-oriented languages such as Java.

Here are three representative approaches that employ contravariance. System $\mathbf{F}_<$ [14] adds subtyping to System **F** in which function types are contravariant in their argument types and there is no dynamic dispatch. Abadi and Cardelli's typed object calculus (see also Sect. 6.3) treats object behaviour directly, using self parameters and self types, but still with contravariance in function types. Similar remarks apply to Bruce's PolyTOIL [12, 13]. Closest to the approach taken here is Castagna's $\lambda\&$-calculus [16, 15] which combines contravariance in function types with covariant method specialisation that is quite similar to that of the simply typed method calculus. A type of the form $P \rightarrow S\ \&\ Q \rightarrow T$ must have the property that if $P < Q$ then $S < T$. Type parameters are not supported. Ocaml [72] uses *row variables* [88] to relate types in the same manner that `Point Colour` is here used to represent coloured points.

An alternative approach is taken by Featherweight Generic Java (FGJ) [49]. Its types are closely identified with its classes, so that the types of methods are not first class. This results in a form of invariance in the types of method arguments. However, class declarations create subtyping relations, so that quantification is by variables having an upper bound, as in $\mathbf{F}_<$.

Chapter 12
Implicit Typing

Abstract The extension calculus provides a bridge between the typed and untyped pattern calculi, and underpins the **bondi** programming language. Its evaluation is type-free, but preserves typing. In turn, this requires that term matching implies type matching, so that patterns must have their most general, or principal types. For static patterns this is easily enforced, but general evaluation may increase or decrease type information, so free variables and functions in patterns are required to be linear, in the sense that they use their arguments exactly once. Central to the type discipline are the rules for typing extensions, which make delicate use of type equations and inequalities. Method specialisation is represented by extensions in which the pattern is an object pattern.

12.1 Extension Calculus

The typed pattern calculus was designed to be as clear as possible. In particular, reduction is confluent and every term has a unique type. However, this has come at the price of a heavy syntax, laden with matchable symbols, types, and the rest. This chapter will lighten the syntax and simplify evaluation, at the cost of some transparency, by introducing the extension calculus, and showing how it can be typed (and subtyped) without changing the terms or evaluation algorithm. Let us take the dynamic pattern calculus of Sect. 5.2 as a starting point.

The first simplification is to eliminate the matchable symbols. Recall that these were introduced to identify symbols in patterns that could not be instantiated. However, the evaluation strategy will guarantee that instantiation occurs before evaluation, so no ambiguity is possible. In other words, every symbol appearing in an evaluated pattern must be available for matching.

The second change is to generalise cases to extensions of the form $[\theta]\ p \to s \mid r$, as described in Sect. 5.5. Although a little more complex, extensions will be used in place of cases, typecases and choices in a typed setting.

The terms of the *extension calculus* are given by the grammar

B. Jay, *Pattern Calculus*,
DOI 10.1007/978-3-540-89185-7_12,

$$\begin{aligned}\{v/x\} &= \mathsf{some}\ \{v/x\}\\ \{c/c\} &= \mathsf{some}\ \{\}\\ \{v_1\ v_2/d_1\ d_2\} &= \{v_1/d_1\} \uplus \{v_2/d_2\}\\ \{v/v_1\} &= \mathsf{none\ otherwise.}\end{aligned}$$

Fig. 12.1 Value matching

$$\begin{array}{lll} t ::= & & \text{(term)}\\ & x & \text{(variable)}\\ & c & \text{(constructor)}\\ & t\ t & \text{(application)}\\ & [\theta]\ t \rightarrow t \mid t & \text{(extension).}\end{array}$$

Free variables of an extension are defined by

$$\mathsf{fv}([\theta]\ p \rightarrow s \mid r) = (\mathsf{fv}(p) \cup \mathsf{fv}(s)) \setminus \theta \cup \mathsf{fv}(r)\ .$$

Evaluation in the extension calculus employs a *big-step operational semantics* rather than a reduction relation. The relation $t \Rightarrow v$ asserts that the term t evaluates to the value v. Working with values rather than arbitrary terms simplifies the rules. The *data values* (meta-variable d) and *values* (meta-variable v) are subsets of the terms given by the grammar

$$\begin{array}{lll} d ::= & & \text{(data value)}\\ & x & \text{(variable)}\\ & c & \text{(constructor)}\\ & d\ v & \text{(compound)}\\ v ::= & & \text{(value)}\\ & d & \text{(data value)}\\ & [\theta]\ v \rightarrow t \mid v & \text{(extension).}\end{array}$$

The data values and values play the role of the data structures and matchable forms of the dynamic pattern calculus. The former are more constrained than the latter in that components are required to be values.

The match algorithm will be simpler than that of the dynamic pattern calculus. First, the evaluation strategy will guarantee that all free variables found in the pattern are to be bound, so there is no need to keep track of the binding symbols. In this sense, the algorithm is more like that of the static pattern calculus in Sect. 4.3. Second, since the pattern and argument are known to be values, there is no need to check for matchable forms. The *value matching* $\{v/v_1\}$ of a value v_1 against a value v is defined by the rules in Fig. 12.1.

It is convenient to redefine the application of a match so that it is applied to a pair of terms, as follows:

$$\frac{}{x \Rightarrow x} \qquad \frac{}{c \Rightarrow c} \qquad \frac{r \Rightarrow d \quad u \Rightarrow v}{r\,u \Rightarrow d\,v}$$

$$\frac{r \Rightarrow [\theta]\, v_1 \rightarrow s \mid v_2 \quad u \Rightarrow v_3 \quad \{v_3/\, v_1\}\, s\, (v_2\, v_3) \Rightarrow v}{r\,u \Rightarrow v} \qquad \frac{r \Rightarrow v_1 \quad p \Rightarrow v_2}{[\theta]\, p \rightarrow s \mid r \Rightarrow [\theta]\, v_2 \rightarrow s \mid v_1}$$

Fig. 12.2 Operational semantics of the extension calculus

$$\begin{aligned} \mathsf{some}\ \sigma\ s\ t &= \sigma(s) \\ \mathsf{none}\ s\ t &= t\,. \end{aligned}$$

The evaluation rules are given in Fig. 12.2.

Theorem 12.1 (Progress). *If t is a term of the extension calculus then there is an evaluation rule which can be applied to it.*

Proof. The proof is by a straightforward induction on the structure of t. The most interesting point is that matching cannot get stuck since it is always defined for values. □

12.2 Linear Types

To provide a type system for the extension calculus that reflects the understanding developed for the typed pattern calculus, it is essential to ensure that term matching implies type matching, which can be achieved if the pattern does not contain any type information beyond that which can be inferred from its term structure.

If the pattern is static then this can be easily enforced during type derivation, but in general, instantiation of free variables in patterns may increase type information, while reduction may lose it. To avoid this, it is necessary to restrict the patterns so that evaluation does not change the type information. That is, patterns will be required to be *linear terms* whose free variables can be replaced by linear terms only.

The *linear type system* has grammar

$$T ::= X \mid C \mid T\,T \mid T \rightarrow T \mid \forall X.T \mid \mathsf{lin}\ T\,.$$

The variables, constants, type applications, function types and quantified types are all as before. The *linear type* $\mathsf{lin}\ T$ represents *linear terms* of type T, as will be defined in the next section. Matchable type symbols are not required because of the evaluation strategy, and match types are not necessary as instantiation of type symbols will be implicit.

12.3 Typing Special Cases

Typing the extension calculus is complicated by the absence of type matching during evaluation. For example, suppose the first projection function $\mathtt{fst} : X * Y \to X$ and the negation $\mathtt{not} : \mathtt{Bool} \to \mathtt{Bool}$ are given and consider the extension

$$[x,y]\ \mathtt{Pair}\ x\ y \to \mathtt{not}\ x \mid \mathtt{fst}.$$

Since the body requires x to be a boolean, the natural typing of the binding symbols is $x : \mathtt{Bool}, y : Y$. However, when this extension is applied to $\mathtt{Pair}\ 3\ 4$ then it will evaluate to $\mathtt{not}\ 3$ which is ill typed. In the typed pattern calculus, matching would involve type matching as well as term matching: as Bool and Int do not unify the matching would fail, and the extension would reduce to $\mathtt{fst}\ (\mathtt{Pair}\ 3\ 4)$. Since terms of the extension calculus do not have any types to match, it follows that this extension cannot be allowed to have a type. To put it more positively, term matching must imply type matching. This can be ensured by requiring patterns to take their most general types. That is, the term context for the pattern $\mathtt{Pair}\ x\ y$ must type x and y by distinct fresh variables X and Y so that $\mathtt{not}\ x$ is ill typed.

Hence, the type derivation rules for patterns must be constrained to ensure that the pattern takes its most general, or *principal* type, using judgements of the form $\Gamma; B \vdash p : P$ where Γ provides a context for the free variables in the pattern, and B provides one for its binding symbols. With this in mind, a natural approach to typing extensions uses the following rule

$$\frac{\Gamma \vdash r : P \to S \quad \Gamma; B \vdash p : P \quad \Gamma, B \vdash s : S}{\Gamma \vdash [\,|B|\,]\ p \to s \mid r : P \to S}$$

(where $|B|$ is the result of removing the types from the term context B).

The rule above is quite safe, but it forces all cases in a pattern-matching function to take the same type. In the typed pattern calculus, cases of different types are combined using typecases of the form $s \# t$ whose branching is determined by type matching. Here, all branching is through extensions, so it is necessary to allow the special case to have a special type.

A more subtle approach is to use type similarity (as defined in Sect. 8.4) to get the rule

$$\frac{\Gamma \vdash r : Q \to T \quad \Gamma; B \vdash p : P \quad \Gamma, B \vdash s : S}{\Gamma \vdash [\,|B|\,]\ p \to s \mid r : Q \to T}\ P \to S \approx Q \to T\,.$$

This works for many examples but does not support the typed λ-calculus! Recall that a λ-abstraction $\lambda x.s$ has type $U \to S$ if s can be given type S in a context where x has type U. In extension calculus, the abstraction above is syntactic sugar for $[x]\ x \to s \mid \mathtt{Nomatch}$. Now the most general type for x is a variable, not an arbitrary type U, so the rule above is too restrictive.

The problem with the type derivation rule above is that the typing of the body s is not taking advantage of the type information provided by the argument. If the body is evaluated then it must be that P and Q are the same type, so this type information should be available when typing the body. The resulting rule is

$$\frac{\Gamma \vdash r : Q \to T \quad \Gamma;B \vdash p : P \quad \upsilon(\Gamma,B) \vdash s : \upsilon T}{\Gamma \vdash [\ |B|\ ]\ p \to s \mid r : Q \to T}\ \upsilon = \{P = Q\}.$$

It is unusual to have a unifier in a type derivation rule, as opposed to one for type inference, but it is a consequence of making types implicit in terms.

Actually, the rule above is not quite enough. Type derivations should be stable under application of a type substitution ρ but this one need not be. If ρP and ρQ have a unifier then all is well, but in general they will not. For example, consider the extension $\lfloor x \rfloor\ x \to ([\,]\ \texttt{True} \to \texttt{not}\ x \mid \lfloor y \rfloor\ y \to y)$. It has type $: X \to X \to X$ since unifying the most general type `Bool` for the pattern with the type variable X forces x to be a boolean so that `not` x : `Bool` is of type X, as required. However, if X is instantiated to `Nat` then it has no unifier with `Bool`. Even more problematic is that `not` x is ill typed. In a rewriting system, the presence of `not` x would be disturbing, but here there is nothing to worry about. After all, `True` cannot match against a natural number, and so `not` x will *never* be evaluated. That is, when P and Q cannot be unified then there is no need to type the body. The corresponding rule is thus

$$\frac{\Gamma \vdash r : Q \to T \quad \Gamma;B \vdash p : P}{\Gamma \vdash [\ |B|\ ]\ p \to s \mid r : Q \to T}\ \{P = Q\}\text{ is undefined.}$$

12.4 Typing the Extension Calculus

Having typed the extensions, now consider the patterns in more detail. If the pattern is static then it is easy to give it a principal type. In general, however, the pattern may contain free term variables and be reduced. Instantiating free term variables may introduce more type information, while reduction may lose it, in either case modifying the principal type. To avoid this, patterns will be required to be *linear terms* in which free variables occur exactly once. Now reduction cannot lose type information. Also, instantiation cannot gain type information provided that the introduced term is itself linear.

A *pattern term context* is a pair $\Gamma;B$ of a term context Γ (for the free variables) and a term context B (for the free matchables).

A judgement of the form $\Gamma;B \vdash t : T$ asserts that t is a *linear term* of type T in the linear context $\Gamma;B$. The type derivation rules for linear terms are given in Fig. 12.3. In a derivation of $\Gamma;B \vdash p : P$ the variables in Γ of linear type may be used any number of times. By contrast, the variables in B must occur exactly once, and must take their most general type. That is, on first appearance, variables in B are assumed to be typed by a fresh type variable, with unification employed to type applications.

$$\frac{}{\Gamma;\vdash x:T}\ x^{\mathsf{lin}\ T}\in\Gamma \qquad \frac{}{\Gamma;\ x^X\vdash x:X}\ x,X \text{ fresh for } \Gamma \qquad \frac{c:\forall\Delta.S}{\Gamma;\vdash c:S}\ \Delta \text{ fresh}$$

$$\frac{\Gamma;B_1\vdash r:R \quad \Gamma;B_2\vdash u:U}{\upsilon(\Gamma;B_1,B_2)\vdash r\,u:\upsilon X}\ \begin{array}{l}\upsilon=\{R=U\to X\}\\ X \text{ fresh}\end{array} \qquad \frac{\Gamma;B,x^U\vdash s:S}{\Gamma;B\vdash [x]\ x\to s\mid \texttt{Nomatch}:U\to S}$$

Fig. 12.3 Linear terms

There is some freedom in deciding how many linear terms to allow. At a minimum, it is necessary to admit the data values built from variables and constructors. At the maximum, one could admit any function which can be proven linear in its argument, including general recursive functions. As a compromise, linear λ-abstractions, of the form $[x]\ x\to s\mid \texttt{Nomatch}$ are allowed.

The judgement $\Gamma\vdash t:T$ asserts that t is a term of type T in the context Γ. The type derivation rules for the terms of the extension calculus are given in Fig. 12.4. The restrictions on free type variables in the rules for extensions are required to ensure that type variables introduced in the typing of the pattern are fresh.

Lemma 12.2. *If there is a derivation of $\Gamma\vdash t:T$ then there is a derivation of $\rho\Gamma\vdash t:\rho T$ for any type substitution ρ.*

Proof. The proof is by induction on the structure of the derivation, applying the various lemmas ensuring stability under substitution. Suppose that the type derivation is for an extension as in the figure, in which $\{P=Q\}$ exists. If $\{\rho P=\rho Q\}$ does not exist then the result is immediate, and otherwise it factors through $\{P=Q\}$ and the result follows by induction. The other cases are routine, given the various lemmas ensuring stability under substitution.

The following lemma implies that any typing of an extension can be assumed to end with one of the two associated rules, rather than by instantiating of bound type symbols.

Lemma 12.3. *Suppose that there are type derivations $;B\vdash v_0:P$ and $\Gamma\vdash v:U$ for values v_0 and v such that the two derivations do not share any free type variables. If $\{v/v_0\}$ is some substitution then there is a type substitution ρ that avoids Γ such that $\rho P=U$ and $\Gamma\vdash\{v/v_0\}x:\rho V$ for each $x:V\in B$.*

Proof. The proof is by induction on the structure of v_0. If it is a variable then the result is immediate. If it is a constructor c then so is v and ρ is given by the type derivation of $v:U$. If v_0 is a compound $v_1\ v_2$ then v is a compound $d\ v_3$. Now apply induction twice to obtain type substitutions ρ_1 and ρ_2 whose union is the required type substitution. □

Theorem 12.4 (Type Preservation). *If there is a derivation of $\vdash t:T$ and there is a value v such that $t\Rightarrow v$ then there is a derivation of $\vdash v:T$.*

$$\frac{\Gamma; \vdash u : U}{\Gamma \vdash u : \mathsf{lin}\, U} \qquad \frac{}{\Gamma \vdash x : T}\; x^T \in \Gamma \qquad \frac{}{\Gamma \vdash c : T}\; c : T$$

$$\frac{\Gamma \vdash t : \forall X.T}{\Gamma \vdash t : \{U/X\}T} \qquad \frac{\Gamma \vdash t : T}{\Gamma \vdash t : \forall X.T}\; X \notin \mathsf{FV}(\Gamma) \qquad \frac{\Gamma \vdash r : U \to S \quad \Gamma \vdash u : U}{\Gamma \vdash r\, u : S}$$

$$\frac{\Gamma \vdash r : Q \to T \quad \Gamma; B \vdash p : P \quad \upsilon(\Gamma, B) \vdash s : \upsilon T}{\Gamma \vdash [|B|]\; p \to s \mid r : Q \to T} \; \begin{array}{l}\mathsf{FV}(Q \to T) \cap \mathsf{FV}(\Gamma; B \vdash p : P) \subseteq \mathsf{FV}(\Gamma) \\ \upsilon = \{P = Q\}\end{array}$$

$$\frac{\Gamma \vdash r : Q \to T \quad \Gamma; B \vdash p : P}{\Gamma \vdash [|B|]\; p \to s \mid r : Q \to T} \; \begin{array}{l}\mathsf{FV}(Q \to T) \cap \mathsf{FV}(\Gamma; B \vdash p : P) \subseteq \mathsf{FV}(\Gamma) \\ \{P = Q\} \text{ undefined}\end{array}$$

Fig. 12.4 Typed extension calculus

Proof. The proof is by induction on the derivation of $t \Rightarrow v$. Without loss of generality the reduction is by successful matching, as in Fig. 12.2 and the type derivation takes the form

$$\frac{\vdash v_2 : Q \to T \quad ; B \vdash v_1 : P \quad \upsilon B \vdash s : \upsilon T}{\vdash [\theta]\; v_1 \to s \mid v_2 : Q \to T} \; \upsilon = \{P = Q\}$$

with $\vdash v_3 : Q$. Note that $\{P = Q\}$ must exist since Lemma 12.3 implies that there is a type substitution ρ with domain within $\mathsf{FV}(\,; B \vdash p : P)$ such that $\rho P = Q$ and $\{v_3/v_1\}x : \rho V$ for each $x : V$ in B. Hence ρ factors through υ by some ρ_1 which can be applied to the derivation of $\upsilon B \vdash s : T$ to get $\rho B \vdash s : T$. Now apply the Substitution Lemma to get $\{v_3/v_1\}s : \upsilon T$ as required. □

12.5 Datum Types

Plentiful examples of terms in the extension calculus will be given in Part III using **bondi**. However, there is an important, and illustrative example that is worth mentioning here. Consider the problem of adding a special case to a function r of type $X \to X$. For natural numbers this is easy. For example, the extension

$$\begin{array}{l} \quad [\,]\; \mathtt{Zero} \to \mathtt{Zero} \\ \mid [x]\; \mathtt{Successor}\; x \to x \\ \mid r \end{array}$$

has type $X \to X$. However, the extension $[x]\; x \to \mathtt{plusint}\; x\; 1 \mid r$ is ill typed since the principal type of x is a variable. The constructors for the type of integers are the unbounded collection of numerals, so it is impractical to give a case for each one. The solution adopted is to introduce a *wildcard* for each primitive type, e.g. `_Int` for integers, that will match any integer value. Now the example above becomes

$$\lambda x.([]\ \_\mathtt{Int} \rightarrow \mathtt{plusint}\ x\ 1 \mid r)\ x\,.$$

A convenient shorthand for this is

$$[x]\ x\ \mathtt{as}\ \_\mathtt{Int} \rightarrow \mathtt{plusint}\ (\mathtt{Int}\ x)\ 1 \mid r$$

in which a pattern of the form p as q requires matching against both p and q. This pattern may also be written as $(x : \mathtt{Int})$ on the understanding that this is a syntactic convenience; no type matching will occur during reduction. A similar approach is taken to floating point numbers, and other datum types.

12.6 Constrained Subtyping

To support implicit subtyping requires a deeper understanding of type inequalities than that required for the method calculus, since there interaction between subtyping and choices was limited to method types. In the extension calculus, however, subtyping arises when trying extend a function of type $Q \rightarrow T$ using a pattern of type P. Without subtyping, ambiguity can arise only if P and Q are unified, but now it arises whenever P is a subtype of Q. Since P and Q are arbitrary types, it is necessary to consider the general problem of solving type inequalities.

A *sub-unifier* of types U and P is a substitution ρ such that $\rho U < \rho P$.

In general, types may have a sub-unifier without having a most general one, since "occurrence errors" need not block the existence of solutions. For example, $C\,X < X$ has solutions given by mapping X to Top or C Top or C (C Top), etc. where each succeeding type is a subtype of the one before, so there is no smallest solution. This situation arises for any inequality $U < X$ where X is covariant in U. By contrast, an inequality of the form $U < X$ in which X is invariant in U (such as U is $X * X$) has a unique solution, given by mapping X to Top.

Even the definition of a most general sub-unifier is problematic as it is unreasonable to require that any other sub-unifier factor through a most general one. For example, the inequality $\mathtt{Int} < X$ is solved by mapping X to either Int or Top but neither substitution factors through the other. A more relaxed approach is to require of a general sub-unifier υ of U and P that, for any other sub-unifier ρ there is a substitution σ such that $\rho U < \sigma\upsilon U < \sigma\upsilon P < \rho P$. However, this is not very useful in practice. In particular, such general sub-unifiers are not unique. For example, the inequality $X < \mathtt{Top}$ has two such, the identity substitution and that mapping X to Top.

The approach adopted here is to parametrise subtyping by *subtyping contexts* (meta-variable Σ) which are sequences of *constraints* of the form $S < T$. Then a judgement of the form $\Sigma \vdash S < T$ asserts that S is a subtype of T in context Σ.

Such subtyping contexts will be added to the typing judgements for terms. To type an extension of a default of type $Q \rightarrow T$ using a pattern of type P requires that the body have type T in a context including the constraint $P < Q$. Such constraints

$$\frac{S < T \in \Sigma}{\Sigma \vdash S < T} \qquad \frac{}{\Sigma \vdash T < \texttt{Top}} \qquad \frac{\Sigma \vdash F < G \quad \Sigma \vdash G < F \quad \Sigma \vdash S < T}{\Sigma \vdash F\,S < G\,T} \qquad \frac{}{\Sigma \vdash T < T}$$

$$\frac{\Sigma \vdash F\,S < G\,T}{\Sigma \vdash F < G} \qquad \frac{\Sigma \vdash F\,S < G\,T}{\Sigma \vdash G < F} \qquad \frac{\Sigma \vdash F\,S < G\,T}{\Sigma \vdash S < T}$$

Fig. 12.5 Constrained subtyping

are exploited by the subsumption rule, which allows a term of type S to be a term of type T if the constraints imply that S is a subtype of T.

The derivation rules for *constrained subtyping* are given in Fig. 12.5. The first rule asserts that Σ implies all of the constraints within it. The next three rules are the analogues of the subtyping rules in Fig. 11.1, except that the identity $F = G$ has been generalised to derivations of $F < G$ and $G < F$. By antisymmetry, if both inequalities hold then F is G. The last three rules are used to draw inferences from complex constraints: if $F\ S < G\ T$ then $F = G$ and $S < T$.

Lemma 12.5. *There is a derivation of* $\vdash S < T$ *if and only if there is a derivation of* $S < T$.

Proof. The proof is by a routine induction on the structure of the derivation.

Lemma 12.6. *If there is a derivation of the judgement* $\Sigma \vdash S < T$ *then there is one of* $\rho\Sigma \vdash \rho S < \rho T$ *for any type substitution* ρ.

Proof. The proof is by a routine induction on the derivation of the premise.

One might now expect to rework the definitions of type invocation and type specialisation to exploit constraints, but this is not so easy. For example, type invocation requires knowing when inequalities are insoluble, which is more difficult when constraints are present. Fortunately, it does not appear to be necessary in practice: the unconstrained definitions are safe, and good enough for the examples of interest.

12.7 Subtyped Extension Calculus

Subsumption is not used when typing linear terms, so their derivation rules are unchanged, but type derivations for terms will use judgements of the form

$$\Sigma; \Gamma \vdash t : T$$

where Σ is a subtyping context, Γ is a term context, t is a term and T is a type. The associated rules are given in Fig. 12.6. They adapt the rules for typing the extension calculus in Fig. 12.4 and add three new rules adapted from the subtyped pattern calculus.

$$\frac{\Gamma; \vdash u:U}{\Sigma;\Gamma \vdash u:\mathsf{lin}\, U} \qquad \frac{}{\Sigma;\Gamma \vdash x:T}\; x:T\in\Gamma \qquad \frac{}{\Sigma;\Gamma \vdash c:T}\; c:T$$

$$\frac{\Sigma;\Gamma \vdash t:\forall X.T}{\Sigma;\Gamma \vdash t:\{U/X\}T} \qquad \frac{\Sigma;\Gamma \vdash t:T}{\Sigma;\Gamma \vdash t:\forall X.T}\; X\notin \mathsf{FV}(\Sigma;\Gamma) \qquad \frac{\Sigma;\Gamma \vdash r:U\to S \quad \Sigma;\Gamma \vdash u:U}{\Sigma;\Gamma \vdash r\,u:S}$$

$$\frac{\Sigma;\Gamma \vdash r:Q\to T \quad \Gamma;B\vdash p:P \quad P<Q,\Sigma;\Gamma,B\vdash s:T}{\Sigma;\Gamma \vdash [|B|]\,p\to s \mid r:Q\to T}\; \begin{array}{l}\mathsf{FV}(\Gamma;B\vdash p:P)\cap\mathsf{FV}(Q\to T)\\ \subseteq \mathsf{FV}(\Gamma)\end{array}$$

$$\frac{\Sigma;\Gamma \vdash s:S \quad \Sigma\vdash S<T}{\Sigma;\Gamma \vdash s:T} \qquad \frac{\Sigma;\Gamma \vdash r:R \quad \Sigma;\Gamma \vdash u:U}{\Sigma;\Gamma \vdash r\,u:U.R}$$

$$\frac{\Sigma;\Gamma \vdash m:M \quad ;B\vdash o:P \quad \Sigma;\Gamma,B\vdash s:S \quad P\Rightarrow S\ll M}{\Sigma;\Gamma \vdash [|B|]\,o\to s \mid m:P\Rightarrow S\,\&\,M}$$

Fig. 12.6 Subtyped extension calculus

Note that the two previous rules for typing extensions have been replaced by a single rule, in which the constraint $P<Q$ has been added to the context. This is possible because the new rule is stable under type substitution; if it should happen that the constraints are no longer solvable then this does not invalidate the rule. Thus, to a function $r:$ `Float` $\to$ `Float` one can still add a case of type `Int` $\to$ `Int`. However, no longer may one add to r a case of type `Int` $\to$ `Bool` since `Int` $<$ `Float` does not imply `Bool` $<$ `Float`. This is probably a good thing. Looking back, it is possible to rework the typed extension calculus to replace the unifiers in its type derivation rules by equational constraints. Further, note that the inequality $Q<P$ is not considered since the nature of linear typing will will imply that Q is P.

The new rules are for subsumption, invocation and *method extensions*. Then an application can be typed by a type invocation, in which case the term may be called an *invocation*. Also, an extension can be typed using type specialisation, in which case it is called a *method extension*, but now the pattern o must restricted, as the following example illustrates.

Suppose that $s:S$ and $t:T$ and $S<T$ and consider the extension

$$\begin{array}{l} \ \ \mathtt{True}\to s\\ \mid \mathtt{False}\to t\\ \mid \mathtt{Nomatch}. \end{array}$$

If the rule for method extensions is unconstrained then this can be given type `Bool` $\to S$ & `Bool` $\to T$. When applied to `False` then the derived type would be S but the result would have type T. To avoid such errors it is necessary that for methods, type matching implies term matching as well as the converse.

Such difficulties will be avoided by requiring that the pattern in a method extension be an *object pattern*. These will have the property that type matching implies term matching.

A constructor is an *object constructor* for a type constant C if it is the unique constructor whose given type is of the form

$$\forall\Delta.T_1 \rightarrow T_2 \rightarrow \ldots \rightarrow T_n \rightarrow C\ S_1\ S_2\ \ldots\ S_k$$

and its actual type is of the form

$$\forall X_1.\ldots.\forall X_n.D * X_n \rightarrow C\ X_1\ \ldots\ X_n$$

for some type D in which X_n is not free. A typical example is

$$\texttt{Point} : \forall X.(\texttt{Float} * \texttt{Float}) * X \rightarrow \texttt{Point}\ X\ .$$

An *object pattern* (meta-variable o) is given by the grammar

$$o ::= x \mid \texttt{Un} \mid \texttt{Pair}\ o\ o \mid c\ o \quad c \text{ is an object constructor}$$

where $\texttt{Un} : \texttt{Unit}$ is the unit constructor of unit type, and $\texttt{Pair} : \forall X.\forall Y.X \rightarrow Y \rightarrow X * Y$ is for pairing.

Lemma 12.7. *Let* $;B \vdash o : P$ *where* o *is an object pattern and let* $\vdash v : V$ *be a closed value. If the type substitution* $\{V \lhd P\}$ *exists then* $\{v/o\}$ *is some term substitution.*

Proof. The proof is by straightforward induction on the structure of o. Let o be of the form $c\ o_1$ where c is an object constructor for some type constant C. Since $\{V \lhd P\}$ exists, the type of v is a data type $C\ V_1\ \ldots\ V_n$ and so the value v must be a data structure. Further, since c is an object constructor, v must be of the form $c\ v_1$. Now apply induction to o_1 and v_1. The other possibilities for o are similar. □

Lemma 12.8. *If there is a derivation of* $\Sigma;\Gamma \vdash t : T$ *then there is a derivation of* $\rho\Sigma;\rho\Gamma \vdash t : \rho T$ *for any type substitution* ρ.

Proof. The proof is by routine induction on the structure of the derivation, given the various lemmas ensuring stability under substitution.

Lemma 12.9. *Suppose that there are derivations* $;B \vdash v_0 : P$ *and* $\Gamma \vdash v : Q$ *of values, where* Q *is not a quantified type, and that these derivations do not share any type symbols. If* $\{v/v_0\}$ *is a substitution then there is a type substitution* ρ *that avoids* $\Gamma \vdash v : Q$ *such that* ρP *is a subtype of* Q *and* $\{v/v_0\}x : \rho V$ *for each* $x : V \in B$.

Proof. The proof is by induction on the structure of v_0. If it is a variable then the result is immediate. If it is a constructor c then so is v and ρ is given by the type derivation of $v : Q$. If v_0 is a compound then so is v. Now apply induction twice to obtain type substitutions ρ_1 and ρ_2. Now $\rho_1 \cup \rho_2$ factors through the unifier used in typing v_0. □

Theorem 12.10 (Type Preservation). *If there is a derivation of* $; \vdash t : T$ *and there is a value* v *such that* $t \Rightarrow v$ *then there is a derivation of* $; \vdash v : T$.

Proof. The proof is by induction on the derivation of $t \Rightarrow v$. Without loss of generality the reduction is by successful matching, as in Fig. 12.2. Suppose that the type derivation takes the form

$$\frac{;\vdash v_2 : Q \to T \quad ;B \vdash v_1 : P \quad P < Q;B \vdash s : T}{\vdash [|B|]\ v_1 \to s \mid v_2 : Q \to T} \quad \begin{array}{l}\mathsf{FV}(\ ;B \vdash p : P) \cap \\ \mathsf{FV}(Q \to T) = \{\}\end{array}$$

with $;\vdash v_3 : Q$. Now Lemma 12.9 implies that there is a type substitution ρ whose domain is within $\mathsf{FV}(\ ;B \vdash p : P)$ such that $\rho P < Q$ and $\{v_3/v_1\}x : \rho V$ for each $x : V \in B$. Hence there is a derivation of $\rho(P < Q;B) \vdash s : T$. Further, since ρ solves $P < Q$ there is a derivation of $;\rho B \vdash s : T$. Now apply the Substitution Lemma to get $;\vdash \{v_3/v_1\}s : T$ as required.

Alternatively, suppose that the extension is a method extension. Then the argument is typed by a type application and so must be a data value. Hence, Lemma 12.7 implies that the method invocation is typed using the special case if and only if matching succeeds. Now proceed as above. □

12.8 Notes

The *constructor calculus* [55] appears to be the first attempt to combine cases having different types in an implicitly-typed calculus. This evolved via a static pattern calculus [58] to the *higher-order typed pattern calculus* [56] in which dynamic patterns were implicitly typed. In turn, this was overtaken by the development of the pure pattern calculus.

It is tempting to include here a formal account of type inference for the extension calculus, in the style of Algorithm W for ML [76, 26]. However, terms of extension calculus do not always have principal types, so there is some choice in the details of the algorithm, and no particular reason to favour the choices developed for **bondi**. The lack of principality has several causes. First, quantified argument types are allowed, and System **F** does not support type inference or indeed type checking [105]. Support for polymorphic recursion arises in various systems (see, e.g. [41]). Further, type inference must here handle general inequalities just to type the application of a function of type $P \to S$ to an argument of type U. Yet, as seen earlier, these do not have most general solutions. The solution adopted in **bondi** is to simplify inequalities as much as possible, making aggressive assumptions when it is safe to do so, e.g. by rejecting some occurrence errors.

In Chap. 11, function types were made invariant in their result types to avoid having to reduce abstractions. Here, however, all reduction is driven by the terms, so that this difficulty does not arise. Hence, one may allow that $S < T$ implies both $U \to S < U \to T$ and $\forall X.S < \forall X.T$ without introducing new difficulties. This proves convenient when typing methods. In the style above, a method taking parameters of type D must be given a type of the form $D * P \Rightarrow S$ but in **bondi** this will have the more convenient type $P \Rightarrow D \rightarrow S$. In particular, the body of the method, of type $D \rightarrow S$, can be given by an extension.

Part III
Programming in bondi

Chapter 13
Higher-Order Functions

Abstract This chapter introduces Part III and **bondi**, focusing on its approach to higher-order functions. It is short because functions alone can't express much.

13.1 From Calculus to Programming Language

Having developed the pattern calculus as a theory, it is time to consider how it can be exploited in programming, using the **bondi** programming language as the medium. **bondi** implements the extension calculus of Chap. 12 with its type-free evaluation rules. To this core is added algebraic data types in the style of functional programming, queries in the style of relational databases, dynamic patterns, imperative features such as assignment and loops, and object-oriented classes. It may well prove that some, or all of the new sorts of polymorphism can be supported by the evolution of an existing language, but the desire to combine a variety of programming styles without biasing towards one or the other is best achieved by making a fresh start. The presentation is driven by examples, since theoretical issues were addressed in Parts I and II.

This chapter introduces the language itself, and its use in the functional style, including let-declarations. The chapter is short, primarily because one cannot do very much with functions alone. Chapter 14 introduces algebraic data types, and the corresponding pattern-matching style, in which each pattern is headed by a constructor. Its novelty arises from the ability to combine cases having different types, as illustrated by functor polymorphic programs. Chapter 15 introduces path polymorphic queries, in which patterns may be headed by a binding symbol. Chapter 16 illustrate the use of dynamic patterns. Chapter 17 introduces imperative features, supporting state through assignment to references. Now path polymorphism can be used to define iterators, though some care is required to avoid infinite loops generated by cycles. Chapter 18 combines subtyping and state to support object-oriented programming. It concludes with the motivating example of Chap. 1.

B. Jay, *Pattern Calculus*,
DOI 10.1007/978-3-540-89185-7_13,

13.2 Let-Terms

bondi provides an interactive environment. When started, some preliminary output is followed by the message

```
Welcome to bondi version 2.0
No warranty expressed or implied
See README for details
type '%quit;;' to exit
~~
```

The ~~ is the prompt, representing the waves at Bondi Beach in Sydney, Australia. All inputs are terminated with a double semicolon. For example, typing `1+2;;` after the prompt displays

```
~~ 1+2;;
it: Int
it = 3
~~
```

The system inputs the term (or program) `1+2` which is inferred to be an integer of type `Int` and have value `3`. The identifier `it` is used here to refer to a nameless value. The infix function `+` is not actually a primitive operation, but rather a generic operation, as will be described in Chap. 15. The trailing prompt is omitted from now on.

bondi supports function definitions as follows

```
~~ fun x -> x+1;;
it: Int -> Int
~~ let plusOne x = x+1;;
plusOne: Int -> Int
~~ plusOne 2;;
it: Int
it = 3
```

The first term `fun x -> x+1` corresponds to the abstraction $\lambda x.x+1$. Its type is `Int -> Int`. Since it is an abstraction its value is not printed. The `let` binding binds `plusOne` to the same λ-abstraction, with the bound variable x now appearing on the left.

Higher-order functions are defined in exactly the same way. For example,

```
~~ let twice f x = f (f x);;
twice: (a -> a) -> a -> a
~~ twice plusOne 3;;
it: Int
it = 5
```

The function `twice` applies its first argument twice to its second argument. It has a polymorphic type, as indicated by the type variable `a`. Recursion is supported by the syntax `let rec`. For example

```
~~ let rec (factorial: Int -> Int) n =
  if n <= 1
  then 1
  else n*(factorial (n-1));;
factorial: Int -> Int
~~ factorial 5;;
it: Int
it = 120
```

Generally speaking, it is necessary to provide explicit types for recursive functions since the possibility of polymorphic recursion makes it harder to infer types, as will be demonstrated in Sect. 15.2.

The function `twice` above is parametrically polymorphic in that the type variable a can be instantiated to any type. A more subtle example is given by the polymorphic identity

```
let identity x = x in identity identity 3;;
```

The second occurrence of `identity` takes the type `Int -> Int` while the first occurrence takes the type `(Int -> Int) -> Int -> Int` so that it can act on the function `identity`. Thus, unlike the parameter `f` of `twice`, the two occurrences of `identity` have different instantiations of their type parameter.

13.3 Notes

bondi is not very well documented, but the source code and some examples are available [10]. The current interpreter is written in Ocaml [72], a member of the ML family of languages, and reuses many of its syntactic conventions.

Chapter 14
Algebraic Data Types

Abstract Algebraic data types are the natural target of pattern-matching functions. When the type is parametric then the pattern-matching functions typically support parametric polymorphism. In addition, **bondi** supports generic functional programming by introducing a small family of primitive, or representing data types, which can be used to define generic functions such as `map`, with one case for each primitive constructor. Each resulting case has a different type, so type specialisation is involved, too. During a type declaration, additional cases can be added to existing functions.

14.1 Type Declarations

A type declaration either declares a type synonym or an algebraic data type. An example of algebraic data types are binary product types. The product type of pairs is declared as part of the standard prelude using the declaration

```
~~ datatype Binprod a b = Pair of a and b;;
Pair: a -> b -> a * b
```

It introduces the type constant `Binprod` and term constructor `Pair` whose type is as displayed. Since pairs play such an important role, they have their own syntax. For example,

```
~~ Pair 2 3;;
it: Int * Int
it = (2,3)
~~ (3,4);;
it: Int * Int
it = (3,4)
```

Here the infix `*` is used to represent `Binprod` and the infix comma is used to represent `Pair`. The output `(2,3)` for `Pair 2 3` is obtained by modifying the function

B. Jay, *Pattern Calculus*,
DOI 10.1007/978-3-540-89185-7_14,

toString as explained in Sect. 14.5. The input (3,4) for a pair is hardwired into the parser. Future work may well see the parser written in **bondi** too.

An example of a type synonym is

```
~~ type Cmplex = Float * Float ;;
type Cmplex = Float * Float
```

in which complex numbers are exactly pairs of floats. Here is how it can be used

```
~~ let (z: Cmplex) = (3.3,4.4);;
z: Float * Float
z = (3.3,4.4)
```

Type inference checks that (3.3,4.4) is indeed of type Cmplex but reports the type Float * Float, which is not especially helpful. Another difficulty is that operations cannot be made to treat complex numbers differently from any other pairs of floating point numbers, as used to define, say an interval on the number line.

By contrast, an algebraic data type of complex numbers is given by the declaration

```
~~ datatype Complex = Cartesian of Float and Float;;
Cartesian: Float -> Float -> Complex
```

Here is an example:

```
~~ let z = Cartesian 1.1 2.2;;
z: Complex
z = Cartesian 1.1 2.2
```

Now the complex values cannot be confused with other pairs of floats.

Algebraic data types may employ type parameters, as in

```
~~ datatype List a = Nil  | Cons of a and List a ;;
Nil: List a
Cons: a -> List a -> List a
~~ [1,2,3];;
it: List Int
it = [1,2,3]
```

The parser supports syntax in which lists are represented by comma-separated sequences of entries, enclosed in square brackets. This syntax is also incorporated into the printing of lists, as defined in the standard prelude.

Here is a data type that is not already known to the system

```
~~ datatype Tree a = Leaf of a | Node of Tree a and Tree a ;;
Leaf: a -> Tree a
Node: Tree a -> Tree a -> Tree a
~~ let tr1 = Node (Leaf 3) (Leaf 4);;
tr1: Tree Int
tr1 = Node (Leaf 3) (Leaf 4)
```

Here is an example with two type parameters, of *coproduct* (or sum) types, declared by

```
~~ datatype Coproduct a b = Inl of a | Inr of b ;;
Inl: a -> Coproduct a b
Inr: b -> Coproduct a b
~~ Inl 3;;
it: Coproduct Int a
it = Inl 3
```

Now let us define some polymorphic functions on these new types.

14.2 Pattern-Matching Functions

The usual means of accessing data of algebraic type is by pattern matching. For example, the projections of pairs can be written as the cases

```
~~ let fst = | (x,y) -> x;;
fst: a * b -> a
~~ let snd = | (x,y) -> y;;
snd: a * b -> b
~~ fst (2,3);;
it: Int
it = 2
```

Each case begins with a vertical bar `|`. Sequences of cases can be combined to form pattern-matching functions. For example, to avoid dividing by `0` use `safeDivInt` defined by

```
~~ let safeDivInt n =
| 0 -> Exception "divide by 0"
| m -> n divideint m
;;
safeDivInt: Int -> Int -> Int
~~ safeDivInt 4 2 ;;
it: Int
it = 2
~~ safeDivInt 4 0 ;;
it: Int
it = Exception "divide by 0"
```

The exception `Exception "divide by 0"` is given by applying the constructor

```
~~Exception;;
it: a
it = Exception
```

to the string "divide by 0". Exceptions can be handled by pattern matching against the constructor Exception.

In the examples so far, all cases have had the same type. In general, **bondi** takes a more liberal view, allowing cases to have different types provided that no ambiguity can arise concerning the type of the result.

Here is a simple example. The booleans True,False : Bool are given as constructors.

```
~~ let isZero =
| 0 -> True
| 0.0 -> True
| _ -> False;;
isZero: a -> Bool
~~ isZero 0;;
it: Bool
it = True
~~ isZero 0.0;;
it: Bool
it = True
~~ isZero Pair;;
it: Bool
it = False
```

isZero tests for being either the integer 0 or the floating point 0.0. Type inference handles the cases in reverse order. The final case discards its argument (represented by the wildcard _) and returns a boolean, and so has type a -> Bool. The second case has type Float -> Bool which is a specialisation of a -> Bool (as defined in Sect. 11.4). The first case is similar. It is interesting to observe what happens if the the last case is deleted, as in

```
~~ | 0 -> True
| 0.0 -> True ;;
Warning: useless pattern detected
it: Float -> Bool
```

Now the overall type is Float -> Bool, being the type of the last case. Note that the first case has type Int -> Bool whose argument type Int cannot be unified with Float. While not strictly illegal, this case cannot ever be evaluated, and so a warning is displayed. Further, reversing these two cases will produce a function of type Int -> Bool. Since the typing is so sensitive to the choice and ordering of cases, it is good style to include an explicit type when cases of different types are involved, as in

```
~~ let (isZero: a -> Bool) =
| 0 -> True
| 0.0 -> True
| _ -> False;;
isZero: a -> Bool
```

Now deleting or permuting cases cannot change the type.

Similar to `isZero` is the test for pairs

```
let isPair =
| Pair _ _   -> True
| _ -> False ;;
isPair: a -> Bool
```

Testing for integers, however, is not so easy, since there is not a single constructor for them all. Various alternatives have been considered, but the preferred option is to create another wildcard `_Int` which matches integers only. For example, consider

```
let isInt =
| _Int -> True
| _ -> False ;;
isInt: a -> Bool
~~ isInt 3;;
it: Bool
it = True
~~ isInt True;;
it: Bool
it = False
```

Similarly, there are wildcards `_Float` and `_Char` and `_String` for floats, characters and strings.

```
 (| _Char -> True) 'a';;
it: Bool
it = True
~~ (| _String -> True) "abc";;
it: Bool
it = True
```

In general, one would like to use the integer, not just detect its presence, as in

```
fun x -> (| _Int -> x +1) x
```

This function first tests its argument to see if it is an integer, then uses it again in the body of the case. A convenient syntax for this is given by patterns of the form `p as q` such as

```
| _Int as x -> x +1
```

in which matching succeeds if the argument matches both `_Int` and `x`. Yet more syntactic sugar is exploited by the example

```
let incrInt =
| (x :Int) -> x+1
| x -> x
```

Its first case is syntactic sugar for the one already given above. Note that the type `Int` does *not* appear during execution, so that this use of types in patterns is strictly limited to those where the type has a characteristic pattern, such as `_Int`. This concept will reappear when considering object-oriented classes.

14.3 Polymorphism in Data

The main use of parametric polymorphism in functional programming has been to define functions that are tailored to some given structure, independent of the type of data that is stored within them. For example, the projections `fst` and `snd` act on arbitrary pairs. Similarly, data of coproduct type is accessed by case analysis, given by the higher-order function

```
 let (alt: (a -> c) -> (b -> c) -> Coproduct a b -> c) f g =
| Inl x -> f x
| Inr y -> g y
;;
alt: (a -> b) -> (c -> b) -> Coproduct a c -> b
~~  alt (fun x -> x+1) (fun y -> 0) (Inl 3);;
it: Int
it = 4
~~  alt (fun x -> x+1) (fun y -> 0) (Inr True);;
it: Int
it = 0
```

Similarly, a typical list program is that for appending lists.

```
~~ let rec (append: List a -> List a -> List a) =
| Nil -> fun y -> y
| Cons x xs -> fun y -> Cons x (append xs y)
;;
append: List a -> List a -> List a
~~ append [1,2,3] [4,5];;
it: List Int
it = [1,2,3,4,5]
```

It uses recursion as well as pattern matching. Mapping over lists is given by

```
~~ let rec (mapList : (a -> b) -> List a -> List b) f =
| Nil -> Nil
| Cons x xs -> Cons (f x) (mapList f xs)
;;
mapList: (a -> b) -> List a -> List b
~~ mapList plusOne [1,2,3];;
it: List Int
it = [2,3,4]
```

Similarly, mapping over binary trees is given by

```
~~ let rec (mapTree: (a -> b) -> Tree a -> Tree b) f =
| Leaf x -> Leaf (f x)
| Node x y -> Node (mapTree f x) (mapTree f y)
;;
```

```
mapTree: (a -> b) -> Tree a -> Tree b
~~ mapTree plusOne tr1;;
it: Tree Int
it = Node (Leaf 4) (Leaf 5)
```

14.4 Generic Functional Programming

The mapping functions above for List and Tree can be generalised to a single function map by representing data types in terms of a small family of primitive constructors. For most purposes, it is enough to employ the following primitives:

```
datatype Konstant a b = Evr of a ;;
datatype Identity a = Ths of a ;;
datatype ParamProduct f g a = ParamPair of f a and g a ;;
datatype Okay f a = Ok of f a ;;
datatype Nested g f a = Nest of g (f a);;
datatype Represent a b c = Tag of a -> b and a c ;;
```

Evr is used to represent structures without any data. Ths represents a single piece of data. ParamPair combines data structures. Ok recognises a data structure. Nested handles nested structures. Tag is used to add labels to structures. The functions deconstruct and reconstruct are used to convert data structures into their primitive representations and back again. For example,

```
deconstruct [] print;;
it: Unit
Tag Nil_name (Evr Un)
```

shows that the empty list is given by the structure Evr Un (having no data) tagged by the name Nil_name associated to Nil. Deconstruction produces something whose exact type is not known in advance, and so has an existential type as described in Chap. 7. That is, deconstruct [] is a function that takes as argument a polymorphic function, such as print that is able to handle whatever type turns up in the existential.

Converse to deconstruct is reconstruct, as in

```
~~ reconstruct(Tag Nil_name (Evr Un));;
it: List a
it = []
```

which rebuilds the original structure. Similarly,

```
~~ deconstruct [2] print;;
it: Unit
Tag Cons_name (ParamPair (Ths 2) (Ok []))
~~ reconstruct (Tag Cons_name (ParamPair (Ths 2) (Ok [])));;
it: List Int
it = [2]
```

```
~~ let rec (map : (a -> b) -> c a -> c b) =
let rec (map0: (a -> b) -> c a -> c b) f =
| Evr x -> Evr x
| Ths x -> Ths (f x)
| Ok x -> Ok (map f x)
| ParamPair x y -> ParamPair (map0 f x) (map0 f y)
| Nest x -> Nest (map (map f) x)
| Tag n x -> Tag n (map0 f x)
in
fun f x -> reconstruct (deconstruct x (map0 f))
;;
map: (a -> b) -> c a -> c b
```

Fig. 14.1 Generic mapping

Note that deconstruction only proceeds to one level, so that `Ok` is applied to the empty list, not its representation.

```
~~ deconstruct (Leaf 3) print;;
it: Unit
Tag Leaf_name (Ths 3)
~~ deconstruct tr1 print;;
it: Unit
Tag Node_name (ParamPair (Ok (Leaf 3)) (Ok (Leaf 4)))
```

These representations can now be used to define generic functions that act on any structures upon which `deconstruct` can be applied. For example, the mapping functions above for `List` and `Tree` can be generalised to a single function `map` defined in Fig. 14.1. Although the presence of the existential type is unusual, it has little material effect: where one might expect to write `map0 f (deconstruct x)` the actual program uses `deconstruct x (map0 f)` in which `map0 f` is the argument instead of the function.

However it is achieved, the use of `map` is quite straightforward. For example,

```
~~ map plusOne [1,2,3];;
it: List Int
it = [2,3,4]
~~ map plusOne tr1;;
it: Tree Int
it = Node (Leaf 4) (Leaf 5)
```

In the same style, one can define generic versions of left and right folds and zipwith as in Fig. 14.2. For example, `foldleft (+) 0 [1,2,3]` evaluates to 6, as does `foldright (+) [1,2,3] 0`. Similarly, `zipwith plus ([1,2,3], [4,5,6])` evaluates to `[5,7,9]`.

```
~~ let rec (foldleft : (a -> b -> a) -> a -> c b -> a) =
let rec (foldleft0: (a -> b -> a) -> a -> c b -> a) f z =
| Evr x -> z
| Ths x -> f z x
| Ok x -> foldleft f z x
| ParamPair x y -> foldleft0 f (foldleft0 f z x) y
| Nest x -> foldleft (foldleft f) z x
| Tag n x -> foldleft0 f z x
in
fun f z x -> deconstruct x (foldleft0 f z)
;;
foldleft: (a -> b -> a) -> a -> c b -> a

~~ let rec (foldright : (a -> b -> b) -> c a -> b -> b) =
let rec (foldright0: (a -> b -> b) -> c a -> b -> b) f =
| Evr x -> fun z -> z
| Ths x -> f x
| Ok x -> foldright f x
| ParamPair x y -> fun z -> foldright0 f x (foldright0 f y z)
| Nest x -> foldright (foldright f) x
| Tag n x -> foldright0 f x
in
fun f x z -> deconstruct x (foldright0 f) z
;;
foldright: (a -> b -> b) -> c a -> b -> b

~~let rec (zipwith: (a * b -> c) -> d a * e b -> d c) =
let rec (zipwith0: (a * b -> c) -> d a * e b -> d c) f =
| (Evr x,_) -> Evr x
| (Ths x,Ths y) -> Ths (f(x,y))
| (Ok x,Ok y) -> Ok(zipwith f (x,y))
| (ParamPair x1 x2, ParamPair y1 y2) ->
        ParamPair (zipwith0 f (x1,y1)) (zipwith0 f (x2,y2))
| (Nest x,Nest y) -> Nest (zipwith (zipwith f) (x,y))
| (Tag m x, Tag n y) -> Tag m (zipwith0 f (x,y))
in
fun f -> | (x,y) ->
     reconstruct (deconstruct x (fun x1 ->
                  deconstruct y (fun y1 -> zipwith0 f (x1,y1))))
;;
zipwith: (a * b -> c) -> d a * e b -> d c
```

Fig. 14.2 Some generic functional programs

14.5 Adding Cases to Existing Functions

Using algebraic data types, it is easy to write new functions for existing types, but it often happens that one would like to add a new case to an existing function, e.g. to modify `isZero` so that it is true of the complex number `Complex 0.0 0.0`. The direct solution is to redeclare `isZero` by

```
let isZero =
| Complex 0.0 0.0 -> True
| 0 -> True
| 0.0 -> True
| _ -> False;;
```

but this creates a *new* term which is systemically distinct from the old one. In particular, any functions that have already been defined using `isZero` will continue to refer to the old program, not the new one. Better would be to modify the existing function by adding a case using the syntax

```
isZero += Complex 0.0 0.0 -> True .
```

This would be equivalent to overwriting the old program with the pattern-matching function displayed above.

Of course, changing the meaning of `isZero` in this way violates *referential transparency*, the principle that the meaning of a term is determined at its point of declaration, not its point of use. Referential transparency of `isZero` is protected, however, since the additional case above produces an error message, namely

```
term error: isZero is not extensible
```

Rather, such additions are only allowed if the original declaration is marked as being extensible, as in

```
let ext isZero =...
```

using the keyword `ext`. Then we have:

```
~~ isZero += | Complex 0.0 0.0 -> True;;
it: Unit
it = Un
```

In general, such extensions may change the behaviour of existing programs, so it is good style to limit them to the declarations of the type whose values are being affected. The program syntax is thus

```
~~  datatype Complex = Cartesian of Float and Float
with
isZero +- | Cartesian 0.0 0.0 -> True
;;
Cartesian: Float -> Float -> Complex
isZero: Complex -> Bool
```

A more interesting example of adding a case concerns the function

```
~~toString;;
it: a -> String
```

which converts an arbitrary term into a string. Then the print function is defined by

```
let (print: a -> Unit) x = printstring (toString x);;
print: a -> Unit
~~ print (Cartesian 1.1 2.2);;
it: Unit
Cartesian 1.1 2.2
```

A more familiar syntax for complex numbers represents the number above by `1.1 + 2.2i` where `i` is the square root of `-1`. This can be introduced by adding a case to `toString` in the type declaration, in

```
~~ datatype Complex = Cartesian of Float and Float
with
isZero += | Cartesian 0.0 0.0 -> True
and toString += | Cartesian x y ->
    (toString x) ^ "+" ^ (toString y) ^ "i"
;;
Cartesian: Float -> Float -> Complex
isZero: Complex -> Bool
toString: Complex -> String
~~Cartesian 1.1 2.2;;
it: Complex
it = 1.1+2.2i
```

In this example, note how the new case introduces new recursive calls to `toString`. In turn, these will call the new version of `toString` not the old one.

To repeat, the newly added cases must exploit the new constructors of the declared type. For example, the following code produces an error

```
~~ datatype Gotcha a = Gotcha of a
with
toString += | (x,y) -> "Gotcha!"
;;
Gotcha: a -> Gotcha a
error: added cases must use a new constructor
```

Hence it is not possible to change the input-output behaviour of existing programs by adding cases to existing functions within data type declarations. The only effect may be to increase execution time caused by new match failures. This property is called *behavioural continuity*. New behaviours can be added, but old ones cannot be changed. Although intuitively clear, it has not been fully formalised.

14.6 The Expression Problem

The expression problem can be stated as follows. Algebraic data types allow new functions to be defined on existing types. Object-oriented classes allow new types to be supported by existing functions. How can both sorts of generalisation be supported simultaneously? The solution developed here is to use additional cases and method specialisation: new cases can be added to existing functions or methods provided that the new types specialise the old types, and the new pattern involves one of the new constructors. The former restriction ensures type safety: the latter restriction ensures a variant of referential transparency. Informally, it follows that

New data type or class declarations cannot affect the results of old programs.

To be precise, the referents of identifiers do change when cases are added, but this only adds new behaviours without changing any existing ones. In this sense, referential transparency is replaced by *behavioural continuity*.

To formalise this as a theorem would require that the notions of type and class declaration be formalised within the calculi, along with the process of adding cases.

14.7 Notes

Algebraic data types have played a central role in functional programming since the 1970s, possibly beginning with [37]. They play a core part of the ML programming language [77, 94] and Haskell [40] whose implementation was elucidated in [83]. Pattern matching has been central to their exploitation. Various papers have formalised patterns headed by constructors. For example, the *pattern-matching calculus* [65] characterises different approaches to match failure. Connections to logic were explored in [17, 66]. Efficient implementation of pattern matching was developed by Simon Peyton Jones [85].

There is a substantial literature on *generic functional programming* [4, 33, 44, 63]. The earliest accounts are probably PolyP [50, 62] and **P2** [54, 61]. The former led to Generic Haskell [45] based on Ralf Hinze's work [43]. The latter developed into Functorial ML [60] (joint work with Bellè and Moggi) and then the constructor calculus [55] and the first pattern calculus [58]. Generic Haskell uses a preprocessor to produce specialised terms for a generic function on each type where it is used. **P2** and its successors employ representations to reduce all mapping to a finite collection of cases, so that `map` can be compiled once and for all. In 2000–1, the author developed an account [55] of functor polymorphism (see also Chap. 8) using pattern matching with patterns headed by constructors. This developed into a typed pattern calculus [58] which incidentally supported the static patterns employed here.

Chapter 15
Queries

Abstract This chapter introduces generic numerical operations, for addition, negation, etc. and also generic queries such as `select` and `apply2all`, that generalise the standard queries of relational database programming.

15.1 Numerical Functions

Various arithmetic operations can be generalised to act on arbitrary data structures by placing them within path polymorphic functions. Perhaps the simplest example is negation, given by

```
~~ let rec (negate : a -> a) =
     | (x:Int) -> negateint x
     | (x:Float) -> negatefloat x
     | x y -> (negate x) (negate y)
     | x -> x
;;
negate: a -> a
~~ negate 3;;
it: Int
it = -3
~~ negate [1.1,2.2,3.3];;
it: List Float
it =  [-1.1,-2.2,-3.3]
```

Integers and floats are negated using their primitive operations. Compounds are negated component-wise: atoms are unchanged. For example, to negate `Cartesian 1.1 2.2` (as introduced in Sect. 14.1) is to negate both `Cartesian 1.1` and `2.2` which is to negate all three of `Cartesian` and `1.1` and `2.2`.

Some detail of the type inference for `negate` can be exposed by switching to the mode `specialise` by

B. Jay, *Pattern Calculus*,
DOI 10.1007/978-3-540-89185-7_15,

```
%show specialise;;
```

Now declaring negate displays the types of each case, in reverse order.

```
~~ let rec (negate : a -> a) =
     | (x:Int) -> negateint x
     | (x:Float) -> negatefloat x
     | x y -> (negate x) (negate y)
     | x -> x
;;
specialising at a ...
specialising at b ...
specialising at Float ...
specialising at Int ...
negate: d -> d
```

Here is an example in which specialisation fails

```
~~ let (either0 :  Coproduct a b -> b) =
| Inl x -> x
| Inr y -> y
;;
specialising at Coproduct a b ...
type error: ty_7251 and ty_7250 don't unify
```

The second case has the correct typing, but the first case does not, since the result type is (the internal representation of) a when it should be b. The error message may appear strange, since it is usual to be able to unify type variables. However, the type of the pattern is fixed when inferring a type for the body (as described in Chap. 12) and so a and b are both fixed. The solution in defining either is to give it a more precise type, as in

```
~~ let (either :  Coproduct a a -> a) =
| Inl x -> x
| Inr y -> y
;;
specialising at Coproduct a a ...
specialising at Coproduct b c ...
either: Coproduct d d -> d
```

Then the additional type information can be hidden by

```
~~ %hide specialise;;
~~ let (either :  Coproduct a a -> a) =
| Inl x -> x
| Inr y -> y
;;
either: Coproduct a a -> a
```

```
~~ let rec (equal : a * b -> Bool) =
| (x1 x2,y1 y2) -> equal (x1,y1) && equal(x2,y2)
| (x,y) -> x eqcons y
;;
equal: a * b -> Bool
~~ let ((==) : a -> a -> Bool) x y = equal (x,y);;
==: a -> a -> Bool
~~ let (!=) x y =  not (x == y);;
!=: a -> a -> Bool
```

Fig. 15.1 Generic equality

Even more general than negation is equality. At the level of constructors this is given by the infix operation `eqcons` which is `True` when both its arguments are the same constructor.

```
~~ Leaf eqcons Leaf;;
it: Bool
it = True
~~ Leaf eqcons Nil;;
it: Bool
it = False
```

Note that there is no need for the arguments to have the same type. `eqcons` underpins the generic equality given in Fig. 15.1. In words, two data structures are equal if either they are both compounds and have equal components, or they are the same constructor. For example,

```
~~ [1,2,3] == [1,2,3];;
it: Bool
it = True
~~ 3 == 4;;
it: Bool
it = False
~~ tr1 == tr1;;
it: Bool
it = True
~~ Inl 3 == Inr 4.4;;
it: Bool
it = False
```

As with `eqcons` the arguments need not have the same type. Indeed, this cannot be enforced anyway, as the final example above shows: both `Inl 3` and `Inr 4.4` have the same type `Coproduct Int Float` but their corresponding components `3` and `4.4` do not. There are occasions when such generality is welcome, but for common purposes, it is safer to require that both arguments have the same type, as when defining `(==)` above. Note the use of the brackets when defining `(==)`. They indicate that `==` is to be written infix.

```
~~ let rec (plus : a * b -> a) =
| ((x:Int),(y:Int)) -> x plusint y
| ((x:Float),(y:Float)) -> x plusfloat y
| (x1 x2,y1 y2) -> plus (x1,y1) (plus(x2,y2))
| (x,y) -> if x eqcons y then x else Exception "plus"
;;
plus: a * b -> a
~~ let ((+): a -> a -> a) x y = plus(x,y);;
+: a -> a -> a
```

Fig. 15.2 Generic addition

Following this approach, the generic addition is defined in Fig. 15.2. For example,

```
~~ [1,2,3] + [4,5,6];;
it: List Int
it = [5,7,9]
~~ z + z;;
it: Complex
it = Cartesian 2.2 4.4
```

where `z` is `Cartesian 1.1 2.2` as before.

15.2 Polymorphic Recursion

The simplicity of the program for `negate` disguises an important point, namely that the recursive calls to `negate` are polymorphic. Consider `negate (u v)` for some compound `u v`. In general, the types of `u`, `v` and `u v` are all different, so each call to `negate` requires a different type. That is, the typing `negate: a -> a)` actually asserts that `negate` has quantified type `all a. (a -> a)`.

When the quantifiers are required for a function argument then they must be given explicitly. For example, in Chap. 13 the self-application of the identity function was given by the let-term

```
let identity x = x in identity identity 3
```

This functionality can also be given by the term

```
let (self_apply: (all a. (a -> a)) -> b -> b) f x = f f x;;
self_apply: (all a.a -> a) -> b -> b
~~ self_apply (fun x -> x) 3;;
it: Int
it = 3
```

The explicit type for `self_apply` is necessary since it is typed before considering its argument function. A slightly more interesting example is given by

```
~~ let rec (select: (all a . (a -> List b)) -> (c -> List b)) f =
    | z y -> append (f (z y)) (append (select f z) (select f y))
    | y -> f y
;;
select: all a.(a -> List b) -> c -> List b
```

Fig. 15.3 Generic search

```
~~ let (apply2both: (all a. (a -> Bool)) -> b -> Bool) test =
| (x,y) -> test x && test y
| x -> test x
;;
apply2both: all a.(a -> Bool) -> b -> Bool
~~
apply2both isZero (0,0.0);;
it: Bool
it = True
~~ apply2both isZero 3;;
it: Bool
it = False
```

In the case for a pair, the test is applied to both components of the pair, whatever their types might be. This is possible because the argument `test` has quantified type `all a.(a -> Bool)`. Note how the type information need only be given once: instantiation of the type of `test` at each application is handled by type inference. This style of polymorphism is central to the generic queries that follow.

15.3 Searching and Modifying

The program for selecting is defined in Fig. 15.3. For example,

```
~~ let (isInt: a -> List Int) =
| (x:Int) -> [x]
| _ -> []
;;
isInt: a -> List Int
~~ select isInt;;
it: a -> List Int
~~ select isInt tr1;;
it: List Int
it = [3,4]
~~ select isInt [(1,2.2),(3,4.4)];;
it: List Int
it = [1,3]
```

There are subtle restrictions on the interaction between selecting and type variables. For example, to select all of the leaves from within a structure containing trees, requires a function `isLeaf` but its return type is not clear. Each tree may have leaves of a different type, so that the resulting list has entries of different types. Since **bondi** supports subtyping, this can be given by

```
~~ let (isLeaf : a -> List Top) =
| Leaf x -> [x]
| _ -> [];;
isLeaf: a -> List Top
~~ isLeaf (Leaf 3);;
it: List Top
it = [3]
~~ isLeaf (Leaf 4.4);;
it: List Top
it = [4.4]
```

in which the result type is a list of arbitrary things. Now

```
~~ select isLeaf (Leaf 3,Leaf 4.4);;
it: List Top
it = [3,4.4]
```

produces a mixed list, as expected. Note that this result is not acceptable as a program, however, since **bondi** assumes that this input contains a type error:

```
~~ [3,4.4];;
type error: Float and Int don't unify
```

If this term is required then more type information must be given, as in

```
~~ [(3:Top),(4.4:Top)];;
it: List Top
it = [3,4.4]
```

By quantifying the type variable `c` in the type of `select` and renaming it to be the type symbol a one can also express this type as

```
(all a . (a -> List b)) -> (all a . (a -> List b))
```

so that the type of the argument and the result are the same. This reflexivity makes it easy to combine `select` terms into ever more complex forms. For example, they can be nested, as in

```
~~ select isInt (select isLeaf (1, Leaf (2,3.3), Leaf 4));;
it: List Int
it = [2,4]
```

picks out the integers that are within leaves. That is, the inner `select` creates a mixed list with entries `(2,3.3)` and `4` whose integers form the list `[2,4]`. Of course, one can combine these selects into a single function

```
~~ let selectIsIntInLeaf x = select isInt (select isLeaf x);;
selectIsIntInLeaf: a -> List Int
```

so that the use of the top type disappears from the overall type.

There are various ways to iterate selections. For example,

```
~~ let rec (select_high:
                (all a.(a -> List b)) -> (c -> List b))
      f =
        | z y ->
              let xs = f (z y) in
              if xs == []
              then append (select_high f z) (select_high f y)
              else xs
        | y -> f y
;;
select_high: all a.(a -> List b) -> c -> List b
~~ select isLeaf (Leaf (Leaf 3), Leaf 4.4);;
it: List Top
it = [Leaf 3,3,4.4]
~~ select_high isLeaf (Leaf (Leaf 3), Leaf 4.4);;
it: List Top
it = [Leaf 3,4.4]
```

`select_high` stops searching as soon as it finds something, compared to `select` which is exhaustive. Again,

```
~~ let rec (select_low:
                (all a.(a -> List b)) -> (c -> List b))
      f =
        | z y ->
              let xs = append (selects f z) (selects f y) in
              if xs == []
              then f (z y)
              else xs
        | y -> f y
;;
select_low: all a.(a -> List b) -> c -> List b
~~ selects_low isLeaf (Leaf (Leaf 3), Leaf 4.4);;
it: List Top
it = [3,4.4]
```

`select_low` only keeps results from the deepest level. Various other combinations are possible. If desired, one can build algebraic types to represent various combinations of search criteria.

Closely related to searching is modifying. In a functional setting this is not in-place updating, but rather creates a new data structure alongside the old one. In-place update requires the imperative features of Chap. 17. The basic function is

```
~~ let rec (apply2all : (all a. (a -> a)) -> b -> b) f =
| x y -> f (apply2all f x (apply2all f y))
| x -> f x;;
apply2all: all a.(a -> a) -> b -> b
```

Fig. 15.4 Applying to all

apply2all as described in Fig. 15.4. Here is an example that adds one to integers within a structure

```
~~ let (anyPlusOne : a -> a) =
| (x:Int) -> x + 1
| x -> x
;;
anyPlusOne: a -> a
~~ apply2all anyPlusOne [(1,2.2),(3,4.4),(5,6.6)];;
it: List (Int * Float)
it = [(2,2.2),(4,4.4),(6,6.6)]
```

Just like `select`, the result type of `apply2all` can be quantified so that it is the same as the argument type, and so more complex, and iterated versions of update can be applied.

15.4 Notes

Most programming languages have tried to simplify the use of arithmetic functions across a variety of types of integers and floats, be they short, long, exact, etc. One option is to use type inference to disambiguate. SML [94] does this for addition of integers from that of floats, but cannot add lists of integers. Haskell [84] has a type class `Num` of types that support arithmetic. Once `Int` and `Float` are in the class then so are `List Int` and `Int * Float`, etc. by careful handling within the compiler. Object-oriented languages commonly have classes for such operations but they do not lift to `List Int`, etc. There does not appear to be an existing language that captures all of these possibilities in a uniform manner.

The generic queries are closest in spirit to those of the SQL language for relational databases, though the latter are restricted to tables rather than arbitrary data types. Similar expressive power is added to Haskell using the "scrap your boilerplate" approach [68, 69, 70]. Also, the explicit use of quantified types in programs is reminiscent of Haskell [84].

Chapter 16
Dynamic Linear Patterns

Abstract This chapter introduces dynamic patterns, and the associated linear types and terms. Basic examples include the linear equality, and the generic eliminator. Further potential is discussed.

16.1 Generic Elimination

Here are some examples that illustrate the potential, and some limitations of dynamic patterns. Further examples are under development elsewhere.

As well as the path-polymorphic equality introduced in Sect. 15.1 one may define equality for linear terms using a dynamic pattern, by

```
~~ let linequal = fun x --> | {} x -> True | y -> False;;
linequal: lin a -> b -> Bool
```

It is called `linequal` since the first argument must be a linear term, as indicated by the long arrow `-->` in the abstraction. The resulting type `lin a -> b -> Bool` requires its first argument to be of type `lin a`, i.e. to be a linear term of type `a`. In the first pattern `| {} x -> True` the braces `{}` indicate that the pattern is dynamic. Since they contain no symbols, the case does not have any binding symbols, and so `x` is a free variable in the pattern. The second case `| y -> False` is a static pattern, just as before. This equality program uses its first argument as the pattern to match against its second argument. As with `equal`, the types of the two arguments need not be the same. This proves useful when comparing components. Here are some examples and counter examples.

```
~~ linequal [1,2,3] [1,2,3];;
it: Bool
it = True
~~ linequal 4 (2+2);;
it: Bool
it = True
```

B. Jay, *Pattern Calculus*,
DOI 10.1007/978-3-540-89185-7_16, © Springer-Verlag Berlin Heidelberg 2009

```
~~ linequal (2+2) 4;;
term error: + not a linear variable
```

In the first example, the list `[1,2,3]` of type `List Int` is also recognised as a linear term, of type `lin (List Int)`. The error arises in the third example because 2+2 is not a linear term.

The *generic eliminator* is given by

```
~~ let elim = fun (x: lin (a -> b)) --> |{y} x y -> y;;
elim: lin (a -> b) -> b -> a
```

In the pattern `x y` above, the symbol `x` is free and `y` is bound. The first argument to `elim` must be a linear term, as indicated by the long arrow `-->`. Here are some examples.

```
~~ elim Cons;;
it: (List a -> List a) -> a
~~ elim Cons (Cons 3);;
it: Int
it = 3
```

`elim Cons` removes the constructor `Cons` from `Cons 3`. Here is a more interesting example.

```
~~ lin singleton x = [x];;
singleton: a -> List a
~~ elim singleton [3];;
it: Int
it = 3
```

The declaration `lin singleton x = [x]` is a form of let-declaration in which `singleton` is declared to be a linear term, and thus suitable for use in a dynamic pattern. Note that the inferred type is of `singleton` as a linear term; as a term its type would be `lin (a -> List a)`.

Linear terms must use their argument exactly once. Counter-examples include

```
~~ lin null x = [];;
term error: x is a missing binding symbol
~~ lin two x = (x,x);;
term error: x is a duplicate binding symbol
~~ lin idBool x = if True then x else True ;;
term error: cond(True)(x)(True) is not linear
```

The conditional above must fail since its reduction will lose type information. Another constraint is that linear terms are required to have their most general type. The most common example of this restriction in practice concerns wildcards, as in

```
~~ let f = fun x --> fst x;;
f: a * b --> a
~~ f _;;
type error: ty_4921 and ty_4919 * ty_4920 don't unify
```

This error message exposes the internal representations of the type variables, a and b and the type of _ in the hope that this will prove useful. The program `elim _` produces a similar error, due to the risk that it will expose type information that should remain hidden, as described in Sect. 9.1.

Here is the pathological example that can cause problems if binding symbols are handled ambiguously, but is here quite safe.

```
~~ let pathology = fun x -->  | {} (fun x -> x) x -> True ;;
pathology: lin a -> a -> Bool
~~ pathology [] [];;
it: Bool
it = True
```

The reduction of `(fun x -> x) x` proceeds without incident.

16.2 Salaries or Wages

It often happens that the same semantic concepts are represented in different ways. For example, the *salaries* developed earlier may also be represented as *wages* given by the declarations:

```
datatype Currency =  AUSD | EURO | USD | YUAN;;
datatype Wage = Wage of Currency and Float ;;
```

Now wages can be increased using

```
let incrWage f = | Wage c s -> Wage c (f s);;
```

A more general approach is to define

```
let incr_salary salary f = | {x} salary x -> salary (f x);;
```

in which the representation of the float inside the salary or wage is given by a free variable `salary`. Then, for example, we have

```
incr_salary (Wage EURO) twopercent (Wage EURO 1.0);;
```

Of course, this example is rather fragile, since the operation being performed may have a different algorithm in each case. For this, object-orientation is required, as developed in Chap. 18.

16.3 Notes

The original **bondi** used linear terms as in the extension calculus. This was followed by experiments in dynamic typing, before returning to the original idea.

Chapter 17
State

Abstract State is represented by references, built using a constructor `Ref`. As well as the usual imperative features, such as for- and while-loops, **bondi** supports a generic iterator, a path polymorphic function that executes a command at each step. Cycles can be avoided by using references to references as backward links, and avoiding these during iteration.

17.1 References

Turing machines compute by reading and writing squares of a tape. Let us generalise the tape to a *store* in which *locations* have *values* that can be read and written. **bondi** uses references to handle locations. These can be created, assigned and read, but their destruction is handled implicitly, using garbage collection. The basic machinery is illustrated by the following example in **bondi**.

```
let x = Ref 3 in
x = !x + 1;
!x;;
it: Int
it = 4
```

The constructor `Ref` has type

```
Ref;;
it: a -> ref a
```

where `ref` a is a new type form, of *references* to values of type a. Note that `ref` is *not* a type constant, even though `Ref` is a constructor. This choice means that type variables cannot be instantiated to `ref` but that pattern matching on references is still possible. The syntax $!x$ represents the value stored at location x, which is obtained by applying the case `Ref` $x \to x$. The semicolon is used to sequence a command followed by a term; it can be expressed using λ-abstraction.

B. Jay, *Pattern Calculus*,
DOI 10.1007/978-3-540-89185-7_17,

The *assignment* x=!x+1 changes the value of x to be one more than the old value of x. It is important to note that attempting to assign to a location whose type is quantified produces an error, as in

```
let x = Ref Nil in
  x = Cons 1 !x;
  x = Cons True !x;        (* ill typed! *)
  !x
term error: x is too polymorphic to be assignable
```

Without the restriction, the result would be the mixed list Cons True (Cons 1 Nil).

The actual display on screen is handled by another primitive operation called printstring which takes a string argument and produces a command, as in

```
printstring "abc";;
it: Unit
abc~~
```

The generic printer in **bondi** is given by applying printString to the result of toString in

```
~~ let print x =  printstring(toString x);;
print: a -> Unit
```

Commands have type Unit whose only constructor is Un : Unit. This may also be written as (). As well as these fundamental commands, **bondi** also supports while-loops and for-loops. For example, here are two more accounts of the factorial function

```
~~let factorial n =
let x = Ref n in
let res = Ref 1 in
while (!x > 0) do
  (res = !res * !x; x = !x - 1);
!res
;;
factorial: Int -> Int
~~ factorial 5;;
it: Int
it = 120
```

and

```
~~ let factorial2 n =
let res = Ref 1 in
(for i = 1 to n do res = !res * i);
!res;;
factorial2: Int -> Int
~~ factorial2 5;;
```

```
datatype LinkedList a = LLnode of ref a and ref (LinkedList a)
with
toString += | LLnode v n as z ->
 let rec (aux: a -> String) =
 | LLnode v1 (Ref (Exception "nil")) -> toString !v1
 | LLnode v1 n1 -> (toString !v1) ^ "," ^ (aux !n1)
 | _ -> ""
 in
 "[" ^ (aux z) ^"]"
;;
LLnode: ref a -> ref (LinkedList a) -> LinkedList a
```

Fig. 17.1 Linked lists

```
it: Int
it = 120
~~ factorial2 (-7);;
it: Int
it = 1
```

Note that for-loops halt if the lower bound is higher than the upper bound.

17.2 Linked Lists

In imperative languages such as C, complex data structures are built from assignable locations. For example a linked list consists of a number of nodes, each of which has a reference to the node value and another to the next list entry. In **bondi** these can be defined using data type declarations involving references, as in Fig. 17.1. As well as the declaration of the constructor `LLnode` there is a new case for the function `toString` used in printing. Here are some examples

```
let llnil  = | Un -> Ref (Exception "nil");;
llnil: Unit -> ref a
~~ let n0 = LLnode (Ref 0) (llnil()) ;;
n0: LinkedList Int
n0 = [0]
~~ let n1 = LLnode (Ref 1) (Ref n0);;
n1: LinkedList Int
n1 = [1,0]
~~ let n2 = LLnode (Ref 2) (llnil()) ;;
n2: LinkedList Int
n2 = [2]
~~ let n3 = LLnode (Ref 3) (Ref n1);;
n3: LinkedList Int
n3 = [3,1,0]
```

Unlike lists in the functional style, it is easy to add entries in the middle of a linked list, as follows

```
let (insert : LinkedList a -> LinkedList a -> Unit) =
| LLnode v1 n1 -> | LLnode v2 n2 ->
n1 = !n2;
n2 = LLnode v1 n1
;;
insert: LinkedList a -> LinkedList a -> Unit
~~ insert n2 n3;;
it: Unit
~~ n3;;
it: LinkedList Int
it = [3,2,1,0]
```

The insertion of `n2` at `n3` has made `n2` the next of `n3`, and changed the next of `n2` to be `n1`.

One can define mapping for these lists by pattern matching on `LLnode` but a more general approach is to use a generic iterator. A first attempt is given by

```
let rec (iter0: (all a. (a->Unit)) -> b -> Unit)  f z =
f z;
(
 | z y -> (iter0 f z); (iter0 f y)
 | y -> ()
) z
;;
iter0: (all a.a -> Unit) -> b -> Unit
```

In structure it is very similar to `apply2all` except that it does not recreate a data structure, but merely sequences the commands associated to the components, in a form of depth-first traversal. For example, define

```
let anyIncr =
| (Ref (x:Int)) as z -> z = !z + 1
| _ -> ()
;;
anyIncr: a -> Unit
~~ iter anyIncr n3; n3;;
it: LinkedList Int
it = [4,3,2,1]
```

Doubly linked lists can be defined in a similar fashion to linked lists, in Fig. 17.2. Now each node has a previous, as well as a next, node. For example,

```
~~ let makeDLnode x =
  DLnode x (Ref (Exception "nil"))
       (Ref (Ref (Exception "nil")));;
```

```
datatype DLinkedList a = DLnode of ref a and ref (DLinkedList a)
        and ref (ref (DLinkedList a))
with
toString += | (DLnode v n p) as z ->
 let rec (aux: a -> String) =
 | DLnode v1 (Ref (Exception "nil")) _ -> (toString !v1)
 | DLnode v1 n1 _ -> (toString !v1) ^ "," ^ (aux !n1)
 | _ -> ""
 in
 "[" ^ (aux z) ^"]"
;;
```

Fig. 17.2 Doubly linked lists

```
makeDLnode: ref a -> DLinkedList a
~~ let n0 = makeDLnode (Ref 0);;
n0: DLinkedList Int
n0 = [0]
~~ let n1 = makeDLnode (Ref 1);;
n1: DLinkedList Int
n1 = [1]
~~ let n2 = makeDLnode (Ref 2);;
n2: DLinkedList Int
n2 = [2]
~~ let n3 = makeDLnode (Ref 3);;
n3: DLinkedList Int
n3 = [3]
```

Insertion is given by

```
~~ let (d_insert : DLinkedList a -> DLinkedList a -> Unit) =
| DLnode v1 n1 p1-> | DLnode v2 n2 p2 ->
        n1 = !n2;
        p1 = Ref (DLnode v2 n2 p2);
        n2 = DLnode v1 n1 p1
;;
d_insert: DLinkedList c -> DLinkedList c -> Unit
~~ d_insert n1 n0 ;;
it: Unit
~~ d_insert n2 n1 ;;
it: Unit
~~ d_insert n3 n2 ;;
it: Unit
~~ n0;;
it: DLinkedList Int
it = [0,1,2,3]
```

```
let rec (iter: (all a. (a->Unit)) -> b -> Unit)  f z =
f z;
(
 | Ref (Ref _) -> ()
 | z y -> (iter f z); (iter f y)
 | y -> ()
) z
```

Fig. 17.3 The generic iterator

As it stands, the program `iter0 anyIncr n0` will not terminate, since the iterator will go to previous nodes as well as next nodes. To avoid this, the previous nodes are given by a reference to a reference, or *pointer* not just a reference. Now it suffices to block iteration over pointers, using the iterator defined in Fig. 17.3. Now

```
~~ iter anyIncr n0 ;;
it: Unit
~~ n0;;
it: DLinkedList Int
it = [1,2,3,4]
```

17.3 Notes

The approach to references is taken from ML [77]. Other approaches to adding state to λ-calculus include the Algol-like languages [79], and the IO-monad of Haskell [86].

Chapter 18
Object-Oriented Classes

Abstract Object-oriented classes in **bondi** are able to support all the usual features through pattern matching, since the canonical pattern for an object in a superclass also matches against objects in the subclass. The language provides a natural account of specialised methods, binary methods and type parameters. All the various forms of polymorphism work together in a natural manner.

18.1 Classifying Objects

An object may be thought of as a self-contained package containing both data and functions, both fields and methods. Being self-contained, the exact number and nature of its attributes is determined by the object, and not the environment in which it sits. This gap between the expectations of the environment and the capacities of the object is bridged by subsumption, by allowing the actual (or dynamic) type of an object to be a subtype of the expected (or static) type. Independence of objects is further enhanced by allowing them their own internal state. Thus, the existing machinery for subtyping and state will suffice to support object-orientation.

Further, since many objects share the same algorithms for methods, it is natural to collect objects into *classes* that share a suite a methods. That is, each object has its own internal state for its fields, while methods are held in the class. Then the collection of fields can be described by an algebraic data type upon which the methods act by pattern matching. That is, a method is given by a method extension, with its type given by a choice between function types, as described in Sect. 11.7.

The resulting approach is able to handle many of the tricky issues that have arisen in supporting object-orientation, including polymorphism in argument types and in return types, and especially ad hoc subtyping in return types. It achieves all of this while also supporting type parameters and the various other sorts of polymorphism. Each feature is illustrated by reworking examples from previous chapters.

B. Jay, *Pattern Calculus*,
DOI 10.1007/978-3-540-89185-7_18, © Springer-Verlag Berlin Heidelberg 2009

```
class Name  {
name : String;
get_name = { | () -> !this.name }
set_name = { fun n -> this.name = n }
with
toString += | Name x y -> toString !y
}
```

Fig. 18.1 Names

18.2 Classes

Example 18.1. Names

Classes in **bondi** use a type variable to represent any unknown fields. A simple example is the class Name given in Fig. 18.1 to which the system response is:

```
class Name {
name: Name[a] -> ref String
get_name: Name[a] -> Unit -> String
set_name: Name[a] -> String -> Unit
toString: Name[a] -> String
}
```

This declaration introduces a new type constant Name. A typical name will have type Name T for some type T that types any additional fields that a name may have. This will typically be written Name $[T]$ for reasons that will become clear when considering subclasses. If T is Unit then this may be further abbreviated to Name[]. This is the type of a new name. Further, if T is Top then it may be written as Name. The sole constructor for names is

```
Name : a -> ref String -> Name[a]
```

though its explicit use in programs is not really necessary or encouraged. The attributes of the class are the field name and the methods get_name and set_name. The keyword this refers to the object under discussion. The dot notation, as in this.name, is used to invoke methods. The type of each attribute is shown in the response. However, attributes are not themselves programs. For example,

```
~~ name;;
term error: name is an attribute
```

However, they can be converted into functions by η-expanding, as in

```
~~ let nameName x = x.name;;
nameName: Name -> ref String
```

The significance of this will be clearer when considering subclasses in Sect. 18.3. The addition of new cases is just as in algebraic data types, as described in Sect. 14.5.

```
class Person {
name : String;
position : Int;
friends : List Person;
get_name = { | () -> !this.name }
set_name  = { fun n -> this.name = n }
get_position = { | () -> !this.position }
set_position = { fun p -> this.position = p }
get_friends = { | () -> !this.friends }
set_friends = { fun p -> this.friends = p }
move = { fun d -> this.set_position (this.get_position() + d) }
moveClone = { fun d ->
        let res = clone this in
        res.set_position (this.get_position() + d);
        res }
closer  = { | (x:Person) ->
if this.get_position() <=  x.get_position()
then (this : Person)
else (x : Person)
}
with
toString += | (x:Person) -> x.get_name ()
}
```

Fig. 18.2 Persons

This mechanism allows generic functions such as `toString` to be given new cases, as well as allowing method specialisation, as will be described in Sect. 18.3.

New names can be created using `new Name` as in

```
~~ let fred = new Name in
fred.set_name("Fred");
fred;;
it: Name
it = Fred
```

Example 18.2. Persons

A slightly richer class, describing a person, is given in Fig. 18.2. The `Person` class has fields for a name, a position, and a list of friends. The output is not displayed. The friends may be of any sort, and so have type `List (Person[Top])`. The methods are for getting and setting the name and position, for moving the position, for making a clone at a new position, and for comparing persons according to their position. The method `moveClone` uses the built-in operation `clone` to make a shallow copy of `this`. It has type

```
Person[a] * Int -> Person[a]
```

whose return type `Person[a]` is exactly the same as that of the invoking object. By contrast,

```
closer: Person[a] -> Person[b] -> Person[Top]
```

takes an object (of type Person[a] for some a) and an argument which is some other sort of person (of type Person[b] for some b) and, since either of them could be the result, produces a person of unknown class (of type Person[Top]). These two methods illustrate the expressive power that comes from using type variables to represent different possibilities. Alternative types for such binary methods include

```
Person[a] * Person[b] -> Person[b]
Person * Person[b] -> Person[b]
Person * Person -> Person[]
Person * Person -> Person
```

Excluded from this list is the type Person[a] * Person[a] -> Person[a] since this is not a method type, as explained in Chap. 11.

Objects in the class are created using the keyword new as before. For example,

```
~~ let homer = new Person;;
homer: Person[]
homer = void
~~ homer.set_name("Homer");
homer.set_position(5);
homer.set_friends([]);
homer.move 3;
(homer,homer.get_position())
;;
it: Person[] * Int
it = (Homer,8)
```

Another interesting point is that the classes Name and Person both have a field name. This does not corrupt any existing programs since name is not itself a program and the function nameName is unaffected. However, the same syntax used to define nameName will now have a different meaning

```
~~ let personName x = x.name;;
personName: Person -> ref String
```

since the type is determined by the latest case for name which is now given by the Person class. To access the earlier meaning requires some additional type information, as in

```
~~ let nName (x:Name) = x.name;;
nName: Name -> ref String
```

Internally, the type of the attribute name is now

```
(Person -> ref String) & (Name -> ref String)
```

but this method type cannot be accessed directly in **bondi** since it is dynamic: new choices may be added at any time.

```
class ProperPerson extends Person {
proper : String;
get_proper = { | () -> !this.proper }
set_proper  = { fun n -> this.proper = n }
get_name = { | () -> super.get_name() ^ " " ^ (this.get_proper()) }
with
toString += | (x:ProperPerson) ->
match x.get_name () with
| Exception "void" -> "name is void"
| str -> str
}
class ProperPerson {
proper: ProperPerson -> ref String
get_proper: ProperPerson -> Unit -> String
set_proper: ProperPerson -> String -> Unit
get_name: ProperPerson -> Unit -> String
}
```

Fig. 18.3 Proper persons

18.3 Subclasses

Example 18.3. Proper Persons

Now let us consider a *subclass* of Person of people that have a proper name given in Fig. 18.3. The keyword extends is used to indicate the subclass relationship. As before, the new class has its own term constructor

```
ProperPerson : a * ref String -> ProperPerson a
```

but this does not mention the type Person. Rather, the interpretation of new is changed to produce something of type ProperPerson[] which is syntax for

```
Person (ProperPerson Unit)
```

That is, a proper person is a person whose extra field has type ProperPerson a for some type a. By doing things in this way, there is no need to add a subtype relationship between ProperPerson and Person: every proper person is a person automatically. For example, the typical pattern for a proper person is

```
Person (ProperPerson _ _) _
```

It is easy to add new methods, such as get_proper. Of more interest is to modify an existing method. Here get_name combines the get_name method of its superclass (the Person class) with the proper name. Since the new function can apply to arguments of the old function, there is now a risk of ambiguity, but in both cases the result is a string, so specialisation is okay. Note that the function toString has not been changed, but invokes the method get_name which has been specialised in the subclass to print the proper name as well as the given name. The latter is accessed using the keyword super. Its effect on evaluation is to reject the first pattern that matches and use the next one. Here is an example.

```
~~ let harry = new ProperPerson;;
harry: ProperPerson[]
harry = name is void
harry.set_name("Harry") ;
harry.set_position(0);
harry.set_proper("Joy");
harry;;
~~ it: ProperPerson[]
it = Harry Joy
```

This example illustrates *dynamic dispatch* in that the meaning of get_name is determined at the point of evaluation, not the point of its introduction. This can be further illustrated by considering a mixed list of friends, as in

```
~~ let  honey = new Person;;
honey: Person[Unit]
honey = void
~~ honey.set_name ("Honey") ;
honey.set_position 1;
honey.set_friends [(homer:Person),harry];
let f x (y: Person) = x ^ y.get_name() ^ ", " in
honey.get_name()^" knows "^
    (foldleft f "" (honey.get_friends()));;
it: String
it = "Honey knows Homer, Harry Joy, "
```

Note that the type of homer must be explicitly coerced to Person since otherwise type inference will try to create a list whose entries are of type Person[]. Here the method get_name is applied to each person in the list of friends, with the choice of specialisation determined by pattern-matching on the structure of the person object. Note the easy interaction between the structure polymorphic foldleft and the method get_name.

18.4 Specialised Methods

Example 18.4. Points and Circles

Now let us consider how subtyping may appear in result types, by redeveloping the points and circles of Sect. 11.7 using classes instead of data type declarations. The class of points is given in Fig. 18.4.

Colours can be given by a data type declaration

```
datatype Colour = Colour of Int
with toString += | Colour x ->
```

```
class Point {
x_coord : Float;
y_coord : Float;
get_x_coord = { |() -> !this.x_coord }
set_x_coord = { fun d -> this.x_coord =  d }
get_y_coord = { |() -> !this.y_coord }
set_y_coord  = { fun d -> this.y_coord =  d }
is_good = { this.get_x_coord() >= 0.0 }
with
toString += | Point z (x,y) ->
  "Point("^ (toString !x) ^ "," ^(toString !y)^ ")"
 }

class ColourPoint extends Point {
colour : Colour;
get_colour = { |() -> !this.colour }
set_colour = { fun x -> this.colour = x }
with
toString += | (x: ColourPoint) ->
  "CPoint("^ (toString (x.get_x_coord())) ^ "," ^
  (toString (x.get_y_coord())) ^ "," ^
  (toString (x.get_colour())) ^")"
}
```

Fig. 18.4 Points and coloured points

```
(| 1 -> "red"
 | 2 -> "green"
 | 3 -> "blue"
 | y -> "Colour "^(toString y))
x
;;
let red = Colour 1;;
let green = Colour 2 ;;
let blue = Colour 3;;
```

and these can be used in defining the class of coloured points in Fig. 18.4.

Now consider the classes of circles and coloured circles defined in Fig. 18.5. The centre of a circle is a mystery point. However, the method `get_centre` of a coloured circle is specialised to produce a coloured point, and so has specialised type

```
ColourCircle[a] -> Unit -> ColourPoint[]
```

as well as `Circle[d] -> Unit -> Point`. Note that if the `centre` was made to have type `Point[]` then this method specialisation would not work. That is, some care is required in defining the superclass to allow this later specialisation. Here is an example.

```
let x = new ColourCircle in
```

```
class Circle {
centre : Point;
radius :Float;
get_centre  = { |() -> !this.centre }
set_centre = { fun x -> this.centre = x }
get_radius = { |() -> !this.radius }
set_radius  = { fun x -> this.radius = x }
}
class ColourCircle  extends Circle {
col : Colour ;
get_col = { |() -> !this.col }
set_col  = { fun x -> this.col = x }
get_centre = { |() ->
let res = new ColourPoint in
res.set_x_coord ((super.get_centre()).get_x_coord());
res.set_y_coord ((super.get_centre()).get_y_coord());
res.set_colour (this.get_col());
res }
}
```

Fig. 18.5 Circles and coloured circles

```
let p = new Point in
p.x_coord = -1.1;
p.y_coord = 2.2;
x.centre = p;
x.col = blue;
(x.centre,x.get_centre());;
it: Point * ColourPoint[]
it = (Point (-1.1,2.2),CPoint(-1.1,2.2,blue))
```

The centre field of x is a mere point, but the `get_centre` method returns a coloured point, whose colour is that of the circle.

18.5 Parametrised Classes

Example 18.5. Linked Lists

Now let us consider type parameters, by defining a class of nodes for linked lists, and then defining a subclass of doubly linked lists, much as in Sect. 17.2. The nodes of the linked lists are given in Fig. 18.6. The declaration creates types of the form `Node <a> [b]` where a represents the type of the node value and b represents the type of any additional fields. The function `toString` is modified to print out the whole list from the node of interest.

Here are some examples.

```
~~ let x0 = new Node <Int>  ;;
```

```
~~class Node <a>   {
value : a ;
next : Node <a>;
getValue  = { |() -> !this.value }
setValue = { fun v -> this.value = v }
getNext = { |() -> !this.next }
setNext = { fun (n: Node <a>) -> this.next = n }
insert = { fun (n: Node<a>) -> n.setNext (this.getNext()); this.setNext n }
with
toString += | (x: Node<a>) ->
 let rec (aux: c -> String) =
 | Node _ (v,Ref (Exception _)) -> toString !v
 | Node _ (v,n) -> (toString !v) ^ "," ^ (aux !n)
 | _ -> ""
 in
 ("[" ^ (aux x) ^"]" , False)
}
class Node {
value: Node<a> -> ref a
next: Node<b> -> ref Node<b>
getValue: Node<c> -> Unit -> c
setValue: Node<d> -> d -> Unit
getNext: Node<e> -> Unit -> Node<e>
setNext: Node<f> -> Node<f> -> Unit
insert: Node<g> -> Node<g> -> Unit
toString: Node<h> -> String
}
```

Fig. 18.6 Nodes

```
x0: Node<Int>[]
x0 = [_void,]
~~ let x1 = new Node<Int>  ;;
x1: Node<Int>[]
x1 = [_void,]
~~ let x2 = new Node<Int>  ;;
x2: Node<Int>[]
x2 = [_void,]
~~ x0.setValue 0;
x1.setValue 1;
x2.setValue 2;
x0.setNext x2;
x0;;
it: Node<Int>[]
it = [0,2,]
~~ x0.insert x1;
x0;;
it: Node<Int>[]
```

```
class DNode <a> extends Node {
previous : ref (DNode <a>);
getPrev = { |()-> !(!this.previous) }
setPrev  = { fun (p:DNode <a>) -> this.previous = Ref (p:DNode <a> ) }
setNext = { | (n:DNode<a>) ->
                super.setNext n;
                n.setPrev this
              | (n:Node<a>) -> super.setNext n
}
}
```

Fig. 18.7 Doubly linked nodes

```
it = [0,1,2,]
~~ let r4 = new Node <Float>;;
r4: Node<Float>[]
r4 = [_void,]
~~ r4.setValue 4.4;
r4;;
it: Node<Float>[]
it = [4.4,]
```

Iteration is illustrated by

```
~~ let anyNode =
| (x:Node <s> b) -> print (x.getValue())
| _ -> ()
;;
anyNode: a -> Unit
~~ iter anyNode x0;;
it: Unit
012~~ iter anyNode r4;;
it: Unit
4.4~~
```

Note how this works with either integers or floats.

Example 18.6. Doubly linked Lists

The doubly linked lists have nodes given in Fig. 18.7. Here is the earlier example modified to produce doubly linked lists.

```
~~ let d0 = new DNode <Int>  ;;
d0: DNode<Int>[]
d0 = [_void,]
~~ let d1 = new DNode<Int>  ;;
d1: DNode<Int>[]
d1 = [_void,]
~~ let d2 = new DNode<Int>  ;;
```

```
d2: DNode<Int>[]
d2 = [_void,]
~~ d0.setValue 0;
d1.setValue 1;
d2.setValue 2;
d0.setNext d2;
d0;;
it: DNode<Int>[]
it = [0,2,]
~~ d2.getPrev();;
d0.insert d1;
d0;;
it: DNode<Int>
it = [0,2,]
~~ d2.getPrev();;
it: DNode<Int>
it = [1,2,]
```

Note that the iterator would not terminate if the field `prev` were of type `DNode<a>` instead of `ref (DNode<a>)` since the iterator is defined to ignore reference to references, as discussed in Sect. 17.2.

This could be used to develop examples of sorting algorithms, etc. that work seamlessly for both linked lists and doubly linked lists. Then the polymorphism in data, path and inclusion are all present simultaneously.

18.6 Building on Standards

Consider the following scenario. Several organisations have agreed to a standard for representing common concepts such as customers, but when these concepts are used in high-level classes then the uniform treatment is lost. Uniformity can be recovered by using path polymorphic functions that act uniformly with respect to all the higher classes. The technique is illustrated using another sort of query, `findOne` in Fig. 18.8, that performs a depth-first search. For example

```
~~ let (isNegFloat: a -> Maybe Float) =
| (x : Float) -> if  x<0.0 then Some x else None
| _ -> None
;;
~~ findOne isNegFloat [1.,2.,-3.,-4.];;
it: Maybe Float
it = Some -3.
```

The `ProperPerson` class defined in Fig. 18.3 is extended to define a class `Customer` in Fig. 18.9. This yields

```
~~ datatype Maybe a = None | Some of a;;
~~ let rec (findOne: (all a. (a -> Maybe b)) ->
                                    c -> Maybe b) f x =
  match f x with
  | Some r -> Some r
  | None ->
     match x with
    |  y z ->
begin
match findOne f y with
| None -> findOne f z
| r -> r
end
    | _ -> None
;;
```

Fig. 18.8 Finding a solution

```
~~let john = new Customer;;
john.set_name "John";
john.set_proper "Smith";
john.set_balance (120.);;
john.get_balance();;

let jane = new Customer;;
jane.set_name "Jane";
jane.set_proper "Doe";
jane.set_balance (-75.);;
jane.get_balance();;
```

and

```
~~ findOne isNegFloat [john,jane];;
it: Maybe Float
it = Some -75.
```

Of course, this loses the identity of the found customer, so define

```
~~ let (isNegCustomer: a -> Maybe Customer) =
| (x : Customer) ->
        if  x.get_balance()<0.0 then Some x else None
| _ -> None
;;
isNegCustomer: a -> Maybe Customer
~~ findOne isNegCustomer [john,jane];;
it: Maybe Customer
it = Some Jane Doe
```

```
class Customer extends ProperPerson {
balance : Float;
get_balance = { | () -> !this.balance}
set_balance  = { fun n -> this.balance = n }
}

class Valued extends Customer {
high_interest : Float;
get_high_interest = { | () -> !this.high_interest}
set_high_interest  = { fun n -> this.high_interest = n }
get_balance = { | () ->
        super.get_balance() + this.get_high_interest() }
}
```

Fig. 18.9 Customers and valued customers

Suppose now that several organisations have agreed to use the customer class, but each uses the class in its own way. For example, Fig. 18.10 defines classes `Bank` and `Division` and `Corporation` which can be used in the following examples.

```
let abc = new Bank;;
abc.set_name "Australian Banking Company" ;
abc.set_customers [john,jane];
findOne isNegCustomer abc;;
```

yields `jane` once again, as does the following

```
let div1 = new Division;;
div1.set_customers [john];
div1.get_customers();;

let div2 = new Division;;
div2.set_customers [jane];
div2.get_customers();;

let corp = new Corporation;;
corp.set_divisions [div1,div2];;

findOne isNegCustomer corp;;
```

Finally, one may create subclasses of `Customer` as in the class `Valued` of valued customers defined in Fig. 18.9. Then

```
let alan = new Valued;;
alan.set_name "Alan";
alan.set_proper "Key";
alan.set_balance (-40.0);
```

```
class Bank {
name : String;
customers : List Customer;
get_name = { | () -> !this.name}
set_name  = { fun n -> this.name = n }
get_customers = { | () -> !this.customers}
set_customers = { fun x -> this.customers = x }
}

class Division {
name: String;
customers: List Customer;
get_name = { | () -> !this.name}
set_name  = { fun n -> this.name = n }
get_customers = { | () -> !this.customers}
set_customers  = { fun x -> this.customers = x }
}

class Corporation {
name : String;
divisions: List Division ;
get_name = { | () -> !this.name}
set_name  = { fun n -> this.name = n }
get_divisions = { | () -> !this.divisions}
set_divisions  = { fun x -> this.divisions = x }
}
```

Fig. 18.10 Banks and corporations

```
alan.set_high_interest 50.0;
alan.get_balance();;

abc.set_customers
    (Cons (alan: Customer) (abc.get_customers()));;

findOne isNegCustomer abc;;
```

once again yields `jane`.

18.7 Updating Salaries

The problem posed at the beginning of this book was to define a function for updating salaries in the most general fashion possible. The solution builds on the classes `Person` and `ProperPerson` introduced in Sect. 18.3.

```
class Employee extends ProperPerson {
salary : Float ;
get_salary = { |() -> !this.salary}
set_salary = { fun s -> this.salary = s}
update_salary = { fun p -> this.salary = !this.salary *(1.0 +p) }
}
```

Fig. 18.11 Employees

Example 18.7. Employees

Nested subclasses are easily defined. For example, an employee is a proper person, as defined in Fig. 18.11. Now the type syntax `Employee[a]` denotes the type

```
Person (ProperPerson (Employee a))
```

for some fresh type variable a without having to specify all of the superclasses of `Employee` explicitly. In the same manner, the pattern `(x:Employee)` is syntactic sugar for the pattern

```
Person (ProperPerson (Employee _) _) _ as x
```

Here is an example of an employee

```
~~ let busy = new Employee;;
busy: Employee[]
busy = name is void
~~ busy.set_name("busy");
busy.set_proper("beaver");
busy.set_salary(2.00);
busy.set_position(7);
busy;;
it: Employee[]
it = busy beaver
```

Building on the class of employees, we can define in Fig. 18.12 a class of managers, who get a bonus that is updated along with salaries. Here is a manager.

```
~~ let lazy = new Manager;;
lazy: Manager[]
lazy = name is void
~~lazy.set_name("Lazy");
lazy.set_proper("B");
lazy.set_salary(4.00);
lazy.set_department("dep1");
lazy.set_bonus(1.00);
lazy.update_salary(0.05);
(lazy,lazy.get_salary(),lazy.get_bonus());;
it: Manager[] * Float * Float
it = (Lazy B,4.2,1.05)
```

```
class Manager extends Employee {
department : String;
bonus : Float ;
get_department = { | () -> !this.department }
set_department  = { fun n -> this.department = n }
get_bonus = { | () -> !this.bonus }
set_bonus  = { fun n -> this.bonus = n }
update_salary = { fun p ->
super.update_salary(p);
this.bonus = !this.bonus * (1.0 + p) }
}
```

Fig. 18.12 Managers

Now declare in Fig. 18.13 a department class that has both a manager and some employees. For example

```
~~ dep1.set_name("dep1") ;
dep1.set_manager(lazy);
dep1.set_employees([busy:Employee ]);
dep1;;
it: Department[]
it = dep1
```

Here is an example of a generic iterator acting on objects.

```
let (update_any_salary: Float -> a -> Unit) p =
| (x:Employee) -> x.update_salary(p)
| x -> ()
;;
```

and its use in the department `dep1`.

```
~~ map (fun x -> (x,x.get_salary())) (dep1.get_employees());;
it: List (Employee * Float)
it = [(busy beaver,2.)]
~~  (dep1.get_manager()).get_bonus();;
it: Float
it = 1.05
~~ iter (update_any_salary 0.5) dep1;
map (fun x -> (x,x.get_salary())) (dep1.get_employees());;
it: List (Employee * Float)
it = [(busy beaver,3.)]
~~  (dep1.get_manager()).get_bonus();;
it: Float
it = 1.575
```

This example combines structure polymorphism, path polymorphism and inclusion polymorphism seamlessly with the stateful representation of objects.

```
class Department {
name : String ;
manager : Manager  ;
employees : List (Employee);
get_name = { |() -> !this.name}
set_name = { fun s -> this.name = s}
get_manager = { |() -> !this.manager}
set_manager = { fun s -> this.manager = s}
get_employees = { |() -> !this.employees}
set_employees = { fun s -> this.employees = s}
with
toString += | (x:Department) -> x.get_name()
}
```

Fig. 18.13 Departments

The final example adds pattern polymorphism and algebraic data types to the mix, and in-place updating. The latter is defined by

```
let rec (update: lin (ref a -> b) -> (a -> a) -> c -> Unit) =
 fun x --> fun f ->
  | {y} x y ->  y = f !y
  | z y -> update x f z; update x f y
  | y -> ()
;;
```

Now consider the data types

```
datatype Worker = Worker of ref String * ref Float
with
toString += | Worker (x,y) -> !x;;
type WorkUnit = List Worker;;
```

and the examples

```
let w1 = Ref (Worker (Ref "Fred",Ref 2.0));;
let w2 = Ref (Worker (Ref "Mary",Ref 3.0));;
let ws = [w1,w2];;
lin salary2 x = Worker (_,x);;
```

Now

```
~~ map (|{y} salary2 y -> !y) ws;;
it: List Float
it = [2.,3.]
~~ update salary2 twopercent ws;;
it: Unit
~~ map (|{y} salary2 y -> !y) ws;;
it: List Float
it = [2.04,3.06]
```

shows the updating of worker salaries.

The same approach applies to the employees class, as follows

```
~~lin salary3 x = Person (ProperPerson (Employee _ x) _) _;;
salary3: ref Float -> Employee
~~ map (fun (x:Employee) -> (x,x.get_salary()))
         (dep1.get_employees());;
it: List (Employee * Float)
it = [(busy beaver,4.59)]
~~ update salary3 twopercent dep1;;
it: Unit
~~ map (fun (x:Employee) -> (x,x.get_salary()))
         (dep1.get_employees());;
it: List (Employee * Float)
it = [(busy beaver,4.6818)]
```

Here the salaries are given by `salary3` that describes an employee. Note that it is necessary here to specify the structure of all the superclasses of `Employee` to describe the pattern. Future work may be able to suppress this, just as has been achieved for defining a new `Employee` object.

Finally, the two ways of describing salaries can be combined. using

```
let rec (update_sal : (Float -> Float) -> a -> Unit) f =
| (x:Department)  -> update salary3 f x
| (WorkUnit _) as x -> update salary2 f x
| z y -> update_sal f z; update_sal f y
| y -> ()
;;
```

This can be applied to an organisation containing a mix of employees and workers, as in `update_sal twopercent (dep1,ws)` which updates the salaries of employees in the department object, and of the workers in the work unit.

This example shows how object-oriented classes and algebraic data types can be mixed freely. The resulting data structures can be handled using functions that are polymorphic in all the ways discussed in the book. Type parameters appear throughout. Functor polymorphism can be used to map over collections of workers or employees. Path polymorphism is used to find employees within an organisation. Pattern polymorphism allows salaries to be represented in different ways within a dynamic pattern. Subclassing allows managers to be treated differently.

Although the shift in theoretical perspective is substantial, these **bondi** examples show that the new approach is quite easily grafted onto existing programming styles. The treatment of algebraic data types and object-oriented classes is quite close to that of popular languages when performing familiar programming tasks, and often easier (as when type inference is employed for object-orientation). Syntactic novelty is generally limited to situations employing new expressive power, as with dynamic patterns. For all that, the full power of this approach is yet to be realised.

18.8 Notes

The **bondi** class syntax is modelled on that of Java. There are so many object-oriented programming languages, based on so many different approaches, that it seems better not to say anything, except that the choice of examples was motivated in part by those in Chap. 3 of Bruce's book on object-orientation [12]. Type inference in object-oriented languages is treated by Palsberg and Schwartzbach [82].

Much remains to be done in representing other programming features, such as communication and networking, but the combination of features already supported by the pattern calculus shows that many of the tensions that arise between programming styles can be eliminated by basing computation on the balanced combination of functions and data structures that is the pattern calculus.

18.2 Notes

Appendix A
Syntax

Abstract This appendix provides an overview of the syntax, but not the semantics, of all the main calculi in the book. Section A.1 considers the untyped calculi. It begins with a figure containing concise grammars of all the calculi. Since these admit significant duplication, the definitions of free variables, substitutions and α-conversion will be given for a grammar obtained as the union of all. A similar approach is used for the types, in Sect. A.2 and the typed terms, in Sect. A.3, except that the individual type grammars have been omitted. Proofs of the lemmas are by routine inductions, and so are omitted.

A.1 Untyped Terms

The grammars of the untyped calculi are given in Fig. A.1. The *free variables* $\mathsf{fv}(t)$ and *free matchables* $\mathsf{fm}(t)$ of an untyped term t are defined in Fig. A.2. The *applications* of a term substitution σ to the free variable (respectively, matchable) symbols of a term is defined in Fig. A.3 (respectively, Fig. A.4). α-conversion is defined in Fig. A.5.

Lemma A.1. *For every substitution σ and term t_1 there is a term t_2 that is α-equivalent to t_1 such that σt_2 and $\hat{\sigma} t_2$ are defined. If t_1 and t_2 are α-equivalent terms*

Pure λ-calculus	$t ::= x \mid t\,t \mid \lambda x.t$
Compound calculus	$t ::= x \mid t\,t \mid \lambda x.t \mid c \mid c\;\texttt{eqa}\;t \mid \texttt{pair?}\;t \mid \texttt{car}\;t \mid \texttt{cdr}\;t$
Static pattern calculus	$p ::= x \mid c \mid p\,p$
	$t ::= x \mid c \mid t\,t \mid p \to t$
Dynamic pattern calculus	$t ::= x \mid \hat{x} \mid t\,t \mid [\theta]\,t \to t$
Extension calculus	$t ::= x \mid c \mid t\,t \mid [\theta]\,t \to t \mid t$

Fig. A.1 Grammars of untyped terms

DOI 10.1007/978-3-540-89185-7_A, © Springer-Verlag Berlin Heidelberg 2009

$$
\begin{array}{rlrl}
\mathsf{fv}(x) &= \{x\} & \mathsf{fm}(x) &= \{\} \\
\mathsf{fv}(\hat{x}) &= \{\} & \mathsf{fm}(\hat{x}) &= \{x\} \\
\mathsf{fv}(c) &= \{\} & \mathsf{fm}(c) &= \{\} \\
\mathsf{fv}(r\,u) &= \mathsf{fv}(r) \cup \mathsf{fv}(u) & \mathsf{fm}(r\,u) &= \mathsf{fm}(r) \cup \mathsf{fm}(u) \\
\mathsf{fv}(\lambda x.s) &= \mathsf{fv}(s) \setminus \{x\} & \mathsf{fm}(\lambda x.s) &= \mathsf{fm}(s) \\
\mathsf{fv}(c \texttt{ eqa } t) &= \mathsf{fv}(t) & \mathsf{fm}(c \texttt{ eqa } t) &= \mathsf{fm}(t) \\
\mathsf{fv}(\texttt{pair? } t) &= \mathsf{fv}(t) & \mathsf{fm}(\texttt{pair? } t) &= \mathsf{fm}(t) \\
\mathsf{fv}(\texttt{car } t) &= \mathsf{fv}(t) & \mathsf{fm}(\texttt{car } t) &= \mathsf{fm}(t) \\
\mathsf{fv}(\texttt{cdr } t) &= \mathsf{fv}(t) & \mathsf{fm}(\texttt{cdr } t) &= \mathsf{fm}(t) \\
\mathsf{fv}(p \to s) &= \mathsf{fv}(s) \setminus \mathsf{fv}(p) & \mathsf{fm}(p \to s) &= \mathsf{fm}(p) \cup \mathsf{fm}(s) \\
\mathsf{fv}([\theta]\, p \to s) &= \mathsf{fv}(p) \cup (\mathsf{fv}(s) \setminus \theta) & \mathsf{fm}([\theta]\, p \to s) &= (\mathsf{fm}(p) \setminus \theta) \cup \mathsf{fm}(s) \\
\mathsf{fv}([\theta]\, p \to s \mid r) &= \mathsf{fv}(p) \cup (\mathsf{fv}(s) \setminus \theta) & \mathsf{fm}([\theta]\, p \to s \mid r) &= (\mathsf{fm}(p) \setminus \theta) \cup \mathsf{fm}(s) \\
& \quad \cup\, \mathsf{fm}(r) & & \quad \cup\, \mathsf{fm}(r)
\end{array}
$$

Fig. A.2 Free variables and matchables of untyped terms

$$
\begin{array}{lll}
\sigma(x) & = \sigma x & \text{if } x \in \mathsf{dom}(\sigma) \\
\sigma(x) & = x & \text{if } x \notin \mathsf{dom}(\sigma) \\
\sigma(\hat{x}) & = \hat{x} & \\
\sigma(c) & = c & \\
\sigma(r\,u) & = (\sigma(r))\ (\sigma(u)) & \\
\sigma(\lambda x.s) & = \lambda x.\sigma(s) & \text{if } \sigma \text{ avoids } x \\
\sigma(c \texttt{ eqa } t) & = c \texttt{ eqa } \sigma(t) & \\
\sigma(\texttt{pair? } t) & = \texttt{pair? } \sigma(t) & \\
\sigma(\texttt{car } t) & = \texttt{car } \sigma(t) & \\
\sigma(\texttt{cdr } t) & = \texttt{cdr } \sigma(t) & \\
\sigma(p \to s) & = p \to \sigma(s) & \text{if } \sigma \text{ avoids } p \\
\sigma([\theta]\, p \to s) & = [\theta]\ \sigma(p) \to \sigma(s) & \text{if } \sigma \text{ avoids } \theta \\
\sigma([\theta]\, p \to s \mid r) & = [\theta]\ \sigma(p) \to \sigma(s) \mid \sigma(r) & \text{if } \sigma \text{ avoids } \theta.
\end{array}
$$

Fig. A.3 Substitution for variable term symbols

then $\mathsf{fv}(t_1) = \mathsf{fv}(t_2)$ *and* $\mathsf{fm}(t_1) = \mathsf{fm}(t_2)$. *Further, if* $u_1 = \sigma(t_1)$ *and* $u_2 = \sigma(t_2)$ *are both defined then* $u_1 =_\alpha u_2$. *Similarly, if* $u_1 = \hat{\sigma}(t_1)$ *and* $u_2 = \hat{\sigma}(t_2)$ *are both defined then* $u_1 =_\alpha u_2$.

A.2 Types

The grammar of types is given in Fig. A.6. The *free type variables* $\mathsf{FV}(T)$ and *free type matchable* $\mathsf{FM}(T)$ of a type T are defined in Fig. A.7. The type syntax $\forall_P[\Delta].S$ is *well-formed* if $\Delta \cap \mathsf{FV}(S) \subseteq \mathsf{FV}(P)$. A type substitution is *applied* to the free variables or free matchables of a type using the rules in Fig. A.8. The α*-equivalence* of types is the congruence generated by the relation in Fig. A.9.

$$
\begin{array}{lll}
\hat{\sigma}(x) & = x & \\
\hat{\sigma}(\hat{x}) & = \sigma x & \text{if } x \in \mathsf{dom}(\sigma) \\
\hat{\sigma}(\hat{x}) & = \hat{x} & \text{if } x \notin \mathsf{dom}(\sigma) \\
\hat{\sigma}(c) & = c & \\
\hat{\sigma}(r\, u) & = (\hat{\sigma}(r))\ (\hat{\sigma}(u)) & \\
\hat{\sigma}(\lambda x.s) & = \lambda x.\hat{\sigma}(s) & \text{if } \sigma \text{ avoids } x \\
\hat{\sigma}(c \texttt{ eqa } t) & = c \texttt{ eqa } \hat{\sigma}(t) & \\
\hat{\sigma}(\texttt{pair? } t) & = \texttt{pair? } \hat{\sigma}(t) & \\
\hat{\sigma}(\texttt{car } t) & = \texttt{car } \hat{\sigma}(t) & \\
\hat{\sigma}(\texttt{cdr } t) & = \texttt{cdr } \hat{\sigma}(t) & \\
\hat{\sigma}(p \to s) & = p \to \hat{\sigma}(s) & \text{if } \sigma \text{ avoids } p \\
\hat{\sigma}([\theta]\ p \to s) & = [\theta]\ \hat{\sigma}(p) \to \hat{\sigma}(s) & \text{if } \sigma \text{ avoids } \theta \\
\hat{\sigma}([\theta]\ p \to s \mid r) & = [\theta]\ \hat{\sigma}(p) \to \hat{\sigma}(s) \mid \hat{\sigma}(r) & \text{if } \sigma \text{ avoids } \theta.
\end{array}
$$

Fig. A.4 Substitution for matchable term symbols

$$
\begin{array}{rll}
\lambda x.t =_\alpha & \lambda y.\{y/x\}t & \text{if } y \notin \mathsf{fv}(t) \\
p \to s =_\alpha & \{y/x\}p \to \{y/x\}s & \text{if } x \in \mathsf{fv}(p) \text{ and } y \notin \mathsf{fv}(p) \cup \mathsf{fv}(s) \\
[\theta]\ p \to s =_\alpha & [\{y/x\}\theta]\ \{\hat{y}/\hat{x}\}p \to \{y/x\}s & \text{if } x \in \theta \text{ and } y \notin \theta \cup \mathsf{fm}(p) \cup \mathsf{fv}(s) \\
[\theta]\ p \to s \mid r =_\alpha & [\{y/x\}\theta]\ \{\hat{y}/\hat{x}\}p \to \{y/x\}s \mid r & \text{if } x \in \theta \text{ and } y \notin \theta \cup \mathsf{fm}(p) \cup \mathsf{fv}(s)
\end{array}
$$

Fig. A.5 α-conversion for untyped terms

$$
T ::= X \mid \hat{X} \mid C \mid T\,T \mid T \to T \mid \quad \mid \forall X.T \mid \forall_T[\Delta].T
$$

Fig. A.6 Type syntax

$$
\begin{array}{rlrl}
\mathsf{FV}(X) & = X & \mathsf{FM}(X) & = \{\} \\
\mathsf{FV}(\hat{X}) & = \{\} & \mathsf{FM}(\hat{X}) & = \{X\} \\
\mathsf{FV}(C) & = \{\} & \mathsf{FM}(C) & = \{\} \\
\mathsf{FV}(F\,U) & = \mathsf{FV}(F) \cup \mathsf{FV}(U) & \mathsf{FM}(F\,U) & = \mathsf{FM}(F) \cup \mathsf{FM}(U) \\
\mathsf{FV}(P \to S) & = \mathsf{FV}(P) \cup \mathsf{FV}(S) & \mathsf{FM}(P \to S) & = \mathsf{FV}(P) \cup \mathsf{FV}(S) \\
\mathsf{FV}(\forall X.S) & = \mathsf{FV}(S) \setminus \{X\} & \mathsf{FM}(\forall X.S) & = \mathsf{FM}(S) \\
\mathsf{FV}(\forall_P[\Delta].S) & = (\mathsf{FV}(P) \cup \mathsf{FV}(S)) \setminus \Delta & \mathsf{FM}(\forall_P[\Delta].S) & = \mathsf{FM}(P) \cup \mathsf{FM}(S)
\end{array}
$$

Fig. A.7 Free type variables and matchables of types

Lemma A.2. *For every type substitution ρ and type T_1 there is a type T_2 that is α-equivalent to T_1 such that $\rho(T_2)$ and $\hat{\rho}(T_2)$ are defined. If T_1 and T_2 are α-equivalent types then $\mathsf{FV}(T_1) = \mathsf{FV}(T_2)$ and $\mathsf{FM}(T_1) = \mathsf{FM}(T_2)$. Further, if $U_1 = \rho(T_1)$ and $U_2 = \rho(T_2)$ are both defined then $U_1 =_\alpha U_2$. Similarly, if $U_1 = \hat{\rho}(T_1)$ and $U_2 = \hat{\rho}(T_2)$ are both defined then $U_1 =_\alpha U_2$.*

$$
\begin{array}{rcl}
\rho(X) &=& \rho X \text{ if } X \in \mathsf{dom}(\rho) \\
\rho(X) &=& X \text{ if } X \notin \mathsf{dom}(\rho) \\
\rho(\hat{X}) &=& \hat{X} \\
\rho(C) &=& C \\
\rho(F\,U) &=& \rho(F)\,\rho(U) \\
\rho(U \to S) &=& \rho(U) \to \rho(S) \\
\rho(\forall X.S) &=& \forall X.\rho(S) \text{ if } \rho \text{ avoids } X \\
\rho(\forall_P[\Delta].S) &=& \forall_{\rho(P)}[\Delta].\rho(S) \text{ if } \rho \text{ avoids } \Delta
\end{array}
\qquad
\begin{array}{rcl}
\hat{\rho}(X) &=& X \\
\hat{\rho}(\hat{X}) &=& \rho X \text{ if } X \in \mathsf{dom}(\rho) \\
\hat{\rho}(\hat{X}) &=& \hat{X} \text{ if } X \notin \mathsf{dom}(\rho) \\
\hat{\rho}(C) &=& C \\
\hat{\rho}(F\,U) &=& \hat{\rho}(F)\,\hat{\rho}(U) \\
\hat{\rho}(P \to S) &=& \hat{\rho}(P) \to \hat{\rho}(S) \\
\hat{\rho}(\forall X.S) &=& \forall X.\hat{\rho}(S) \text{ if } \rho \text{ avoids } X \\
\hat{\rho}(\forall_P[\Delta].S) &=& \forall_{\hat{\rho}(P)}[\Delta].\hat{\rho}(S) \text{ if } \rho \text{ avoids } \Delta
\end{array}
$$

Fig. A.8 Type substitutions applied to types

$$
\begin{array}{rcll}
\forall X.S &=_\alpha& \forall Y.\{Y/X\}S & \text{if } Y \text{ fresh} \\
\forall_P[\Delta].S &=_\alpha& \forall_{\{Y/X\}P}[\{Y/X\}\Delta].\{Y/X\}S & \text{if } X \in \Delta \text{ and } Y \text{ fresh}
\end{array}
$$

Fig. A.9 α-equivalence of types

Simply typed λ-calculus	$t ::= x^T \mid t\,t \mid \lambda x^T.t$
System **F**	$t ::= x^T \mid t\,t \mid \lambda x^T.t \mid t\,T \mid \Lambda X.t$
System **FM**	$t ::= x^T \mid t\,t \mid \lambda x^T.t \mid t\,T \mid [\Delta]\,T \to t$
Typecase calculus	$t ::= x^T \mid t\,t \mid \lambda x^T.t \mid t\,T \mid [\Delta]\,T \to t \mid t \,\#\, t$
Query calculus	$t ::= x^T \mid t\,t \mid \lambda x^T.t \mid t\,T \mid [\Delta]\,T \to t \mid t \,\#\, t \mid$
	$c^T \mid c^T\ \mathtt{eqa}\ t \mid \mathtt{fold}(t,t,t)$
Static pattern calculus	$p ::= x^T \mid c^T \mid p\,p \mid p\,T$
	$t ::= x^T \mid c^T \mid t\,t \mid p \to t \mid t\,T \mid [\Delta]\,T \to t \mid t \,\#\, t$
Dynamic pattern calculus	$t ::= x^T \mid \hat{x}^T \mid t\,t \mid [\theta]t \to t \mid$
	$t\,T \mid [\Delta]\,T \to t \mid t \,\#\, t$
Simply typed method calculus	$t ::= x^T \mid t\,t \mid (\lambda x.t)^T \mid t\,T \mid ([\Delta]\,T \to t)^T \mid t.t \mid t \,\&\, t$
Subtyped pattern calculus	$t ::= x^T \mid \hat{x}^T \mid t\,t \mid ([\theta]\,t \to t)^T \mid$
	$t\,T \mid ([\Delta]\,T \to t)^T \mid t \,\#\, t \mid t.t \mid t \,\&\, t$

Fig. A.10 Grammars of typed terms

A.3 Typed Terms

The grammars of the typed calculi are given in Fig. A.10. The *free type variables* $\mathsf{FV}(t)$ and *free type matchable* $\mathsf{FM}(t)$ of a term t are defined in Fig. A.11. A type substitution is *applied* to the free type variables or free type matchables of a term using the rules in Fig. A.12. The *free term variables* $\mathsf{fv}(t)$ and *free term matchables* $\mathsf{fm}(t)$ of a term t are those of the corresponding untyped terms, obtained by erasing all type information. A term substitution is *applied* to the free variables or free matchables of a term using the rules in Fig. A.13. The α*-equivalence* of types is the congruence generated by the relation in Fig. A.14.

$$
\begin{aligned}
\mathsf{FV}(x^T) &= \mathsf{FV}(T)\\
\mathsf{FV}(r\,u) &= \mathsf{FV}(r) \cup \mathsf{FV}(u)\\
\mathsf{FV}(\lambda x^U.s) &= \mathsf{FV}(U) \cup \mathsf{FV}(s)\\
\mathsf{FV}(\lambda x.s)^T &= \mathsf{FV}(s) \cup \mathsf{FV}(T)\\
\mathsf{FV}(r\,U) &= \mathsf{FV}(r) \cup \mathsf{FV}(U)\\
\mathsf{FV}(\Lambda X.s) &= \mathsf{FV}(s) \setminus \{X\}\\
\mathsf{FV}([\Delta]\,P \to s) &= (\mathsf{FV}(P) \cup \mathsf{FV}(s)) \setminus \Delta\\
\mathsf{FV}([\Delta]\,P \to s)^T &= ((\mathsf{FV}(P) \cup \mathsf{FV}(s)) \setminus \Delta)\\
&\quad \cup \mathsf{FV}(T)\\
\mathsf{FV}(s\,\#\,t) &= \mathsf{FV}(s) \cup \mathsf{FV}(t)\\
\mathsf{FV}(c^T) &= \{\}\\
\mathsf{FV}(c^T\ \mathtt{eqa}\ t) &= \mathsf{FV}(t)\\
\mathsf{FV}(\mathtt{fold}(s,t,u)) &= \mathsf{FV}(s) \cup \mathsf{FV}(t) \cup \mathsf{FV}(u)\\
\mathsf{FV}(p^P \to s) &= (\mathsf{FV}(s) \setminus \mathsf{FV}(p)) \cup \mathsf{FV}(P)\\
\mathsf{FV}(\hat{x}^T) &= \mathsf{FV}(T)\\
\mathsf{FV}([\Delta;\theta]\,p \to s) &= \mathsf{FV}(\theta) \cup \mathsf{FV}(p)\\
&\quad \cup (\mathsf{FV}(s) \setminus \Delta)
\end{aligned}
$$

$$
\begin{aligned}
\mathsf{FM}(x^T) &= \mathsf{FM}(T)\\
\mathsf{FM}(r\,u) &= \mathsf{FM}(r) \cup \mathsf{FM}(u)\\
\mathsf{FM}(\lambda x^U.s) &= \mathsf{FM}(U) \cup \mathsf{FM}(s)\\
\mathsf{FM}(\lambda x.s)^T &= \mathsf{FM}(s) \cup \mathsf{FM}(T)\\
\mathsf{FM}(r\,U) &= \mathsf{FM}(r) \cup \mathsf{FM}(U)\\
\mathsf{FM}(\Lambda X.s) &= \mathsf{FM}(s)\\
\mathsf{FM}([\Delta]\,P \to s) &= \mathsf{FM}(P) \cup \mathsf{FM}(s)\\
\mathsf{FM}([\Delta]\,P \to s)^T &= \mathsf{FM}(P) \cup \mathsf{FM}(s)\\
&\quad \cup \mathsf{FM}(T)\\
\mathsf{FM}(s\,\#\,t) &= \mathsf{FM}(s) \cup \mathsf{FM}(t)\\
\mathsf{FM}(c^T) &= \{\}\\
\mathsf{FM}(c^T\ \mathtt{eqa}\ t) &= \mathsf{FM}(t)\\
\mathsf{FM}(\mathtt{fold}(s,t,u)) &= \mathsf{FM}(s) \cup \mathsf{FM}(t) \cup \mathsf{FM}(u)\\
\mathsf{FM}(p \to s) &= \mathsf{FM}(p) \cup \mathsf{FM}(s)\\
\mathsf{FM}(\hat{x}^T) &= \mathsf{FM}(T)\\
\mathsf{FM}([\Delta;\theta]\,p \to s) &= ((\mathsf{FM}(p) \cup \mathsf{FM}(\theta)) \setminus \Delta)\\
&\quad \cup \mathsf{FM}(s)
\end{aligned}
$$

Fig. A.11 Free type symbols of terms

$$
\begin{aligned}
\rho(x^T) &= x^{\rho(T)}\\
\rho(r\,u) &= \rho(r)\,\rho(u)\\
\rho(\lambda x^U.s) &= \lambda x^{\rho(U)}.\rho(s)\\
\rho(\lambda x.s)^T &= (\lambda x.\rho(s))^{\rho(T)}\\
\rho(r\,U) &= \rho(r)\,\rho(U)\\
\rho(\Lambda X.s) &= \Lambda X.\rho(s) \quad \text{if } \rho \text{ avoids } X\\
\rho([\Delta]\,P \to s) &= [\Delta]\,\rho(P) \to \rho(s)\\
&\quad \text{if } \rho \text{ avoids } \Delta\\
\rho([\Delta]\,P \to s)^T &= ([\Delta]\,\rho(P) \to \rho(s))^{\rho(T)}\\
&\quad \text{if } \rho \text{ avoids } \Delta\\
\rho(s\,\#\,t) &= \rho(s)\,\#\,\rho(t)\\
\rho(c^T) &= c^T\\
\rho(c^T\ \mathtt{eqa}\ t) &= c^T\ \mathtt{eqa}\ \rho(t)\\
\rho(\mathtt{fold}(s,t,u)) &= \mathtt{fold}(\rho(s),\rho(t),\rho(u))\\
\rho p \to s &= \rho(p) \to \rho(s)\\
\rho(\hat{x}^T) &= \hat{x}^{\rho(T)}\\
\rho([\Delta;\theta]\,p \to s) &= [\Delta;\theta]\,\rho(p) \to \rho(s)\\
&\quad \text{if } \rho \text{ avoids } \Delta
\end{aligned}
$$

$$
\begin{aligned}
\hat{\rho}(x^T) &= x^{\hat{\rho}(T)}\\
\hat{\rho}(r\,u) &= \hat{\rho}(r)\,\hat{\rho}(u)\\
\hat{\rho}(\lambda x^U.s) &= \lambda x^{\hat{\rho}(U)}.\hat{\rho}(s)\\
\hat{\rho}(\lambda x.s)^T &= (\lambda x.\hat{\rho}s)^{\hat{\rho}T}\\
\hat{\rho}(r\,U) &= \hat{\rho}(r)\,\hat{\rho}(U)\\
\hat{\rho}(\Lambda X.s) &= \Lambda X.\hat{\rho}(s) \quad \text{if } \rho \text{ avoids } X\\
\hat{\rho}([\Delta]\,P \to s) &= [\Delta]\,\hat{\rho}(P) \to \hat{\rho}(s)\\
&\quad \text{if } \rho \text{ avoids } \Delta\\
\hat{\rho}([\Delta]\,P \to s)^T &= ([\Delta]\,\hat{\rho}(P) \to \hat{\rho}(s))^{\hat{\rho}(T)}\\
&\quad \text{if } \rho \text{ avoids } \Delta\\
\hat{\rho}(s\,\#\,t) &= \hat{\rho}(s)\,\#\,\hat{\rho}(t)\\
\hat{\rho}(c^T) &= c^T\\
\hat{\rho}(c^T\ \mathtt{eqa}\ t) &= c\ \mathtt{eqa}\ \hat{\rho}(t)\\
\hat{\rho}(\mathtt{fold}(s,t,u)) &= \mathtt{fold}(\hat{\rho}(s),\hat{\rho}(t),\hat{\rho}(u))\\
\hat{\rho}(p \to s) &= \hat{\rho}p \to \hat{\rho}s\\
\hat{\rho}\hat{x}^T &= \hat{x}^{\hat{\rho}(T)}\\
\hat{\rho}([\Delta;\theta]\,p \to s) &= [\Delta;\theta]\,\hat{\rho}(p) \to \hat{\rho}(s)\\
&\quad \text{if } \rho \text{ avoids } \Delta
\end{aligned}
$$

Fig. A.12 Applying type substitutions to terms

Lemma A.3. *For every type substitution ρ and term substitution σ and term t_1 there is a term t_2 that is α-equivalent to t_1 such that $\rho(t_2)$ and $\hat{\rho}(t_2)$ and $\sigma(t_2)$ and $\hat{\sigma}(t_2)$ are defined. If t_1 and t_2 are α-equivalent terms then they have the same free (type and term) variables and matchables. Whenever a substitution is applicable to both then the results are α-equivalent.*

$$
\begin{array}{rlrl}
\sigma(x^T) &= \sigma x & \hat{\sigma}(x^T) &= x^T \\
\sigma(r\,u) &= \sigma(r)\;\sigma(u) & \hat{\sigma}(r\,u) &= \hat{\sigma}(r)\;\hat{\sigma}(u) \\
\sigma(\lambda x^U.s) &= \lambda x^U.\sigma(s) \text{ if } \sigma \text{ avoids } x & \hat{\sigma}(\lambda x^U.s) &= \lambda x^U.\hat{\sigma}(s) \text{ if } \sigma \text{ avoids } x \\
\sigma(r\,U) &= \sigma(r)\;U & \hat{\sigma}(r\,U) &= \hat{\sigma}(r)\;U \\
\sigma(\Lambda X.s) &= \Lambda X.\sigma(s) \quad \text{if } \sigma \text{ avoids } X & \hat{\sigma}(\Lambda X.s) &= \Lambda X.\hat{\sigma}(s) \quad \text{if } \sigma \text{ avoids } X \\
\sigma([\Delta]\;P \to s) &= [\Delta]\;P \to \sigma(s) & \hat{\sigma}([\Delta]\;P \to s) &= [\Delta]\;P \to \hat{\sigma}(s) \\
& \quad \text{if } \sigma \text{ avoids } \Delta & & \quad \text{if } \sigma \text{ avoids } \Delta \\
\sigma(s\,\#\,t) &= \sigma(s)\,\#\,\sigma(t) & \hat{\sigma}(s\,\#\,t) &= \hat{\sigma}(s)\,\#\,\hat{\sigma}(t) \\
\sigma c &= c & \hat{\sigma}(c) &= c \\
\sigma(c \;\mathsf{eqa}\; t) &= c \;\mathsf{eqa}\; \sigma(t) & \hat{\sigma}(c \;\mathsf{eqa}\; t) &= c \;\mathsf{eqa}\; \hat{\sigma}(t) \\
\sigma(\mathtt{fold}(s,t,u)) &= \mathtt{fold}(\sigma(s),\sigma(t),\sigma(u)) & \hat{\sigma}(\mathtt{fold}(s,t,u)) &= \mathtt{fold}(\hat{\sigma}(s),\hat{\sigma}(t),\hat{\sigma}(u)) \\
\sigma p \to s &= p \to \sigma(s) \text{ if } \sigma \text{ avoids } \mathsf{fv}(p) & \hat{\sigma}(p \to s) &= p \to \hat{\sigma}(s) \\
\sigma \hat{x}^T &= \hat{x}^T & \hat{\sigma}\hat{x}^T &= \hat{x}^T \\
\sigma([\Delta;\theta]\;p \to s) &= [\Delta;\theta]\;\sigma(p) \to \sigma(s) & \hat{\sigma}([\Delta;\theta]\;p \to s) &= [\Delta;\theta]\;\hat{\sigma}(p) \to \hat{\sigma}(s) \\
& \quad \text{if } \sigma \text{ avoids } \Delta;\theta & & \quad \text{if } \sigma \text{ avoids } \Delta;\theta
\end{array}
$$

Fig. A.13 Applying term substitutions

$$
\begin{array}{rll}
\lambda x^U.s &=_\alpha \lambda y^U.\{y^U/x\}s & \text{if } y \notin \mathsf{fv}(s) \\
\Lambda X.s &=_\alpha \Lambda Y.\{Y/X\}s & \text{if } Y \notin \mathsf{FV}(s) \\
[\Delta,X]\;P \to s &=_\alpha [\Delta,Y]\;\{Y/X\}P \to \{Y/X\}s & \text{if } Y \notin \Delta \cup \mathsf{FV}(P) \cup \mathsf{FV}(s) \\
p \to s &=_\alpha \{y^U/x\}p \to \{y^U/x\}s & \text{if } x^U \text{ is free in } p \text{ and } y \notin \mathsf{fv}(p) \cup \mathsf{fv}(s) \\
p \to s &=_\alpha \{Y/X\}p \to \{Y/X\}s & \text{if } X \text{ is local in } p \text{ and } Y \notin \mathsf{FV}(p) \cup \mathsf{FV}(s) \\
[\Delta,X;\theta]\;p \to s &=_\alpha [\Delta,Y;\theta]\;\{\hat{Y}/\hat{X}\}p \to \{Y/X\}s & \text{if } Y \notin \Delta \cup \mathsf{FV}(p) \cup \mathsf{FM}(p) \cup \mathsf{FV}(s) \cup \mathsf{FM}(s) \\
[\Delta;\theta,x^U]\;p \to s &=_\alpha [\Delta;\theta,y^U]\;\{\hat{y}^{\hat{U}}/\hat{x}\}p \to \{y^U/x\}s & \text{if } y \notin \theta \cup \mathsf{fm}(p) \cup \mathsf{fv}(s)
\end{array}
$$

Fig. A.14 α-conversion of terms

References

1. Abadi, M., Cardelli, L.: A Theory of Objects. Monographs in Computer Science. Springer (1997)
2. Aho, A., Kernigan, B., Weinberger, P.: Awk: A pattern scanning and processing language. Softw. Pract. Exper. **9**(4), 267–280 (1979)
3. Baader, F., Nipkow, T.: Term Rewriting and All That. Cambridge University Press (1999)
4. Backhouse, R., Sheard, T. (eds.): Workshop on Generic Programming: Marstrand, Sweden, 18th June, 1998. Chalmers University of Technology (1998)
5. Balland, E., Brauner, P., Kopetz, R., Moreau, P.E., Reilles, A.: Tom: Piggybacking rewriting on Java. In: Proc. of the 18th Conference on Rewriting Techniques and Applications, Lecture Notes in Computer Science. Springer (2007)
6. Barendregt, H.: The Lambda Calculus: Its Syntax and Semantics. North Holland (1984). Revised edition
7. Barendregt, H.: Lambda calculi with types. In: S. Abramsky, D. Gabbay, T. Maibaum (eds.) Handbook of Logic in Computer Science, vol. 2. Oxford University Press (1992)
8. Barthe, G., Cirstea, H., Kirchner, C., Liquori, L.: Pure patterns type systems. In: POPL '03: Proc. of the 30th ACM SIGPLAN-SIGACT Symposium on Principles of Programming Languages, pp. 250–261. ACM Press (2003)
9. Bird, R., Wadler, P.: Introduction to Functional Programming. International Series in Computer Science. Prentice Hall (1988)
10. **bondi** programming language. URL `www-staff.it.uts.edu.au/~cbj/bondi`
11. Breazu-Tannen, V., Kesner, D., Puel, L.: A typed pattern calculus. In: M. Vardi (ed.) 8th Annual IEEE Symposium on Logic in Computer Science (LICS), pp. 262–274. IEEE Computer Society Press (1993)
12. Bruce, K.: Foundations of Object-Oriented Languages: Types and Semantics. The MIT Press (2002)
13. Bruce, K.B., Fiech, A., Schuett, A., van Gent, R.: Polytoil: A type-safe polymorphic object-oriented language. ACM Trans. on Progr. Lang. and Sys. **25**(2), 225–290 (2003)
14. Cardelli, L., Mitchell, J.C., Martini, S., Scedrov, A.: An extension of system F with subtyping. In: T. Ito, A.R. Meyer (eds.) Proc. of 1st Int. Symp. on Theor. Aspects of Computer Software, TACS'91, Sendai, Japan, 24–27 Sept 1991, vol. 526, pp. 750–770. Springer (1991). URL `citeseer.ist.psu.edu/cardelli91extension.html`
15. Castagna, G.: Object-Oriented Programming: A Unified Foundation. Progress in Theoretical Computer Science Series. Birkhäuser (1997)
16. Castagna, G., Ghelli, G., Longo, G.: A calculus for overloaded functions with subtyping. Information and Computation **117**(1), 115–135 (1995)
17. Cerrito, S., Kesner, D.: Pattern matching as cut elimination. Theoretical Computer Science **323**, 71–127 (2004)

18. Church, A.: A set of postulates for the foundation of logic. The Annals of Mathematics **33**(2), 346–366 (1932)
19. Church, A.: An unsolvable problem of elementary number theory. American Journal of Mathematics **58**(2), 345–363 (1936)
20. Church, A.: A formulation of the simple theory of types. Journal of Symbolic Logic **5**(2), 56–68 (1940)
21. Church, A.: The Calculi of Lambda Conversion, *Annals of Mathematics*, vol. 6. Princeton University Press (1941)
22. Cirstea, H., Fernández, M.: Rewriting calculi, higher-order reductions and patterns. Mathematical Structures in Computer Science **18** (2008). Special Issue 03
23. Cirstea, H., Liquori, L., Wack, B.: Rewriting calculus with fixpoints:untyped and first-order systems. In: Proc. of Types '03, International Workshop on Types for Proof and Programs. Turin, Italy, vol. 3085, pp. 147–161. Springer (2003)
24. Clavel, M., Durán, F., Eker, S., Lincoln, P., Martí-Oliet, N., Meseguer, J., Talcott, C.: The Maude 2.0 system. In: R. Nieuwenhuis (ed.) Rewriting Techniques and Applications (RTA 2003), no. 2706 in Lecture Notes in Computer Science, pp. 76–87. Springer (2003)
25. Curry, H.B., Feys, R.: Combinatory Logic, Vol. I. North Holland (1958)
26. Damas, L., Milner, R.: Principal type-schemes for functional programs. In: POPL '82: Proc. of the 9th ACM SIGPLAN-SIGACT Symposium on Principles of Programming Languages, pp. 207–212. ACM (1982)
27. Dybvig, R.K.: The Scheme Programming Language, 3rd Edition. MIT Press (2003)
28. Erwig, M.: Active patterns. In: IFL '96: Selected Papers from the 8th International Workshop on Implementation of Functional Languages, pp. 21–40. Springer (1997)
29. Farber, D.J., Griswold, R.E., Polonsky, I.P.: Snobol, a string manipulation language. J. ACM **11**(1), 21–30 (1964)
30. Faure, G.: Notes on the confluence of PPTS (2008). Private communication
31. F# homepage (2007). URL `http://research.microsoft.com/fsharp/fsharp.aspx`
32. Gamma, E., Helm, R., Johnson, R., Vlissides, J.: Design Patterns: Elements of Reusable Object-Oriented Software. Addison-Wesley (1995)
33. Gibbons, J., Jeuring, J. (eds.): Generic Programming: IFIP TC2/WG2.1 Working Conference on Generic Programming, July 11–12, 2002, Dagstuhl, Germany. Kluwer Academic Publishers (2003)
34. Girard, J.Y.: Interprétation fonctionelle et élimination des coupures dans lárithmétique dórdre supérieur. Ph.D. thesis, Université Paris VII (1972)
35. Girard, J.Y., Lafont, Y., Taylor, P.: Proofs and Types. Tracts in Theoretical Computer Science. Cambridge University Press (1989)
36. Given-Wilson, T.: Interpreting the Untyped Pattern Calculus in **bondi**. Honours Thesis, University of Technology, Sydney (2007)
37. Goguen, J., Thatcher, J., Wagner, E., Wright, J.: Initial algebra semantics and continuous algebras. Journal of the Association for Computing Machinery **24**, 68–95 (1977)
38. Hankin, C.: Lambda Calculi. Oxford University Press (1994)
39. Harper, R., Morrisett, G.: Compiling polymorphism using intensional type analysis. In: Conference Record of POPL '95: 22nd ACM SIGPLAN-SIGACT Symposium on Principles of Programming Languages, pp. 130–141 (1995)
40. HASKELL. `http://www.haskell.org/` (2002)
41. Henglein, F.: Type inference with polymorphic recursion. ACM Trans. on Progr. Lang. and Sys. **15**, 253–289 (1993)
42. Hindley, R., Seldin, J.: Introduction to Combinators and Lambda-calculus. Cambridge University Press (1986)
43. Hinze, R.: A new approach to generic functional programming. In: Proc. of the 27th ACM SIGPLAN-SIGACT Symposium on Principles of Programming Languages, pp. 119–132. ACM Press (2000)
44. Hinze, R. (ed.): Proceedings: Workshop on Generic Programming (WGP 2006): Portland, Oregon, 16th September 2006. ACM Press (2006)

45. Hinze, R., Jeuring, J.: Generic Haskell: Practice and theory. In: Generic Programming, *Lecture Notes in Computer Science*, vol. 2793, chap. 1, pp. 1–56. Springer (2003)
46. Hoffmann, C.M., O'Donnell, M.J.: An interpreter generator using tree pattern matching. In: POPL '79: Proc. of the 6th ACM SIGACT-SIGPLAN Symposium on Principles of Programming Languages, pp. 169–179. ACM Press (1979). DOI http://doi.acm.org/10.1145/567752.567768
47. Horatiu Cirstea, Claude Kirchner: The rewriting calculus — Parts I *and* II. Logic Journal of the Interest Group in Pure and Applied Logics **9**(3), 427–498 (2001)
48. Huang, F., Jay, B., Skillicorn, D.: Programming with heterogeneous structures: Manipulating XML data using **bondi**. In: V. Estivill-Castro, G. Dobbie (eds.) Twenty-Ninth Australasian Computer Science Conference (ACSC2006), *Australian Computer Science Communications*, vol. 48(1), pp. 287–296 (2006)
49. Igarashi, A., Pierce, B.C., Wadler, P.: Featherweight Java: a minimal core calculus for Java and GJ. ACM Trans. Program. Lang. Syst. **23**(3), 396–450 (2001)
50. Jansson, P., Jeuring, J.: PolyP – a polytypic programming language extension. In: POPL '97: The 24th ACM SIGPLAN-SIGACT Symposium on Principles of Programming Languages, pp. 470–482. ACM Press (1997)
51. Jay, B., Jones, S.P.: Scrap your type applications. In: P. Audebaud, C. Paulin-Mohring (eds.) Mathematics of Program Construction, 9th International Conference, MPC 2008, Marseille, France, July 2008, *Lecture Notes in Computer Science*, vol. 5133, pp. 2–27. Springer (2008)
52. Jay, B., Kesner, D.: Pure pattern calculus. In: Programming Languages and Systems, 15th European Symposium on Programming, ESOP 2006, Vienna, Austria, March 27–28, 2006, Proceedings (ed: P. Sestoft), pp. 100–114 (2006). Revised version at `www-staff.it.uts.edu.au/~cbj/Publications/purepatterns.pdf`
53. Jay, B., Kesner, D.: First-class patterns. Journal of Functional Programming **19**(2), 34 pages (2009)
54. Jay, C.: Polynomial polymorphism. In: R. Kotagiri (ed.) Proc. of the Eighteenth Australasian Computer Science Conference: Glenelg, South Australia 1–3 February, 1995, vol. 17, pp. 237–243. ACS Communications (1995)
55. Jay, C.: Distinguishing data structures and functions: the constructor calculus and functorial types. In: S. Abramsky (ed.) Typed Lambda Calculi and Applications: 5th International Conference TLCA 2001, Kraków, Poland, May 2001 Proceedings, *Lecture Notes in Computer Science*, vol. 2044, pp. 217–239. Springer (2001)
56. Jay, C.: Higher-order patterns. unpublished (2004)
57. Jay, C.: Methods as pattern-matching functions. In: Foundations of Object-Oriented Languages, 2004 (2004). `http://www.doc.ic.ac.uk/~scd/FOOL11/patterns.pdf`
58. Jay, C.: The pattern calculus. ACM Transactions on Programming Languages and Systems (TOPLAS) **26**(6), 911–937 (2004)
59. Jay, C.: Typing first-class patterns. In: D. Kesner, M.O. Stehr, F. van Raamsdonk (eds.) Higher-Order Rewriting, electronic proceedings (2006). `http://hor.pps.jussieu.fr/06/proc/jay1.pdf`
60. Jay, C., Bellè, G., Moggi, E.: Functorial ML. Journal of Functional Programming **8**(6), 573–619 (1998)
61. Jay, C., Cockett, J.: Shapely types and shape polymorphism. In: D. Sannella (ed.) Programming Languages and Systems – ESOP '94: 5th European Symposium on Programming, Edinburgh, U.K., April 1994, Proceedings, *Lecture Notes in Computer Science*, vol. 788, pp. 302–316. Springer (1994)
62. Jeuring, J.: Polytypic pattern matching. In: FPCA '95: Proceedings of the seventh international conference on Functional programming languages and computer architecture, pp. 238–248. ACM, New York, NY, USA (1995). DOI http://doi.acm.org/10.1145/224164.224212
63. Jeuring, J. (ed.): Proceedings: Workshop on Generic Programming (WGP 2000): July 6, 2000, Ponte de Lima, Portugal. Utrecht University, UU-CS-2000-19 (2000)
64. Jouannaud, J.P., Rubio, A.: Polymorphic higher-order recursive path orderings. J. ACM **54**(1), 1 (2007)

65. Kahl, W.: Basic pattern matching calculi: A fresh view on matching failure. In: Y. Kameyama, P. Stuckey (eds.) Functional and Logic Programming, Proc. of FLOPS 2004, *Lecture Notes in Computer Science*, vol. 2998, pp. 276–290. Springer (2004). URL `http://link.springer.de/link/service/series/0558/tocs/t2998.htm`
66. Kesner, D., Puel, L., Tannen, V.: A Typed Pattern Calculus. Information and Computation **124**(1), 32–61 (1996)
67. Klop, J.W., van Oostrom, V., de Vrijer, R.: Lambda calculus with patterns. Theoretical Computer Science **398**, 16–31 (2008)
68. Laemmel, R., Peyton-Jones, S.: Scrap your boilerplate: a practical approach to generic programming. In: Proc ACM SIGPLAN Workshop on Types in Language Design and Implementation (TLDI 2003), New Orleans, Jan 2003 (2003)
69. Lämmel, R., Peyton Jones, S.: Scrap more boilerplate: reflection, zips, and generalised casts. In: Proc. of the ACM SIGPLAN International Conference on Functional Programming (ICFP 2004), pp. 244–255. ACM Press (2004)
70. Lämmel, R., Peyton Jones, S.: Scrap your boilerplate with class: extensible generic functions. In: Proc. of the ACM SIGPLAN International Conference on Functional Programming (ICFP 2005), pp. 204–215. ACM Press (2005)
71. Landin, P.J.: The next 700 programming languages. Commun. ACM **9**(3), 157–166 (1966)
72. Leroy, X.: The Objective Caml system release 3.10 – documentation and user's manual (2007). `http://caml.inria.fr/pub/docs/manual-ocaml/index.html`
73. Lloyd, J.W.: Foundations of logic programming (2nd extended ed). Springer (1987)
74. McCarthy, J.: Recursive functions of symbolic expressions and their computation by machine, part I. Commun. ACM **3**(4), 184–195 (1960)
75. McMahon, L.E.: Sed—a non-interactive text editor, pp. 389–397. W. B. Saunders Company, Philadelphia, PA, USA (1990)
76. Milner, R.: A theory of type polymorphism in programming. Journal of Computer and Systems Sciences **17**, 348–375 (1978)
77. Milner, R., Tofte, M.: Commentary on Standard ML. MIT Press (1991)
78. O'Donnell, M.J.: Computing in Systems Described by Equations, *Lecture Notes in Computer Science*, vol. 58. Springer (1977)
79. O'Hearn, P., Tennent, R. (eds.): Algol-like Languages, Vols I and II. Progress in Theoretical Computer Science. Birkhäuser (1997)
80. Oliveira, B.C.d.S., Gibbons, J.: Typecase: a design pattern for type-indexed functions. In: Haskell '05: Proc. of the 2005 ACM SIGPLAN workshop on Haskell, pp. 98–109. ACM Press (2005)
81. van Oostrom, V.: Lambda calculus with patterns. Tech. Rep. IR-228, Vrije Universiteit, Amsterdam (1990)
82. Palsberg, J., Schwartzbach, M.: Object-oriented type systems. John Wiley (1994)
83. Peyton Jones, S.: The Implementation of Functional Programming Languages. Prentice Hall (1987). URL `http://research.microsoft.com/~simonpj/papers/slpj-book-1987/`
84. Peyton-Jones, S.: Haskell 98 Language and Libraries: The Revised Report. Cambridge University Press (2003)
85. Peyton Jones, S., Lester, D.: Implementing Functional Languages: a tutorial. Springer (1992)
86. Peyton Jones, S.L., Wadler, P.: Imperative functional programming. In: POPL '93: Proc. of the 20th ACM SIGPLAN-SIGACT Symposium on Principles of Programming Languages, pp. 71–84. ACM (1993)
87. Pfenning, F., Paulin-Mohring, C.: Inductively defined types in the calculus of constructions. In: Proc. of the Fifth International Conference on Mathematical Foundations of Programming Semantics, pp. 209–226. Springer (1990)
88. Remy, D., Vouillon, J.: Objective ML: An effective object-oriented extension to ML. Theory and Practice of Object Systems **4**, 27–50 (1998)
89. Reynolds, J.: Types, abstraction, and parametric polymorphism. In: R. Mason (ed.) Information Processing '83. North Holland (1985)
90. Robinson, J.: A machine-oriented logic based on the resolution principle. Journal of the Association for Computing Machinery **12**, 23–41 (1965)

91. Rosser, J.: Highlights of the history of the lambda-calculus. ACM Press New York, NY, USA (1982)
92. Scheme homepage. URL http://www-swiss.ai.mit.edu/projects/scheme/
93. Scott, D., Strachey, C.: Toward a mathematical semantics for computer languages. Tech. Rep. PRG-6, Oxford Univ. Computing Lab. (1971)
94. STANDARD ML OF NEW JERSEY. http://cm.bell-labs.com/cm/cs/what/smlnj
95. Syme, D., Neverov, G., Margetson, J.: Extensible pattern matching via a lightweight language extension (2006). URL http://blogs.msdn.com/dsyme/attachment/2044281.ashx
96. Tait, W.: Intensional interpretation of functionals of finite type I. Journal of Symbolic Logic **32**, 198–212 (1967)
97. The Coq Development Team LogiCal Project: The Coq proof assistant reference manual version 8.1 1 (2007). URL http://pauillac.inria.fr/coq/V8.1/refman/
98. The Tom language. http://tom.loria.fr/
99. Turing, A.M.: On computable numbers, with an application to the Entscheidungsproblem. Proc. of the London Mathematical Society **42**, 230–65 (1936)
100. Turing, A.M.: Computability and lambda-definability. J. Symb. Log. **2**(4), 153–163 (1937)
101. Visser, E.: Program transformation with Stratego/XT: Rules, strategies, tools, and systems in StrategoXT-0.9. In: C. Lengauer, et al. (eds.) Domain-Specific Program Generation, *Lecture Notes in Computer Science*, vol. 3016, pp. 216–238. Spinger (2004)
102. Vrijer, R.C.D., Klop, J.W.: Term Rewriting Systems, *Tracts in Theoretical Computer Science*, vol. 55. Cambridge University Press (2003)
103. Wadler, P.: Views: a way for pattern matching to cohabit with data abstraction. In: POPL '87: Proc. of the 14th ACM SIGACT-SIGPLAN Symposium on Principles of Programming Languages, pp. 307–313. ACM Press (1987)
104. Wall, L., Christiansen, T., Orwant, J.: Programming Perl, Third Edition. O'Reilly (2000)
105. Wells, J.B.: Typability and type checking in the second-order λ-calculus are equivalent and undecidable. In: Proceedings, Ninth Annual IEEE Symposium on Logic in Computer Science. IEEE Computer Society Press (1994)
106. Wolfram, S.: Mathematica: a system for doing mathematics by computer 2nd ed. Addison Wesley Longman (1991)
107. Wright, A., Duba, B.: Pattern matching for scheme (1995). URL citeseer.ist.psu.edu/wright95pattern.html

Index

R

S

T

U

V

W

Z